**BY UNITED MEN OF HONOR**

Navigating
Your
Storm

VISIONARY AUTHORS
KEN A. HOBBS II & ASAAD FARAJ

Published by World Publishing and Productions
PO Box 8722, Jupiter, FL 33468
Worldpublishingandproductions.com

ISBN: 978-1-957111-19-3

Library of Congress Control Number: 2023919998

TABLE OF CONTENTS

INTRODUCTION

You are about to set sail into a book, a guide, an inspiration that will allow you to navigate through rogue waves and tumultuous waters brought on by the ugly hurricanes of life threatening to spiral you out of control. Reading this book will guide you to a fresh start—a new course that will change the direction of your heart and give you the ability to see the light of God so you can navigate any storm that comes upon you.

In this book, you will encounter Men of Honor who have stepped up to share with transparency the obstacles they faced, giving you a glimpse of how God works in victorious ways. Through their words and experiences, may your eyes be illuminated to see the storms ahead and be prepared to seek God's guidance through them, realizing and admitting that we all need His strength.

We are each a work in progress, trying to accomplish great and mighty things in our lifetime. But we may need to overcome tremendous challenges before we can ever see a breakthrough. Or we may need to yield to the manifestation of God's power over our own circumstances or those of our loved ones. Whatever raging storm you are currently experiencing, know that it will not last forever. As you read this book, we pray you will profoundly claim victory as God carries you to the other side of the turbulence. We pray that the Holy Spirit will use these stories, allowing you to identify with your fellow brothers in Christ and empowering you to see His glory as you face each wave.

These authors have learned that God wants us to shift our focus and prayers from what we desire to His will for us. When we allow this to happen, things will begin to change. Despite any storm we may encounter, with God, our eyes will start to open to new possibilities. As you read these stories, we know God will trigger your heart to be receptive to the scriptures He has chosen to be placed strategically inside this book. *Navigating Your Storm* will become a help to you, a manual to course a realignment of your heart. In your life, God is always looking ahead, making minor course adjustments here and there so that everything works together for His good.

> *For I am about to do something new.*
>   *See, I have already begun! Do you not see it?*
> *I will make a pathway through the wilderness.*
>   *I will create rivers in the dry wasteland.* (Isaiah 43:19 NLT).

God is a God of new things. We need not worry or stress that any trials or tragedies of life will paralyze us. Look to the wisdom from God's Word poured out in this book. Our sword, God's Word, is clear about giving us a message for today and overcoming any storm that may whip up.

Yet even in the midst of all these things, we triumph over them all, for God has made us to be more than conquerors, and his demonstrated love is our glorious victory over EVERYTHING! (Roman 8:37 TPT, emphasis added).

Storms will come and storms will pass, and the Bible says each day has enough trouble of its own. God's Word tells us in Matthew 6:34 not to worry about tomorrow because tomorrow will worry about itself.

We need to focus on the now and what God wants us to see through the day that is upon us.

Our prayer as Men of Honor writing this book is that God will allow you to be reminded of who He is and what He promises so you can rest in assurance that He is in control of your circumstances. After relating to some of these stories, we pray you will be able to tell God how you feel and acknowledge that His character is good and trustworthy. You will find God in these stories, and it is our hope you will agree with Him that all He says in His Word is true.

Journey with us as a Band of Brothers going through the raging waves of life. Allow God to chart your course through the storms. Then, hold tight to your rudder and look toward the light, because with Him, all things are possible (Matthew 19:26).

As you read, may your life be filled with purpose and provision as you allow God to take you to peaceful and tranquil waters.

> *"If you can?" said Jesus. "Everything is possible for one who believes"* (Mark 9:23 NIV).

KEN A. HOBBS II

Ken A. Hobbs II is a Christ follower devoted to impacting others in para-church ministries, missions, and business, where he leads a marketplace ministry.

Ken is the Founder of United Men of Honor—leading, coaching, and empowering men to lead with integrity and faith in their homes, businesses, and communities. www.unitedmenofhonor. com. His book *United Men of Honor: Overcoming Adversity Through Faith* is a #1 Amazon best-seller.

As a part of the Leadership Team of Band of Brothers, Ken is strongly passionate about the bootcamps, believing they are needed so men do not have to fight their struggles alone. www.BandofBrothersFL.com

Ken Hobbs II is a Senior Vice President / Financial Coach / Multiple Brokerage owner and operator for www.PRImerica.com/kenhobbs2 — impacting communities nationwide with business-building, coaching/ training, personal financial coaching, and services for over 30 years.

Ken is married to his wife Kimberly and actively supports her in Women World Leaders and World Publishing and Productions. www. WomenWorldLeaders.com.

Ken's work also reaches around the world, where he supports Kerus Global Education, African Orphan Care Project, and anti-trafficking/trauma training as an Advisory Board member. www.kerusglobal.org

Ken passionately loves his family and friends.

THE LIGHTHOUSE IN MY STORMS

by Ken A. Hobbs II

Growing up and going through my share of storms, I can now look back and see multiple "Lighthouse Moments" that gave me hope and helped me navigate rough waters. Although the storms we encounter are different, we all have something in common: when we look to God and the Lighthouse Moments He provides, He will lead us to a safe harbor. Although circumstances may appear catastrophic and we may feel in danger of crashing and sinking, if we let Him, our Lord, with His undeniable saving light, will carry us through. I'd love to share my testimony of how God has lit the way for me, and I pray that it makes an impact as you search for the guiding light God has for you.

In *United Men of Honor: Overcoming Adversity through Faith*, I wrote about the four men—my father, stepfather, and two grandfathers—who led me and guided me through some of the toughest times in my life. They reflected God's light and their example, love, care, and courage taught me to look for the lighthouse to guide me through my storms. Allow me to give a quick summary.

My dad's father left an indelible mark on me to find joy in every circumstance. He was tragically killed in a car accident when I was fourteen.

My father showed me what a forgiven man after God's own heart looks like and the true meaning of Revelation 3:20. He pursued me and poured into my life like no other. He suffered from early onset Alzheimer's and passed away two years ago.

Larry, my stepfather, always challenges me to question and learn from anyone. He has shown me how resilient you can be when you love and are committed. Even through the tragic deaths of his only son (at two and a half years old) and both his younger brothers, he has been committed with love to my mother and me.

Finally, my mother's father, Pop Cerullo, who is 97 years old, is my hero and still teaches me today. His unwavering faith and love for the Lord is amazing. Being able to talk, pray, sing, share, preach, and encourage others is a living testimony of Pop's impact in my life. He has been a warrior battling cancer for over twenty years and is still claiming victory every day. He is an example for me, my son, and our family.

God used Pop Hobbs to show me my first Lighthouse Moment. Both my parents remarried when I was five. My dad started his church, and I went from being his focus during and after the divorce to being a distraction, leaving me feeling like the lost child. Both sets of parents fought over me, which was difficult to navigate. I acted in all the wrong ways to get attention, learning that bad behavior was the most effective. My grandfather, Pop Hobbs, showed me the way to the Lord and was an incredible example of our heavenly Father's love and care for me. He was my rock, encouraging me and exemplifying a kind, strong man of God. He was my lighthouse, reflecting God's love for me.

As he cared for me, Pop Hobbs also brightened my life by passing on his love of music to me. He and my mom helped buy my first instrument, an alto saxophone, which I played until college. I traded that saxophone in for a Takamine 12-string guitar that I still have today. With it, I have led worship and played in life groups; I've used it for God's glory and to soothe my own soul when I was hurting.

If you love music like I do, look back to see how it helped you guide your way through the storms of life. Music can be our lighthouse.

My second Lighthouse Moment was the beacon streaming into my life from my other grandfather, Pop Cerullo, who has always been there for me and still is today.

I was eight the year my mother and stepfather moved to Colombia, South America. This was heartbreaking for me, and I did not manage well. I felt rejected and lost. That summer, my mom sent me to stay with Pop Cerullo in Philadelphia, Pennsylvania. They had just sold their home and bought a Winnebago, and I spent the summer zig-zagging across the country with them and my aunt Jennie (who is like a sister and only six years older than me), their dog Pepper, and cat Sandy. This turned out to be an amazing journey and the best memory of my childhood. But it also directed me in my life's calling. From the bonding solidified during that time, Jennie and I still serve together in ministries. God provided a lighthouse of hope to show me the way and lead me to the Father's call on my life.

God always provides a guiding light, even in the darkest challenges. And this Lighthouse Moment was no exception. Although I felt abandoned and alone, God was there, sending me beacons of hope and direction to traverse my storms.

For many, the teenage years are challenging, transitional, and defining. Mine were no exception. My mom returned to South Florida when I was entering middle school, and I moved to live with her under tenuous circumstances. I went from being a preacher's son to being a "Hippie" son.

As a result, I went into full rebellion from any spiritual authority figures in my life. I left a home that burned records to one where I bought whatever records I wanted. I experimented with drugs and delved deep into heavy metal rock and roll music (now called classic rock, but at that time, it was considered extreme!). I started playing in a rock band and was exposed to pornography in many places. I lived the motto of the times—"Drug, sex, and rock and roll."

My mom sent me to California to stay with my grandfather for the summers, which I took as a rejection. But as He always does, God worked everything together for good. My mom's decision turned out to be one of the most impactful times of my life, bringing me to a life-changing, mind-alternating Lighthouse Moment that would guide and help redirect me later in life. At the time, I was a chameleon, not knowing who I was but blending in with whomever I was with. I wanted to be "somebody," but I wasn't sure who or what.

At 14, I was in reckless abandon. I was flunking out of school, put into alternative classes (one step away from expulsion), suspended regularly, acting out, smoking cigarettes, associating with the wrong crowd, and trying drugs. I was trying to live the words of all the rock and roll songs I listened to. I was lost, trying to escape and medicate from my hurts.

My mom recently gave me a few memories she saved, which included my last suspension letter. I read it, shaking my head. I quote from the letter: "Willful disobedience, Serious misconduct, Kenneth gave a degrading/suggestive hand signal to the teacher. Other types of discipline have been used with no measurable success"!

I was close to allowing that to become my life story. I thought of myself as the prodigal son, looking for attention for all the wrong reasons.

Can you relate?

But God! God always provides a lighthouse. And thankfully, He used my father and grandfather to light my way. They pursued me and showed me what Revelation 3:20 truly meant. I knew I had to make a major change, to stop going in the direction I was headed. I needed to turn my life around. When you see a lighthouse in a storm, if you are going the wrong way, you can make a choice and turn your ship around. Like the prodigal, I came to my senses and redirected my energies.

I moved back with my father, stepmom, and three brothers and began to right my ship. I lost Pop Hobbs at the end of that year, making me grateful for his influence and legacy in my life. His death was a defining moment in our family, helping direct me in the career I have now been in for 30 years.

I excelled in the Christian school I began to attend. I made the basketball team and was editor of the yearbook. Working to help pay for my tuition, I graduated in the top three in my class while being voted "most likely to succeed." Those years gave me a chance to grow and directed me to rebrand myself, which carried forward into my adult life. I qualified for a partial scholarship to attend Southern California College. I carried an over-achiever attitude into college and, in the first semester, was voted by my peers to be the first freshman class president from another state. The second semester was quite different. I started to regress, no longer validated by success that I deemed hollow. I began self-sabotaging my life with drinking, girls, and the wrong crowd. I was looking for attention again from the wrong people and places.

Working while taking challenging classes and being rejected by the popular and "good" kids left me feeling alone. I started heading down the wrong path yet again. I was barely getting by when I got the news my baby brother had been fatally struck by a car. He was only two and a half years old.

Where was my lighthouse?

Seeing only storms and feeling tossed about like waves in the ocean, my belief system was rocked. First, my grandfather, a good man, had been killed in a car accident when I was fourteen. "Why God?" Now my baby brother, only two and a half years old. "Why God??"

I came home from college to say goodbye to my brother and attend his funeral. My mind was so dark I could not see any light. I used his death as a reason not to return to college. I worked job after job looking for direction. I finished my teen years living a "Miami Vice" lifestyle—clubbing, drinking, and looking for attention in the wrong places.

My twenties started much as my teen years ended. I spent my time clubbing and going job to job searching for direction, including working as an extra on Miami Vice. I met my first wife, the mother of my son, where? In a club. We started amazingly. We fell in love and rededicated our lives to the Lord, marrying within nine months of meeting. I was twenty, married, and chasing a dream of building a video production company, Travelvision. I even traded a resort video for my honeymoon in North Eleuthera Island, Bahamas, chasing a dream of producing videos for resorts worldwide. It was a great idea, but after producing videos for Resorts International (Now Atlantis) and Chalks Airlines, someone with more money started an in-room TV network called Travelvision Int. My dream was dashed.

Where was my lighthouse?

I went to work for the local affiliate of CNN, ESPN, USA, and MTV. Making mostly local commercials and corporate videos, I helped produce Roger Staubach Rolaids commercials and even produced an idea for the predecessor to the infomercial called "What's New." It was a "Tonight Show" format with interviews and videos promoting new products to sell on TV through an 800 number. As one of the interviewers, I set a man and a car on fire to advertise a new Halon fire extinguisher system and promoted a new water treatment system and a spine align device intended to replace chiropractic care.

I quit my job to chase this dream as a newly married man with a condominium and car payment. Shortly thereafter, Home Shopping Network started, and the infomercial spun off. Yet again, my dream came crashing down—dashed! I had no job, and I just wanted to be somebody.

Where was my lighthouse?

I went to work for the Halon Fire Systems Company as their in-house video producer to make an income. A management team bought the company and my Worldwide Audio and Video company. I was so hopeful to learn how to build and run businesses. The owner took a liking to me, and I became his assistant. I really thought this was my way to become a success, even while going against what my family advised me to do. "Something doesn't sound right..." they said.

Boy, were they right. After two years, my world came crashing down again. Some of the company's principals were arrested, and poof! Everything was gone again.

With no job, I was afraid for my family's security and uncertain about chasing a dream again. I had a one-year-old son, owned a house, and had lost my company car. I did not know how we would survive. At the same time, my son's mom and I were facing severe marital issues and heading to the edge of divorce. But God! My light in this darkness!

I experienced a true Lighthouse Moment as my family and I recommitted to the Lord. He was my guiding light through this storm.

I gave up chasing dreams and took a telemarketing job at Craftmatic Beds. I set appointments, worked the day shift, night shift, and Saturdays, working my way to marketing manager. I came in early, stayed late, missed family events, worked sick, and gave all I had to build someone else's business.

Getting my life back together after losing everything, I bought a fixer-upper home and a 20-year-old car for transportation. Reestablishing my marriage, I was the best father I could be while going through these adversities.

God's Lighthouse Moment brightly illuminated my path to a safe harbor as I led my church family in worship and grew stronger in my walk with the Lord.

After two years, I took my first vacation and came back refreshed and ready to go to work. That is when the owner, my boss, called me into his office and informed me that while I was on vacation, he had given my job to his son. I was offered two weeks' pay and a 401k, which, due to the market, was worth less than what I had put in. Here we go again. I had the worst holidays and could not find a replacement job. I delivered pizzas, worked side jobs, and went to a pawn shop in order to pay bills.

And then I had another Lighthouse Moment. My father encouraged me to try his career of financial coaching again. Although I had started this twice before, I saw no other choice.

My dad supported and coached me to immediate success. I was so driven to be somebody. I earned my $50,000 watch my first full year and my $100,000.00 income ring shortly thereafter. I was completely focused on building my business. I took three mortgages in the first five years, doing whatever I could to stay in business. My son's mom quit her job to care for our son and help administratively with the business. We struggled but made it work. We still had marital issues, but I figured if we could survive those stormy years, we could make it through anything.

My career continued growing as I opened new offices and promoted new partner offices. I found a balanced work life, coaching/managing my son's sports teams as he excelled in athletics. But the stress in my marriage intensified, and my wife separated from the business. I quit smoking, which caused us to grow further apart as I found being around her while she smoked difficult. Next came affair accusations, my 40th birthday, and three literal hurricanes in one year. It was the beginning of the most turbulent storm of my life.

Hurricane Wilma caused extensive damage to our home. We received a sizable insurance settlement in our joint account, and then, Boom, it was gone! My wife took the funds. It was the beginning of the end. After 20 years, our marriage crumbled. For the next two years, I tried everything I could to save it, but to no avail. I could not fix this! The following year, my wife filed for divorce and hired what I call a "man-hater" attorney who requested lifetime alimony.

There was no light in sight. Rocks and waves were everywhere. Why God??

My business began to crumble, I gained 30 lbs., and my son was affected terribly. The divorce was finalized with legal bills over $50k. And I accepted the alimony agreement. I took a second mortgage, got a contract to sell the house, and moved everything into storage after my son's mom moved away. I rented an apartment in Ponce Inlet (Daytona Beach) for five months. The plan was for my son to play football, graduate early, and start college. Then, the house sale fell through, and my business began crumbling as fast as the economy at the end of 2007.

To top it off, my son made some bad decisions and ended up in the hospital. I was at my office three hours away and traveled back as fast as I could. I stayed with him through serious issues that required prayer, counseling, and 24-hour support. I was losing everything again—my wife, house, mental health, business, and almost my son. I worked my business the best I could, but I refused to leave my son alone.

Where was my guiding light now? Was this the end? I needed to be strong for my son to get him through this! As I look back, I now recognize that it was me God was using for my son's Lighthouse Moment.

Our condominium was right next to the Big Red Lighthouse of Ponce Inlet. As the morning sun rose each day, I listened to the waves crash while taking walks on the beach. The walks to the lighthouse became my healing time. My son and I found a local church, worshiped at all services, prayed, went to counseling, and refocused on our new beginnings. He graduated, and we moved back to our house, which hadn't sold. My son decided not to go to college but began working different jobs as a nightclub bouncer and a restaurant server, as he essentially enjoyed two years of spring break.

I went through 50 first dates myself with online dating! Unable to afford alimony, business expenses, and a big house payment, I rented out our home and moved into a small duplex, waiting for the economy to recycle after hitting bottom. Now what? The house went into foreclosure, then modification. We moved back into the house and took in vagabond roommates just to help make ends meet. Where was my light in the darkness??

My family, business partners, and church family supported me through this turbulent time. I cried out to God! Again, Lord?

I prayed Psalm 23 through it all.

The Lord is my Shepherd, I shall not want...He leads me beside the still waters. He restores my soul... though I walk through the valley of the shadow of death, I WILL FEAR NO EVIL (!!!)...Your rod and Your staff, they comfort me (Psalm 23:1-2, 4 NKJV emphasis added).

After four years of wandering, followed by a short-lived relationship that ended abruptly, my son decided to go into the Navy Special Operations for four years and three deployments on aircraft carriers. I am very proud of his service and his resilience to become the man he is today. He recently got married, and they have started their own business. I am so proud of them. God is working in their lives daily.

During one of my sons' deployments, while alone after a rebound relationship, I met the woman of my prayers. She found me on Christian Mingle.

My 3-page profile and a 100% personality match made me stand out. We met at Starbucks, and sparks flew. The day after we met, she traveled far to visit her mom and family. We talked for ten days straight, sometimes all day and all night. We fell in love with each other's story and what we had learned through the trials we had been through.

She is now my "heartmate." We have very different personalities, but have the same heart goals for the Lord, family, and the rest of our journey here on earth. We married in three months and merged our lives together, serving the Lord and each other. We have been married for eleven years and serve in five ministries together, including United Men of Honor and Women World Leaders, which we founded, and Kerus Global Education with my Aunt Jennie. We have traveled and served on orphan care missions, led life groups, written books, and developed many ideas together. My business has grown, and we have walked hand in hand for God's kingdom. She reflects His light to me!!!

God uses people and situations to guide us through our storms of life. In every storm since childhood, I can see now that His light was always there. Sometimes, He shined His light directly, and sometimes indirectly as His light reflected through others.

Looking back at your own life, you might see your own examples of Lighthouse Moments you did not recognize before. But in retrospect, it may become crystal clear to you, too, that God was always there!!!

Jesus is THE lighthouse through any storm. And He is the light shining in the darkness that will safely lead you through. If it were not for His light, my ship would be no more. I am and am becoming the man God wants me to be because of the storms I have endured.

God also positions us to reflect His light and provide Lighthouse Moments for others. May you step out and be a lighthouse for your family, job or business, community, and world. Look to Him, follow His light, and then reflect it for others.

> *Jesus spoke to the people...and said, "I am the light of the world. If you follow me, you will not have to walk in darkness, because you will have the light that leads to life"* (John 8:12 NLT).

ASAAD FARAJ

Asaad Faraj, his wife, Lois, and their three wonderful children—Blake, Billy and Chloe—live in Alva, Florida. He has ownership of 40 plus Primerica Financial Services offices in 14 states that service over 100,000 clients.

Asaad's drive and success in business are fueled by his passion for reaching others for Christ. While serving as an elder at Oakland Church, Asaad is also a Board Member for Aramaic Broadcast Network, where he preaches the Gospel to the world's Arabic population through television. He also serves on the board for The Detroit Youth For Christ, an outreach ministry for urban kids in Detroit.

Asaad has been on 37 major international mission trips where he has shared the Gospel by speaking to and praying for tens of thousands of business leaders, pastors, and everyday citizens. He also speaks here in the U.S. through seminars for churches and businesses. He has a heart for the Great Commission, as evidenced by his giving and his going!

Asaad is the author of *Faith Over Finance*, which explores biblical financial principles and shows how to apply them. His book will teach you to implement godly strategies to overcome all financial challenges and thrive for your creator's glory.

Thriving Through the Storm

by Asaad Faraj

"Life isn't fair!"

I'm sure that's a thought we've all expressed in frustration at one time or another. Especially when everything in our lives is crumbling down at once, and we seemingly have nowhere to turn to for relief.

There was once a time in my life when storms and trials appeared to be too powerful for me to overcome. There I was, 22 years old, living in a one-bedroom apartment in Chicago with my girlfriend of three years. I was struggling financially and weighed down by the pressure of my college studies. On top of that, my girlfriend decided she wanted to date other guys—even while we were still living under the same roof. I couldn't bear to see other guys pick her up on dates while I was home, but I also could not afford to move out.

I was devastated. My heart was shattered. I was alone in Chicago with no family or friends, just acquaintances.

I just wanted it all to stop. The pain, the isolation, the burdens I carried. I didn't have a gun to pick up and point at my head, but I could certainly understand why someone in my state of mind would have considered doing something like that... just to make the misery end.

In that season of despair, I wish I understood spiritual truths—particularly the truth statement that I now keep posted on my phone calendar so I can view it every day: *The joy of the Lord is your strength* (Nehemiah 8:10 NLT).

When you allow someone or something to steal your joy and upset you, you'll find that your strength becomes depleted. That's because your strength comes from your joy, and true joy comes from the Lord.

While I was in Chicago, my family was back in Detroit, trying to keep their struggling grocery business afloat. My parents, both immigrants from the Middle East, moved to the United States in 1973 when I was very young. They started the grocery store shortly after coming to America and had run the business for 19 years.

Unfortunately, the store was going bankrupt, and their house was going into foreclosure. I felt hopeless and helpless, trapped in my own difficult situation and unable to help my parents. I suppose my storm really began to brew out of the financial problems facing my dad's business.

It wasn't fair. Mom and Dad were my heroes and had sacrificed so much to support our family. Twice, my father rescued us from oppressive governments as we escaped religious persecution. Twice, he gave up a high-paying career with executive benefits, including his own driver, so that his children could have a better, more secure future in America.

Dad worked faithfully at his store, Mondays through Saturdays from 9 a.m. to 9 p.m. and Sundays from 9 a.m. to 6 p.m. He was never able to even sit down at work. I have never met a harder worker in my life.

Initially, the store did well, and it meant the world to my family. I began working there on weekends when I was nine years old. My aunt and uncle—who were like second parents to me—were also partners in the business.

But, the neighborhood around my father's business had begun to deteriorate, and the store started to decline. By the time I was in high school, the writing was on the wall. It was just a matter of time before the store went under. Our family was scared to death.

I took this personally because I was the only son in our immigrant family. Nobody said I had to shoulder this burden, but that was the truth I created for myself.

My family had managed to escape from two Middle Eastern countries that were war-torn my entire childhood. So even with the hardships I was facing as a young adult in America, I felt incredibly grateful not to be living in either of those countries. At the same time, I felt indebted to my father. I was not guilted into feeling responsible for the welfare of my family and the business.

Even though I had zero knowledge about the 10 Commandments, I was unknowingly following the biblical command to honor my parents—which is the only one of the 10 Commandments that comes with a promise.

> *"Honor your father and mother. Then you will live a long, full life in the land the LORD your God is giving you"* (Exodus 20:12 NLT).

When I was a senior in high school, I knew I had to do something to support my family. I was 17 years old and felt like the decisions I was going to make next would determine the future for my parents, aunt, and uncle. One wrong move, and we might end up living in the street and eating out of garbage cans.

I remember the morning when I walked out of my bedroom and caught up with my father by the stairs before he left for work. I thought the only way out for my family was for me to get a college degree in a high-paying field.

I looked my father in the eyes, took a deep breath, and popped the big question: "Dad, is there any money saved for me to go to college?"

In the back of my mind, I knew my dad's business had done great in its beginning years despite the recent struggles. That knowledge filled me with hope that I was going to hear what I needed to hear. Perhaps he had set enough money aside for me to attend college! Everything hinged on his reply.

I remember what happened next like it was yesterday. Dad averted his gaze, looked down at his feet, and said, "What about student loans?"

Somehow, I knew those words hurt him 1,000 times worse than they hurt me. He felt totally ashamed, and I felt like my world had crashed and burned.

What should I do next? I saw only one road for me, and it had just imploded.

Even with that disappointment, I forged ahead anyway and researched college degrees. Eventually, I learned one of the highest-paying four-year degrees was electrical engineering. There was just one problem: I was the opposite of a stereotypical engineer. In fact, I never cared how anything worked or had a desire to learn how to fix anything. As a kid, when the chain fell off my bicycle, I would walk it three blocks to my friend's house and have him put it back on.

Nonetheless, I pursued engineering and entered a co-op program at Marquette University in Milwaukee, which required me to work for four months and then attend school for four months until graduation. While

I was working, I took courses at the local community college to graduate faster.

While in school, I also worked two or three jobs. At age 19, I met a girl and ended up living with her to save money on rent during my co-ops in Chicago. But college itself was just a means to an end. I hated what I was studying.

I did the best I could to prepare for what was coming and be in the best position possible. The trouble was, the closer I got to graduating, the faster our family business was deteriorating.

To make matters worse, I had just seven dollars left for food during my last three weeks in college. I had a credit card with a $5,000 limit, but I was determined to maintain a zero balance on it. I used that last seven dollars to buy small boxes of generic brand macaroni and cheese, and that's all I ate for my last three weeks.

Thankfully, I landed a job at a cellular phone engineering company in Chicago. Before I had gotten my first paycheck, my father and uncle asked me if I would charge $5,000 on my credit card to pay the electric bill at the grocery store so the food in the coolers wouldn't go bad and we could keep the doors open. I said yes, and that bought us three more weeks. But it was too late. Eventually, the store shelves were empty, and the business was done.

I guess my college graduation present was two mortgage payments that were not mine and helping to provide for two households in Detroit while supporting myself in Chicago. It didn't take long to figure out that an entry-level engineering salary was nowhere near enough. Oh, and I couldn't afford to move out of my apartment, even as my girlfriend was dating other guys.

Looking back through the lens of spiritual maturity, I would've advised myself then to recognize that God had brought me through other storms before.

The truth is, I was blessed simply because I was alive. I was born in Basra, Iraq, where the law of the land stated that each male had to serve in the military once they turned 18. If it wasn't for God's hand to direct my family to leave the country, that would've been my destiny.

I just happened to turn 18 the same month the Gulf War began. Remember that conflict? That was the first war you could watch on CNN. Iraq invaded Kuwait, prompting the United States to unleash its military might on the Iraqis through Operation Desert Storm. Much of the U.S. attack centered on the same region I was born in. They called it shock and awe!

As we watched the news, we saw the explosions of mortars and missiles lighting up our TV screen like a Fourth of July celebration and learned about the vast casualties inflicted on the Iraqi army. I could have been one of those dead soldiers if it wasn't for the goodness of God. He was at work, and I didn't even realize it. He was also at work through what happened next in my life.

Shortly after I began my new job, I was working out at the Chicago Health Club in Schaumburg when I met a guy who invited me to hear about a business opportunity and learn how to earn additional income. I said yes immediately, but I was afraid. It required meeting with people to help them with their finances and training agents to do the same. One minor issue: I was the most shy, quiet, and introverted person I knew, and I had no background or experience in the financial industry or knowledge about the programs, products, or concepts offered by the company.

I was in an impossible situation. Again, I had no knowledge of Bible verses, but I wish I had known this one.

> *Jesus looked at them intently and said, "Humanly speaking, it is impossible. But not with God. Everything is possible with God"* (Mark 10:27 NLT).

It was now December 1991. This new financial company I was working with part-time was having a convention in Fort Worth, Texas. At this point, I hadn't made any money with the company, and I was just starting my engineering job. It didn't make any logical sense for me to attend the convention, but I knew I had to go.

At the convention, I had a strange but amazing spiritual encounter. During the awards ceremony, a young man who was just 26 years old came up to accept several awards. He was doing extremely well in his business, and I admired him because he was close to my age. When it was his time to speak to the crowd, he pounded the podium and screamed these words: "JESUS CHRIST CHANGED MY LIFE FOREVER!"

At that very moment, I froze. Time stood still. I don't know how to explain it except to say that my spirit was awakened.

Mind you, I was raised in a Catholic household and went to church often, so I heard about Jesus every week. But I did not know the Bible. Our family prayed to God, but we did not know Him.

After hearing the young man's testimony, things changed rapidly for me. For the next two weeks, I would lay awake at night, tossing and turning as my spirit man hungered and thirsted for more. I had no idea how to quiet the restlessness I felt.

On December 28, 1991, I was invited to a pizza party on a Saturday night at my business mentor's apartment in a suburb of Chicago. I didn't expect anything "spiritual" to happen there, but what immediately transpired after I walked in the door would start a chain of events that would change my life for eternity.

A couple I had never met before walked up to me and asked me a riveting question. They asked, "If you died right now, do you know where you would spend all of eternity? Would it be heaven, or would it be hell?"

I remember having a desire to be sarcastic and respond with something like, "Well, nice to meet you, too." But I did not dare. Somehow, I recognized it as a holy moment. I responded with something like, "I'm not sure, but I think heaven."

They asked me, "Why?"

I responded with an uncertain tone with something like, "I guess it's because I've never murdered anybody or stolen anything of value."

Without hesitation, they asked me another question, "Would you like to know 100% for sure?"

Then I responded, "Wouldn't everybody?"

Without hesitation, they offered, "Come to our house tonight, sleep on our couch, and come to church with us in the morning!"

So, I did just that. I remember sitting through their church service as the pastor was preaching, thinking to myself how interesting and relevant the message was. It was something I had never experienced in church before.

Immediately after the service, the pastor approached me and asked if I wanted to have lunch with him and the couple who invited me. Of course, I said, "Yes!"

He then asked me if I knew what it meant to be a Christian. I thought that was an odd question since I had attended a Catholic junior high school, a Catholic high school, and a Catholic university. I thought I knew, but I didn't!

For the next few hours, he opened the Bible and began to unveil truths I never heard before. God's Word was healing to my soul and brought peace and joy into my heart.

Then, the pastor asked me if I wanted to say a prayer to make Jesus my Lord and Savior. I got on my knees, repeated a simple prayer, and then opened my eyes, suspecting something would be different, but I wasn't sure what.

Like my pastor says now, the old me was dead, and a new me lives instead. Biblically speaking, I became a new creation in Christ.

Around 30 hours later, I experienced the first evidence of this transformation. This all went down in the days before New Year's Eve. I had already made plans to go out with my friends to drink and womanize at the bars in downtown Chicago.

I remember so clearly ordering a beer at a bar and just having a few sips. I remember looking at the women around me, but what used to be attractive to me was not anymore. I called it an early night, as I felt like a fish out of water.

When I was with the pastor a few days before, he had given me a Bible as a gift. My family grew up having a Bible in our house, but we just never opened it. But now, I developed a thirst and hunger for God's Word through reading the Bible. It was different than any other book I had ever read. It was nourishment to my soul and my spirit. This was more evidence that my life had changed.

> *Do not waste time arguing over godless ideas and old wives' tales. Instead, train yourself to be godly. "Physical training is good, but training for godliness is much better, promising benefits in this life and in the life to come." This is a trustworthy saying, and everyone should accept it. This is why we work hard and continue to struggle, for our hope is in the living God, who is the Savior of all people and particularly of all believers* (1 Timothy 4:7-10 NLT).

My challenges did not disappear overnight, but God clearly had begun to move! One of my business mentors, who had just become a brother in Christ to me, allowed me to sleep in his home. God placed a grace on me for my side business to work long hours during the night and on weekends and earn the income necessary to help my parents. The best way to describe what has happened to me since can be summed up in this scripture, Ephesians 3:20 (NLT): *Now all glory to God, who is able, through his mighty power at work within us, to accomplish infinitely more than we might ask or think.*

For anyone who is going through a difficult season and navigating a storm of despair, I would give you this advice: Pray for Jesus to be the center of your relationships and the one who thinks through your spirit and speaks through your lips. Ask for Him to be the guide of all your steps and the protector of all you love. Most of all, allow Him to be your provider and chief counsel for all decisions. Amen!

NAVIGATING YOUR PAST

by Asaad Faraj

There is an often-used statement in the world of investments: "Past performance is no guarantee of future results." There's a reason this "warning label" is included in every document that discusses the performance of a particular fund or strategy. Because when it comes to financial markets, circumstances can change—sometimes quickly and unexpectedly.

When it comes to believers, the same warning label should apply. But instead, it should say: "Past failures provide no indication or limitation for future successes."

One of my favorite sayings is that God does not call the qualified; He qualifies the called!

If you ever feel unqualified for a task, reflect on the story of Gideon!

> So Israel was reduced to starvation by the Midianites. Then the Israelites cried out to the LORD for help... The angel of the LORD appeared to him and said, "Mighty hero, the LORD is with you!"... "But Lord," Gideon replied, "how can I rescue Israel? My clan is the weakest in the whole tribe of Manasseh, and I am the least in my entire family!" (Judges 6:6, 12, 15 NLT).

God saw Gideon differently than Gideon saw himself! Gideon saw himself as insignificant, full of fear, the runt of the litter in the poorest family in a community reduced down to nothing!!

In other words, Gideon told God, "You could not have picked a lesser man to call a mighty man of valor!!"

That's the funny part...look at 6:12 again. God did NOT say Gideon was a mighty man of valor. He said, "The Lord is with you!"

Have you ever felt incapable of doing what God called you to do?

Extend both of your arms to the side. Your left hand represents how you see yourself. Your right is how God sees you. And your body now makes a cross, which represents that what Jesus has done for you reconciles the two views!

Anyone plus God is more than capable!

> *The LORD said to him, "I will be with you. And you will destroy the Midianites as if you were fighting against one man"* (Judges 6:16 NLT).

God does not suggest we forget about our past failures, He commands us to! God does not pour new wine into old wineskins.

> *"Forget the former things; do not dwell on the past. See, I am doing a new thing! Now it springs up; do you not perceive it? I am making a way in the wilderness and streams in the wasteland"* (Isaiah 43:18-19 NIV).

Dwelling on things of the past is the comparison of running through the airport with two large suitcases and a carry-on. Give your past to the Lord, and no longer carry the burdens He will take from you.

When we allow God to redeem our past failures and believe all that He says about us, He rewards us with a testimony to share with others. Instead of focusing on what we have messed up, let's focus on God's resolution in our life. Use His forgiveness, grace, and mercy as fuel to launch into the future He has prepared for you as you shine a light on His glory.

. . . .

MICHAEL JENKINS

Michael Jenkins calls Jupiter, Florida, home. He has been a devoted husband to Julie for over 27 years and is a loving father of three wonderful children: Sarah (23), Emily (21), and Matthew (17). His life is a testament to the power of faith, family, and hard work.

With a heart dedicated to serving the Lord, Mike is a devout Christian who radiates love for Jesus in every aspect of his life. Professionally, he serves with Hope Media Group and WayFM, a national contemporary Christian music and media ministry. As a Senior Vice President and General Manager of the radio station in West Palm Beach, he combines his passion for media and ministry. He works daily with business owners, bridging the gap between faith and entrepreneurship.

Mike's hobbies include running, working out, keeping a pristine yard, and relaxing to a Tampa Bay Buccaneers game with his dogs Ginger and Marlo by his side.

As you read his chapter, you will recognize that Mike's insights into leadership, faith, and perseverance offer a guiding light to those facing the challenges of life's tempests.

To connect, contact him at mjenkins@hopemediagroup.com

THE LIGHT
IN THE STORM

by Michael Jenkins

"I think it's time for you to go."

The words hung in the air for just a moment, and then the weight of them hit me like a punch in the stomach. I had known things were not going well with my new boss (understatement of the year), but I didn't think they were going that bad.

The casualness of the moment caught me off guard. I had friends and colleagues who had lost jobs before, but I never imagined what it would be like when it happened to me. I always imagined being "let go" would be somewhat more dramatic. It wasn't. I was allowed to resign and keep some shred of dignity, but my manager's nonchalant manner as he changed my life and career seemed surreal.

Only two years earlier, one of my company vice presidents had approached me with an offer to become the Director of Sales for this television station in Little Rock, Arkansas. At the time, I lived in Tampa with my wife Julie and our three kids: Sarah, Emily, and Matthew. Florida was my home. I grew up there. My family was there. My wife's family was there. Our entire community—from church to friends and our kids' friends—was there. Needless to say, it was not an easy decision to leave what I knew, a place where we were all comfortable, to move across the country. However, this was an incredible opportunity. I had worked toward this goal and invested countless hours learning the business of television sales and how to be a good leader in the industry.

So, we said yes to the job and the journey.

We shared the "exciting" news with our kids—only to see the tears flow. My wife and I took them to my daughter's favorite restaurant to tell them we would be leaving. We had moved back to Florida from Ohio only two years earlier, and I had promised them that would be our final move. After telling them we would be moving again, my 8-year-old daughter proclaimed I had lied to her. The thought of those words still stings. Both daughters broke down in tears, ran to the van with my wife following behind (in tears), and I was left with our preschool-aged son. I asked him how he was doing and if he was okay. His main concern was if we were going to bring the dog. I love boys! So much for the family's excitement about my new opportunity.

Less than a week later, I was on the road from the Sunshine State and the beach to Arkansas, The Natural State. It was a new adventure. My family had finally started to warm to the idea of a new home. We researched schools, neighborhoods, and activities. My wife and I had met in Tulsa, Oklahoma, so we were familiar with that part of the country.

I was leaving a great job as the local sales manager in charge of new business development for the CBS station in Tampa. I knew I would miss my incredible boss, great staff, and other valued business relationships built on mutual respect. But, at the same time, I was excited to step into this new leadership role and felt confident I had the expertise my new station needed.

One of my primary reasons for taking the job in Little Rock was Larry, my new station manager. I highly respected this new boss, a former news anchor with a skill set far different than mine. He readily shared that sales was not his strong point, and he had complete confidence in me as I took over a sales department that needed a fresh start and new leadership. The previous manager had only been in the position for a year and had unexpectedly died. The sales department was in shambles, and I was hired to bring much-needed leadership. Larry was a true man of God. He read the Bible in his office daily and kept it in plain sight. He wasn't afraid to quote scripture. We shared the same faith and values. He was also very good at his job. He hired good people and let them do their jobs. I respect that a lot.

Larry was so good at his job that the company promoted him to a new market less than a year later. The person who had recruited me to be an integral member of his staff and who respected me, gave me the latitude to do my job, and trusted me was now gone. What followed began one of the most turbulent storms of my life.

It took almost a year for the company to hire a new general manager. He came from a very small market, but his station had done well. Still, his reputation in the industry wasn't great. He was reputed to be difficult to work with—and that proved to be true. Within the first week, he made it clear his approach to management was very different from mine. For example, he quickly determined that my long-tenured local sales manager wasn't a good fit for the job and needed to go. He then "suggested" that I reorganize my staff because the sales department needed more "hands-on" management, which surprised me as we were exceeding our goals. Seeking to control the salespeople's schedules, he even put a bell at the entrance to the sales area. Each morning, he would ring the bell to signal that all the salespeople were to leave the office to go on calls.

As I look back now, it was during this point in my career that I began to feel like the disciples on the boat in Matthew, chapter 14. Jesus had sent them out on the lake. As they were rowing across, a storm began to rock their boat. How many times has this happened to you? You get away from Jesus, and suddenly, your boat gets rocked. The story gets even better. Jesus saw they were floundering, and He began to walk on the water toward them. Matthew 14:25 says, *Shortly before dawn, Jesus went out to them, walking on the lake. Verse 26 continues, When the disciples saw him walking on the lake, they were terrified. "It's a ghost," they said and cried out in fear* (Matthew 14:25-26 NIV). So not only were they terrified, but the only source of salvation was walking toward them—and they thought He was a ghost. I can certainly identify. I was sent out from a place of comfort with the best intentions and hopes. A storm came up in the form of my new boss, and the seas got very rough. I wasn't as mature in my faith and didn't realize at the time that Jesus had sent me out for a specific purpose and was not going to forsake me. The entire time I was dealing with my issues, He was walking toward me.

As my time with my new boss continued, my boat (and my world) rocked and crashed through the waves. I had no idea where my situation was headed, but it looked dark, and I felt like a rocky shore was waiting for me. I had moved my family halfway across the country, away from our support system, and put my kids in a school system that was in disarray and where they knew no one, all for a job that was now heading south. Much like the disciples in the story from the gospels, I thought I could row my way out of my storm. Mark records that Jesus *saw the disciples straining at the oars* (Mark 6:48 NIV). I felt like I was straining at the oars, too! Nothing I seemed to do was good enough.

Then things went from bad to worse.

My father has always been an anchor in my life. Growing up, he was my hero, but the issues he dealt with were severe. A serious heart condition, times of abject poverty, and, in his later years, being a full-time caregiver to my mom were just some of the storms he navigated. As I was dealing with my work-related storm that threatened so many other areas of my life, I got a call from my sister that my dad was facing his own disturbance: he was in the hospital, and his health was rapidly failing. For some context, this wasn't the first time I had heard this, but this time seemed different. There was a more serious tone than ever before. My anchor was starting to give way. My dad's health continued to deteriorate, and a few days later, my sister called again, this time saying my dad wanted to talk to me. His voice was labored and weak. As I write this over ten years later, I can hear every word he said to me as if we spoke just a few minutes ago. He told me he loved me and that he was proud of me. My dad went to heaven shortly after. I read once that losing your parents makes you feel like a ship without a rudder. That was my feeling that day and in the days to follow.

As we prepared to return to Florida for my dad's funeral, I called my boss to tell him what had happened. He said he was very sorry and wanted to know how long we would be gone. I told him I was unsure but that we would try to be back in a few days. I could hear the irritation in his voice, which would become a constant refrain in my head during our trip home to bury my dad. Not only had I lost my remaining parent, I felt my career slipping away.

While we were at my dad's house in the days following his passing, I felt the amazing love of family. Friends I had not spoken to in years reached out after reading my Facebook post about my father. It was like coming up for air and being able to breathe for the first time in months. My dad and mom valued family above all else. No visit could end without a "Please come back soon. We love you. Be safe." The feeling that my priorities were off-center was becoming readily apparent.

After my father's funeral, I returned to work to receive condolences from friends and co-workers. I felt supported by almost everyone. It was a short-lived period of calm in an otherwise turbulent time. Within a week, Michael, my boss, was challenging everything I was doing. It seemed more intense than before and almost like he was punishing me for taking four days off to bury my dad. The pressure was unrelenting.

Less than three weeks later, my storm shifted to a full-fledged hurricane with my boss's eight words: "I think it's time for you to go." As I stated earlier, I felt it was coming but was still stunned.

I remember the station's business manager, who was the witness to my dismissal, asking if I was alright. It seemed like an absurd question, but he didn't know what else to say. I asked if I could finish out the week. The answer was no. Not only that, I couldn't finish out the day. I was allowed to make the announcement of my "resignation" effective immediately to the staff and then was to leave. I could come back on the weekend to clean out my office. In a daze, I walked to my office to get my keys, and then I stood beside my boss to deliver the news to my staff. I wish I could remember what I said. It certainly wasn't thought out or delivered well.

Then it was over. Just like that, our two-year journey that had started with such promise was over.

Our home sat at the top of a hill that looked down into our neighborhood. In the fall, it was an amazing view as the leaves changed. I drove home that day, uncertain how to tell my wife and kids what had happened. I was a failure. I wondered if that's how Peter felt when he stepped out of the boat to walk to Jesus on the lake when a moment of fear sent him plunging beneath the waves. Did he feel like a failure? He knew he was walking to JESUS. The same Jesus he had watched perform miracles and raise people from the dead. And yet, Peter still doubted. Jesus told him to "Come" (Matthew 14:29 NIV), so Peter stepped out of the boat and did what no other man has done before or since—he walked on the water! After a few steps, his human side came back with full force, and he went from being the "walking on the water guy" to needing a lifeguard! Jesus' next words had to sting. *"You of little faith. Why did you doubt?"* (Matthew 14: 31 NIV). OUCH! That was me. A Ye of Little Faith, Doubter, Total Failure, who had to face his family without a plan and no idea where the next paycheck was coming from.

I was the sole source of income for my family and had been for over a decade. And, like many men, a huge part of my identity was tied to my career. For over 25 years, I had worked to climb the corporate ladder. My suits were bought with the goal of impressing my managers. I never said no to work projects, business trips, dinners away from home, drinks with colleagues or co-workers—all in the name of climbing the ladder. I didn't realize it, but I was navigating away from God and to a job that could only provide a paycheck.

If you have ever lived through a hurricane, as I have in South Florida, you know that the clearest sky you will ever see is right after the storm passes. Your world can get rocked, and then one ray of sunshine appears. Then another, and then another. Soon, you have the most brilliant blue sky and bright sunlight. Not to be all meteorological, but hurricanes pull all the moisture out of the atmosphere, leading to a clear sky. My ray of sunshine was waiting for me inside the door of our home. My wife, Julie, has been my safe harbor since we started dating. It's her nature to be calm, cool, and collected (most of the time). The day I lost my job, she was not only my port in the storm, but also my fortress. She didn't flinch when I told her. There was no worry in her voice as we discussed the next steps. It may have been there, but it didn't show. We discussed how to tell the kids that we would probably have to move again. She was amazing (and still is as I write this 11 years later). The next rays of sunshine were our kids—Sarah, Emily, and Matthew. As upset as they had been to leave our home in Tampa, now they were calm, cool, and collected as we told them we might have to move again.

Slowly but surely, God was moving my faith, removing my pride, and redefining who I was and who I wanted to be. This storm had started months before with my failure in judgment to move us as the waves loomed large, my failure to provide what I thought my company was asking of me, and my failure to live up to the expectations someone else had of the position I was in. Notice the use of the word MY in the previous sentence. That's (reasonably) intentional on my part because, at that point, everything was about me. But the truth is that the most accurate things ever said about any of us are spoken by God. In my storm, I was navigating the waters of pride, isolation, and ignorance. God was trying to tell me the same things that Julie told me that faithful day. I am loved, I matter, and I am so much more than a job description or title on a business card.

Not only was God moving me and my heart, but He was literally moving us as a family. The loss in Little Rock became a win in West Palm. Just a few weeks later, God provided an amazing job opportunity for me back in the Sunshine State. We rented a house about a mile from the beach, found a wonderful church family, and, finally, a place to call home. All the storms weren't over, but, like Peter, I had stepped out in faith, struggled in fear, and found the hand to save me by putting mine in the Savior's.

It's been 11 years since God navigated us through that storm of life. The following years have not always been easy, but I now know that my worth is not just in a paycheck. After working at another television station job, I was called to work in full-time ministry with a Christian radio group. I would have never guessed that my career would take this turn. But when I turned it over to God and said, "Here I am. Send me." (Isaiah 6:8 NIV), boy did He ever. I now get to serve alongside some of the most incredible people I have ever known and have developed friendships I will have for the rest of my life. Each day, I know that what I do will serve His kingdom and not just a group of shareholders.

In addition, the three little rays of sunshine are not so little anymore. They are superstars. I recently had a conversation about resilience with my now-adult daughter, who lives about six hours away. I always worried about how moving our kids so much affected them. In my mind, I worried they might not have roots that others who grew up in one place might have. My daughter told me our experiences taught her she could live anywhere and be okay. They taught her how to make friends and fit in. I couldn't be more proud of all of them.

Finally, as I think about this storm and how it helped shape the last decade of my life, I have to give credit to my wife, Julie. She was my first mate, who pointed out the lighthouse—God, who is always present to provide safety and direction even on the darkest night. When you are lost in a storm, find a crew who will lead you to the light. We are not made to go through life alone. Your storm, while it may feel like it, is never unique. Someone else has gone through it and survived. God saw it coming long before you did, and He is shining brightly, ready to help you navigate your storm.

ALLEN L. THORNE

Allen L. Thorne is an accredited Safety Manager in corporate construction and a developing Recovery Pastor in South Florida.

Allen and his beloved wife, Stacy Jo, live in Stuart, Florida, with their daughter Jocelynne, their pampered pups, Leia and Lilo, and their Calico cat, Tinkerbell.

Aside from building their professional and ministerial lives together, Allen and Stacy enjoy live music and theater productions, spending time with local friends, and traveling to visit family in Georgia, South Carolina, and Ohio.

With over ten years of sobriety, Allen has learned to appreciate the Lord's divine "teachable moments" that have enhanced his ministerial, personal, and professional life.

Allen has recently earned his degree in Ministerial Leadership and currently follows the Lord's calling in writing and revising *Reviving Recovery: Unbound. Unbound* combines the Word and Spirit in a paradigmatic shift to lead participants to a transformational Spirit-led deliverance.

Jesus' Truth transformed Allen's "yes" into his *"truth"* identity. He lives passionately to share Christ's freedom from a pliable heart for the Lord, an openness to His divine perspective, and an embrace of new or renewed beliefs so the Spirit's renewing of our hearts and minds may transform us!

FROM AGNOSTIC TO AUTHORITY

by Allen L. Thorne

The difference between cognitive knowledge and experiential belief cannot be overstated. The former merely offers behavioral modification opportunities, while the latter is the root of all thoughts and actions. Thus, to transform from the inside out, our core beliefs must shift experientially before our thoughts and actions alter. For example, perhaps we experienced abuse throughout our lives from which we harbor lie-based beliefs. Revealing such abuse in conventional counseling and being told that it's not our fault, while true, is only adding information. It doesn't affect the experiential belief carried from the abusive experience. We can say "It's not my fault" all we want, but until we encounter a "lie-altering/truth-providing" experience, our beliefs, emotions, and ensuing actions remain the same. Hence, our authentic beliefs either advance or hinder our healing progression. The following tells the tale of a lost boy found for God's purposes and the paradigm shift that ensued from victory amid the same divinely created man.

To begin, I was raised in a somewhat dysfunctional Ohioan home. As a three-tour Vietnam veteran, my father was a rage-consumed alcoholic. Conversely, my mother modeled sacrificial love as she consistently placed others before herself. Amid Dad's violence, she was my loving haven.

I cannot say that our lives together were all bad. However, in reflection, from unavoidable late-night arguments through his physical homestead destruction to his alcohol-drenched tirades, these formidable years are when the fear took hold of my young, impressionable soul.

Further, we lived in the open country, where I had plenty of room to escape the fearful household. I spent most of my time alone roaming the countryside fields or aimlessly riding back roads on lonesome adventures amid the strip mines, train tracks, and cow fields. Fortunately, I had quite an imagination and entertained myself as I *"isolated"* in the great wide open.

Additionally, not long after my brother Michael arrived, my parents decided we would begin attending church. At eight years old, I did not know what to expect since I had no concept of God or the man they called Jesus. All I knew was that church cut into my countryside adventure/escape time. Sunday school was awkward. Because I *"isolated"* most of the time, I was not interested in making friends. The lessons confused me, and the love and kindness I heard about appeared only in that book. However, Sundays and Wednesdays began to improve when I shifted to a classroom with a more relatable husband-and-wife teaching team. Dad worked with the husband, and our families began meeting for home Bible studies and fellowship. I became friends with their son and daughter, and things were looking up everywhere except home. Despite newly learned information and Dad's appearance when others were around, there was minimal to no change when it was just us at home. He ruled the house with an iron fist, thus fear ensued.

Moreover, my grandmother losing her cancer battle didn't help Dad's mindset. Just before Mamaw's passing, Dad took me aside and insisted that I accept Jesus as my Savior. There wasn't much explanation, just a command to profess my submission to Jesus that Sunday. Hence, full of confusion,

I said the prayer with the other kids. The daunting red room heard me fall behind the teacher's pace as I stammered through the prescribed recitation. I wondered if God had heard my words and what they all meant. Nonetheless, it was a good day because, at least for a little while, Dad was pleased that I did what I was told. Something shifted that day because I began to feel like I belonged at church. I gained a few AWANA buddies, and our families enjoyed substantial time together. Son-shine rays peered through the darkness, and all appeared well until Mamaw passed away.

Mamaw held our family together. She had a way with Dad that no one else had. As a witness to his mournful sobbing over her body, Mom asserted that it wouldn't be long until he was gone. At nine years old, I didn't understand. Nevertheless, she was right. Not long after our grand matriarch's passing, Dad's adulterous affair was revealed, and he decided he was leaving home in pursuit of my supposedly compassionate Sunday school teacher. The woman who stood with her husband each Sunday and welcomed our family into their home for biblical fellowship was having an affair with my father. What?!? How could this be? She was my friend. More than that, she was Mom's friend! She represented the Truth; until she swiftly became the liar's portrait. Two people's deceptive domestic deconstruction over carnal desires selfishly shifted seven other lives forever, and as far as I could determine, it all developed from the church. How could God let this happen? Why was my newfound belonging place's Son-shone brilliance blotted out by the liar's deception?

In addition, why would the church's so-called safe haven offer no consolation for my distressed mother? Amid such emphatic betrayal, I witnessed Mom's intensified sorrow and mourned over the heinous fact that the one person who was so *"there"* for my baby brother and me was so unfathomably devastated. John's Gospel records Jesus' affirmation that *"The thief comes only to steal and kill and destroy; I have come that they may* have life and have it to the full" (John 10:10 NIV). The *truth* of my faith's infancy stages crumbled beneath deceptive lies—thus magnifying the prior while the latter's would-be truth diminished with the rest of organized religion's experiential lies. Scorned by the church and blinded by the pain of what God allowed to happen, we never returned to the church.

Meanwhile, amid the ruins, satan's lies were the only believable perceptions at the time. My soul's adversary convinced me that I was not worthy of belonging; I was not worthy of my daddy's love and affection; I, as his first-born son, was not good enough for him to stay and raise me, or even raise me from afar; we were not worthy of his support. Moreso, however, satan's greatest lie that I carried higher than the rest for the following three decades was that God does not care about me and was never there for me. That's fine! I don't need God!

Further, my father fully abandoned us in 1980, leaving Mom with an old, dilapidated house and no support whatsoever for his now *three* sons. Between Mom's absolute best effort and our extended family's strong assistance, we never missed a meal. However, I do recall wondering from where it may come several times. Hence, the aforementioned lies, combined with blatant paternal abandonment and a poverty mindset, established the standard for my foreseeable future. In a complete absence of faith, satan aimed to keep me bound in shortsighted victimhood's ensuing despair for as long as he could.

> *The enemy pursues me, he crushes me to the ground; he makes me dwell in the darkness like those long dead. So, my spirit grows faint within me; my heart within me is dismayed* (Psalm 143:3-4 NIV).

Moreover, I would be remiss not to recognize Mom's sacrificial loving life laid down for her boys. In such desperate times, she gave us everything she had and then some. She never gave up, and she loved all three of us despite the challenges we presented. Even though we never returned to any church, her faith saw us through life's inevitable challenges. Her tutorial love and affection knew no boundaries; I am eternally grateful for that. I love you, Mom! Thank you.

Nevertheless, even as "there" as Mom was for me, a fear-ridden lie-based belief structure overruled her loving attempts to rescue my well-being as a deeply wounded child. Thus, my feeble attempts to subdue the fearful pain underneath began. In a skewed belief structure that denounced anything greater than myself, self-medication began early via food. Likewise, I found solace in that crazy rock and roll music, which was soon accompanied by pornography and the like. Whatever entertained my escape was worth pursuing *more*. However, regardless of how much *"more"* became, the unaddressed pain underneath always required that much more. The shrieking pain pierced my soul and marred my spirit; thus, life's challenges spiraled downward as addiction took hold of me too early.

Additionally, my search for belonging led to sports. I found my place as an over-achieving powerlifter. Such seemed like a win-win-win for me; for a time, I felt like I belonged in the gym, the extreme physicality burned off the calories from eating my feelings, and my achievements gained Dad's attention. He came around when I gave him something to see. However, as stated, it only seemed like a winning situation. Truthfully, even though I enjoyed powerlifting, I only played ball because it gained Dad's attention. He came to all of my games, which helped us build a new relationship over time. However, my sense of belonging was short-lived until I began drinking with the team and other schoolmates. *"It's about time that you started drinking with us,"* was acceptance's call to the new *"more"* idol that introduced me to my other side via false courage and shallow confidence.

Furthermore, through the next twenty-seven years, alcoholic agnosticism's slippery slope ignited darker addictions to cover the torment produced by the ignored pain beneath. Because I believed I was not worthy of love and belonging, I idolized numb fun over the potential true love of the one girl who loved me more than I'd ever know. In hindsight, she was divinely hand-picked for me. However, amid the victim mentality, I was incapable of receiving or reciprocating her love. Hence, after an inconsistent long-term relationship, we went our separate ways in the early nineties. Likewise, such a detrimental mindset fueled an unrelenting series of hard falls, each one seemingly landing me deeper in the pit than the last.

Moreover, through several drug and intoxicated driving charges, a geographical escape, one failed drug-induced marriage, and a near-death overdose experience, the love of my dear mother never failed. Likewise, relations with Dad improved year over year as he consistently bailed me out more than he should have. Even as grateful as I was for his financial help through these dismal times, our fear, guilt, and shame fueled consistent failure in taking down the ten-ton elephant in the room. Perhaps someday, courage will prevail to slaughter the problematic pachyderm.

Further, in the early 2000s, even as the party life was in full swing, I was wearing thin. Self-sufficiency was between falling short and failing miserably. I was working with a faith-filled project manager who was led to tell me about Jesus after a late night out. I was nearing the end of myself and willing to consider new perspectives. Likewise, I respected our working and personal relationship; thus, I listened attentively to the testimony of Christ's love, grace, and mercy. Similarly, he assured me that God, without a doubt, had heard my prayer in 1978 and was waiting for me to come back His way.

> *Let the wicked forsake their ways and the unrighteous their thoughts. Let them turn to the Lord, and He will have mercy on them, and to our God, for He will freely pardon* (Isaiah 55:7 NIV).

Additionally, to gain my full attention, God provided persistent, glorious authority glimpses. He first taught me to pray and believe *for* healing when He saw Mom through heart surgery that no one thought she would survive. He then reunited me with the girl who loved me so many years before. Even as I was still an addicted mess, He knew what He was doing, and He would see our unlikely family through several valleys. He declares, *"As the heavens are higher than the earth, so are My ways higher than your ways and My thoughts than your thoughts"* (Isaiah 55:9 NIV). Likewise, as I faced jail time over another intoxicated driving charge, my knees came down, and I, of my own volition, received Christ as my Savior. Only a few days later, I sat in the courtroom amid a confident prosecutor and a frustrated attorney when the Son-shine ray showed through the room's only small window and landed in front of me. A peace fell over me as God assured me He had already handled my situation. Moments later, all charges were dropped.

This blessing came from God—whom I had distanced myself from all my life. In His divinely powerful authority, He extended life, sent love, and provided freedom. Life, love, and freedom were great ways to start a journey I never planned to take. Paul affirms in Galatians, *It is for freedom that Christ has set us free. Stand firm then, and do not be burdened again by the yoke of slavery* (Galatians 5:1 NIV). I'd like to say that life was smooth sailing from there. However, even as gratefully astonished as I was, I was new in my faith and learning through an immensely stubborn heart still bound by debilitating lie-based beliefs. Hence, as much as I desired to *stand firm,* I was only sprinkling a little Jesus on my otherwise intoxicated existence. Fortunately, He is a patient Father and did not fail me in the falling. Instead, He gave me endless opportunities to live and learn from a plethora of face-plant failures over the next several years.

As swiftly as Stacy and I were married, addiction just as swiftly nearly ended our lives together. Nevertheless, the Lord did not reunite us only to have a hapless addiction destroy His plan. Thus, since 2013, transformational challenges ensued through stringent Christ-centered recovery. Sanctification requires sobriety! In blurred vision's absence, His clear vision taught me to see with the eyes of my heart as He introduced and extinguished the lies underneath that bound me for a lifetime. Through His progressive process and with His perfect love, God smothered fearful lies of not being good enough to be loved or belong. Over time, His perfect love drove out all fear and empowered me to receive His forgiveness *earnestly,* allowing me to forgive myself. For as I, in Christ, am entirely forgiven by my Creator, who am I not to forgive myself? Such genuine forgiveness empowers all who freely receive to freely distribute authentic forgiveness. Forgiveness changes everything!

Additionally, the Lord's Word commands love and forgiveness from the Father through Jesus Christ. Matthew's Gospel depicts Jesus' perspective when He affirms, *"For if you forgive other people when they sin against you, your heavenly Father will also forgive you. But if you do not forgive others their sins, your Father will not forgive your sins"* (Matthew 6:14-15 NIV). Similarly, Mark's Gospel records Jesus' greatest two commandments: *Love the Lord your God with all your heart and with all your soul and with all your mind and with all your strength...[and] love your neighbor as yourself* (Mark 12:30-31 NIV). Likewise, John's Gospel depicts love as Christ's disciples' pinnacle attribute as Jesus asserts, *"By this everyone will know that you are my disciples, if you love one another"* (John 13:35 NIV). Further, Jesus affirms His God-given authority in His pre-ascension proclamation that *"All authority in heaven and on earth has been given to me"* (Matthew 28:18 NIV). Luke's Gospel acknowledges the distribution of Jesus' authority to His disciples as He declares, *"I have given you authority to trample on snakes and scorpions and to overcome all the power of the enemy; nothing will harm you"* (Luke 10:19 NIV). Therefore, as a disciple under His authority, He calls me to operate in His authority as I love and forgive others. Some time ago, as I sat befuddled by why I was still so angry after much recovery progress, God told me I had to forgive my father. Even as our loving relationship appeared all right and I had journaled and discussed forgiveness with mentors, the Lord noted that I had not authentically forgiven my father directly. Wow! Sometimes, revelation is just that simple. It was time to go elephant hunting.

My arrival at Dad's Ohio home was shrouded in mystery until I revealed why I had come. I told him that through several years of recovery, the Lord had revealed fear's roots amid my childhood's violence and abandonment. The room's tension elevated as tears welled in our eyes, and he said, *"I know."*

In Christ's confident authority, I informed him that I did not come to condemn him but to forgive him entirely. I placed my hand on his shoulder, looked him in the eyes, and said, *"Dad, I forgive you."*

At that moment, the Holy Spirit swept the room of all tension. During hours of continued conversation, my father disclosed that our talk revealed more about how to handle emotional challenges with his father than he had received in twenty-plus years of counseling. Such goes to prove that the Holy Spirit can do in a moment what we could miss over a lifetime. In His authority, *we overcame all the enemy's power.* The elephant is dead! Praise God!

Even as I spent most of my life burdened by satan's lies, blame, resentment, and ensuing addictions, I was never out of my Savior's reach.

Even as I denied and blasphemed my Creator's holy name, He never stopped pursuing me. He was only waiting for me to turn around.

Even as I fell for the enemy's lies and allowed him to nearly kill and destroy me, Jesus stayed near, knowing I'd be back to receive His abundant life (John 10:10)!

Even as the enemy sought to harm me, God turned death's mess around to life's message for such a time as this (Genesis 50:20).

Likewise, even as I was tangled in deceit's web, God demonstrated His love for me. While I was a sinner still, Christ died for me (Romans 5:8)! He drew me in and justified me in His righteousness so that I could be saved from God's wrath (Romans 5:9).

Because God *is* truth, He traded the world's lies for His truth as He experientially shifted my belief structure! He says I am worthy of His love and belong to Him. He called me out of futile agnostic bondage and put me under His authority so I could operate in His Spirit to go forth and present His freedom to those yet wandering.

And if He could do it for me, He can do it for you, too.

Praise Him!

Navigating Through Unforgiveness

by Ken A. Hobbs II

The storm begins brewing when someone you know hurts you. If you don't release it as God instructs, the clouds of bitterness, anger, and pain roll in and darken the sky with unforgiveness. The poison of an unforgiving heart makes you a prisoner of your past and opens the door to alienate you from the full and rich fellowship God desires for you. Forgiveness is difficult for our flesh to grasp, which is why it's so vital in these situations for us to draw close to God. When we harbor unforgiveness, It becomes more challenging to see the sunlight appear. It gets deeply hidden within the storm because you're hiding yourself inside the impending darkness of a begrudging attitude and unforgiving spirit.

There is no doubt about it: people have the potential to hurt us in ongoing ways. They hurt us with ego, resentment, jealousy, arguments, gossip, and more. We are told in God's Word to reconcile with those who have something against us. We can't allow the control of hurt, anger, or resentment to keep us from forgiveness. Holding on to pain caused by the heart of unforgiveness prevents us from making things right with others. As issues such as health challenges, isolation, or broken fellowship with God rise inside you from the storm of unforgiveness, clouds of ominous gloom hang about your person. The storm can rage so viciously that you often can't even pinpoint where you became trapped. You become accustomed to living in the black clouds. You retreat from happiness because the imminent storm consumes your behavior. Forgiving someone or the offense that wronged you may seem impossible, but it isn't. Because with God, all things are possible. He is always there to give us the strength we need to follow His will.

> *For if you forgive others their trespasses, your heavenly Father will also forgive you, but if you do not forgive others their trespasses, neither will your Father forgive your trespasses* (Matthew 6:14-15 ESV).

> *I can do all things through him who strengthens me* (Philippians 4:13 ESV).

If you wholeheartedly ask God to give you the strength to forgive someone, He will do it. And when you seek forgiveness from someone else, it may take asking that person several times. But you must start somewhere. Even when you feel someone has wronged you, begin by praying and searching your own heart. Then humble yourself and request their forgiveness for your part in the issue. If they do not wish to be part of the process, you may find your thoughts drifting back to your own anger and hurt—this is where the storm could keep you trapped inside. Don't allow it to. Release your unforgiveness to God, or you may not see the sunrays appear ever again.

As a Man of Honor, it is imperative to release pride and forgive as your heavenly Father has forgiven you. No one is perfect. We each make mistakes daily, and it can take time to realize our mistakes and change them. This could be the case for the other person who has wronged you. When someone does not accept your humble heart requesting forgiveness, allow God to handle them. Navigating through forgiveness is a natural process we must approach with the proper heart attitude. That is what God expects from us. Think of it as building a muscle of forgiveness that must be strengthened by doing the right thing each time you use it. It is right to condition this muscle by following the Word of God and doing as He tells us: *Be kind to one another, tenderhearted, forgiving one another, as God in Christ forgave you* (Ephesians 4:32 ESV).

The Bible tells us the number one reason we should forgive others is simply because God forgave us! Because He loves us so much, He is ready to forgive us when we sincerely ask Him for forgiveness. The more we draw "closer to God," the stronger we will become when it comes to forgiving in a world full of hurtful people. No one is perfect, not even us. That is why we need a Savior. How many times have we hurt God? If you're honest, you will admit you fall short every day. We all make mistakes because none of us are perfect human beings. Yet, we expect God to forgive us.

God knows it is not easy to live in our fleshly bodies where we must interact daily with other imperfect people. Yet God gave us scriptures that tell us to tolerate the weakness of others.

> *Tolerate the weakness of those in the family of faith, forgiving one another in the same way you have been graciously forgiven by Jesus Christ. If you find fault with someone, release this same gift of forgiveness to them* (Colossians 3:13 TPT).

Let's not try to think about settling the score or being right. God will avenge; it's His place, in His time, to do so. You are a child of the living God; He loves you more than you could comprehend. He also loves all His creation. Is the person who wronged you one of His creations, too?

He doesn't take the offense of one of His sons or daughters lightly. He will apply His justice where He will. But it is up to God as to when and where and how.

> Beloved, don't be obsessed with taking revenge, but leave that to God's righteous justice. For the scriptures say: "If you don't take justice in your own hands, I will release justice for you," says the Lord (Romans 12:19 TPT).

Forgive as God has forgiven you, and know that He does not want you tossed about inside a storm of unforgiveness. Forgive the situation. Forgive the person. Even if your feelings and emotions don't align with your decision, ask God for His help and keep seeking a heart of forgiveness until they do. This is all an act of obedience. When you can follow what God's Word says by navigating this storm, you will be released from the dark clouds of unforgiveness into a bright sun-soaked sky of freedom

. . . .

CHRISTIAN MAYBERRY

Christian Mayberry is undoubtedly one of the most outgoing and charismatic young men you could ever meet. He lives in Oklahoma, where, ten years ago, he was the victim of a devastating ATV accident and suffered a severe traumatic brain injury. The driver of the ATV was drunk and fled the scene while leaving Christian unconscious in a ditch for over three hours before getting help. During that time, Christian died and went to heaven, where the Lord told him he was going to have a platform to help bring thousands to Him!

For nearly a year, Christian was paralyzed on his left side and continued to face untold challenges in his journey toward recovery. While he could have become bitter and full of hate, Christian chose to forgive those who were involved. Because of that decision, he has been touching lives for the last ten years!

Christian shares his testimony and the power of love and forgiveness in churches, schools, and literally everywhere he goes. And he could not love it more! He has a unique ability to make people feel loved and happy! One of the ways he does this is by giving them a great big smile and a Christian Mayberry hug!

How I Navigated My Storm to Victory

by Christian Mayberry

On September 1, 2013, I was just a normal 16-year-old boy starting my junior year in high school. I played football and had just started my first job. But on that day, my "normal" life was forever changed.

A teammate from football invited me to the river to ride four-wheelers. I ended up on a four-wheeler with my teammate's mom, who was drunk. She crashed the vehicle, and I suffered a traumatic brain injury (TBI). She had no injuries. But she fled instead of getting me immediate help, leaving me in a ditch for three hours before calling for help. During that time, I died and went to heaven—visualize a place where everything was perfect, peaceful, and happy. Right there before me was the King of kings and Lord of lords! He told me He loves me and then asked if I would like a hug as He opened His arms and embraced me! There are truly no words to describe this. All I can say is Jesus is love, pure love! He put His arms around me. He told me that I would one day have a platform and bring thousands to Him. While there, I saw three of my grandparents, whom I had never met. And I met my sister Vanessa. She opened her arms wide as she ran up to me, saying, "Christian!"

Over three hours later, my broken body arrived at the hospital. My mom was out of the country with my sister Mia, who had taken her to Cancun to celebrate Mom's birthday on their very first mother-daughter trip.

My only injury was a TBI, but that was enough to change life as I knew it. It was touch and go for weeks; no one knew if I would survive. The doctors had to remove a piece of skull the size of a grapefruit on both sides of my head to relieve the pressure on my brain to save my life.

After three or four weeks, I started to open my eyes. They tell me I would only stare. I couldn't speak a word. As excited as my family was that I had opened my eyes, the reality hit hard that it really was as if I were still asleep.

After a month in the hospital, the doctors told my parents there was nothing more they could do. My parents were in shock and disbelief as they were instructed that my next step was to go to a rehabilitation facility. With an enormous amount of stress, my parents found and decided on a facility. On October 3, I left St. John's Hospital in Tulsa, Oklahoma, by ambulance, headed for the Children's Center in Bethany, Oklahoma, to begin treatment.

On October 4, 2013, my rehab started. In reality, however, I wasn't aware of anything. My entire left side was paralyzed. My eyes were open, but they tell me it was as if I wasn't present. I remained there for the next 2 1/2 months. The head doctor told my mom it would literally take a miracle to get me back, which wasn't the first time she heard that. The doctor had no problem stating this in my room in front of me. Thank goodness I don't remember it. But my mom pointed to me and said, "You remember the name Christian Mayberry—because we are going to get our boy back!"

Mom never let another doctor, nurse, or visitor say anything negative in front of me again!

Four years later, the coolest thing happened when we returned to the children's hospital. I was able to consciously meet several of the nurses and staff who had taken care of me—including the doctor who had told Mom it would take a miracle to get me back. It was such an amazing day! They couldn't believe I was the same young man who had left there four years earlier! I reminded the doctor what she had told Mom. She remembered that well. She knew this was an absolute miracle!

After 2 1/2 months in Bethany, we were told there was nothing more that could be done for me at that facility. I left in about the same shape I was in when I arrived.

We returned to Tulsa to have the bone plates surgically put back in both sides of my head. But the shunt they placed in my head got infected, causing me to be very sick. Several weeks after being in the hospital, I had a massive seizure. In an instant, doctors and nurses filled my room. Mom said it was incredibly scary— one of the most frightening times during my recovery. The next morning, the doctors told my parents they had come very close to losing me all over again—BUT GOD!!

My mom and dad stayed with me 24/7. Dad always insisted that Mom and Grandma—if she was in town—go to the Hospitality House to get some sleep. This incredible facility takes in families from out of town who are caring for their critically injured or sick loved ones at the hospital. One night, my dad had a heart attack while trying to sleep in my room. This turned out to be the first of three heart attacks, which were later followed by three strokes. The third stroke and the third heart attack were massive, putting him in a nursing home in March 2016. Later, he contracted COVID-19 twice and suffered two broken hips. We lost my dad, John, on August 8, 2022.

Before I got hurt, my dad had been in excellent health. He exercised and ate right. And as long as he could be, he was right there with me every step of my recovery, encouraging and cheering me on. He always reminded me that I can do all things through Christ who strengthens me (Philippians 4:13). I miss him so much every day! My dad taught me that giving up wasn't an option—that no matter how challenging a situation, with God, all things are possible! (Matthew 19:26). My dad never met a stranger he didn't like. Mom tells me I'm the same exact way.

Finally, the infection left my body, and once again, it was time to leave the hospital for another rehab. Mom and Dad were told on a Friday that they had to have a place to take me by the following Monday when I would be discharged—that was the very weekend my dad had his first heart attack. So, Mom was in the middle of this deadline to get me out of the hospital when suddenly, she had to deal with Dad being in the hospital as well. She searched high and low while door after door slammed shut.

But her perseverance paid off. A rehabilitation facility in Tulsa finally accepted me. By that time, it had been six months since I was hurt. I was just starting to say a few words but was still paralyzed on my entire left side, fed through a peg tube, and wearing diapers. During the next six weeks, rehabilitation did little to help me as I was barely responsive. Soon, the same question arose: Where is he going next? Years later, my mom told me she spent this time constantly on the phone and the computer, frantically searching. With no other rehab possibilities, my parents were given just two options—either take me to a nursing home or take me home. They wanted neither, insisting I receive further rehabilitation. But there were no viable facilities in Oklahoma, and my insurance wouldn't pay for me to go out of state, so the options remained to take me home or to a nursing home. So, with my mom kicking, screaming, and praying every step of the way, I ended up in an awful situation in a nursing home in Fort Smith, Arkansas.

My mom vowed I would be out of that nursing home and in proper rehab within a week. Unfortunately, I was there for six months. Without proper rehabilitative treatment, I was just wasting away.

My parents still never left my side. Dad slept every night in a chair or on the floor of my room, and Mom remained with me every day. She spent most of her time trying to get me out of the nursing home. She would take a chair into the bathroom so I couldn't hear her, doing her best not to let me hear her on the phone as she begged, fought, cried, or did whatever else it took. One day, she reached out to our State Representative, John Bennett. She told him what was happening, that our Medicaid wouldn't pay for me to go out of state. That was a turning point.

State Representative Bennet came to meet me. Sometime later, he told us that when he left the nursing home and got in his car, the Lord told him to do whatever it would take to get me out of that nursing home! The Lord told him I would have a platform and bring thousands to Him. That is exactly what the Lord had told me while I was in heaven!

Bennet took action. He, along with Senator Mark Allen, paid a visit to Medicaid. At the same time, Mandy McLaughlin Pursell, an investigative reporter who had become interested in my story, reached out to Julie Weintraub in Tampa, whose foundation is Hands Across The Bay. Julie is still my amazing advocate! She has blessed me so!! After Medicaid got a visit from the State Representative and the Senator and a phone call from Julie Weintraub, Mom received a phone call from the head of Medicaid saying that they would pay for me to go wherever Mom wanted to take me for as long as I needed to be there. And they would pay for my medical flight! Wow, this was such a victory! With our many family, friends, and huge Facebook family, literally thousands of people were praying for this victory—and it came through. Thank you, Jesus!!! I can't tell you what a win this was! Finally, I was getting out of the awful nursing home and getting real rehab—for as long as I needed it! God is so good!!

I can never express my gratitude for the joy, love, and blessings that our Facebook family has brought to our family. The same goes for Representative Bennett, Senator Allen, and Julie Weintraub! I owe so much to these three! They became like family to me. John is now my pastor at Lee Creek Assembly of God. You talk about coming full circle; how amazing is it that the Lord told him I would have a platform and bring thousands to Him, and then years later, I would have the privilege of attending this man's church and giving my testimony in front of his congregation. Now that's God! And to my Facebook followers, I can't imagine this journey without all your love, support, and, most of all, prayers! Mom would always read me your inspiring comments and beautiful prayers. It would and still does put a great big smile on my face. I thank you from the bottom of my heart! I love each and every one of you!

In September 2014, one year after I was hurt, I began treatment at the Florida Institute for Neurologic Rehabilitation in the small town of Wachula, Florida. It was there that I started the painful process of walking. At first, I had to have help to even try to stand. But in time and with a lot of pain, discouragement, screaming, and, of course, prayer, the steps started becoming easier and easier. And I improved in other areas, too. Soon, I was doing things like getting back on my cell phone, brushing my teeth, and eating by myself—all things they said I would never do. BUT GOD! God had been with me from the day I got hurt, and He wasn't done yet! With God's help and a lot of determination, I was finally taking many steps! After about two and a half years post-accident, I could, cautiously and slowly, walk on my own. Again, the doctors had initially told my parents this would most likely never happen. BUT GOD!! I knew I could do all things through Christ, who gave me strength! We knew, and everyone watching knew this was the miracle we had been praying for! I was finally up and on my feet!! God had given me the miracle of saving my life, and now He was giving me so much more!

I wanted to tell the world what the Lord had done. I wanted to share about the miracle of my healing, and I also wanted everyone to know how I had died that night and Jesus Himself held me in His arms! God fulfilled my longing.

While I was in Wachula, I met two pastors who both invited me to give my testimony in their churches. Wow—me, sharing my testimony in front of an entire congregation? I was thrilled! I was going to be able to give all the glory to God publicly! Until that time, I would give my testimony to anyone who would listen, anywhere, anytime! Now, God had opened the door for me to speak in churches! Would this be my platform that would bring thousands to Christ? This was so exciting! I gave my testimony in both of the churches. I never knew I could love anything so much. I knew the enemy tried to take me out, but my God had saved me to do this—to show people, even in their darkest times, that if they would trust God, they too could see their miracle!

Nearly one year after arriving in Florida, we headed home to Oklahoma. I had arrived on a medical flight on a gurney, but now I was leaving behind my wheelchair and flying home on a commercial flight. It was August 6, 2015, and I hadn't been home in nearly two years—since September 1, 2013. I experienced so many emotions going home. It should have been nothing but joy and excitement, but honestly, there was a great deal of dread as well. All my friends had graduated high school and moved on. I was 16 years old when I left, just starting my junior year and playing football. Now everything had changed. The job I had to work so hard to get was gone, and high school was no more. The driver's license I had been about to get now wouldn't happen. When I got home, reality hit; it came crashing down on my head. Nothing was the same. I will tell you, depression hit me hard! There were many times I would just break down, yelling and screaming, "Why did I ever come back from heaven?" But God! With God, all things are possible!

My parents helped me understand that I had to forgive the woman who crashed that night and left me alone, dying in the ditch. At first, this was very hard, but I knew I had to. I knew if God was going to continue to help me, I had to forgive her and everyone else who was there that night. Only God could help me do this. And He did! I knew He had forgiven me for all my sins and wouldn't forgive me if I didn't forgive those who sinned against me. I want you to know that if you have unforgiveness in your heart, pray to understand the true power of forgiveness. There is nothing like the freedom that comes when you give it all to Jesus. That is absolutely the key to getting through your storm—and life in general!

My parents also taught me the importance of speaking life into every situation. *The tongue has the power of life and death* (Proverbs 18:21 NIV). Trust me, there were many times I had to work on this, and I still do.

I also learned I needed to praise God like never before. Praising Him is another key. At times, this can be so easy, but not always. We can't just praise Him when things are good. We also need to praise Him during our darkest times. I learned this would pull me through faster than anything. For me, there is nothing like praising the Father in song. I can't encourage you enough: the darker your storm, the more you need to praise God and speak life into every part of your situation. There will be many times you don't feel like doing this! Ask God to help you. Soon, it will start to flow; it will become easy! Something that has truly helped me in this journey is to do my best to be grateful for everything! This is so very powerful!

I have said over and over that if I could take all of this back and just erase everything that happened, I wouldn't do it! Yes, there were definitely times in my meltdowns when I wanted to go back to the life I once had. But I truly wouldn't. God has been so good to me! He has blessed me in too many ways to count! I've danced with the stars in Tampa, sailed the Caribbean as the Inspiration Ambassador with Buddy Cruise, and worked with Jered Allen as he is creating a documentary on my story. They tell me I've touched and encouraged so many lives! Yes, my life has completely changed, but there are so many ways it has changed for the better!

If you are in the middle of a storm, I want to encourage you to do your best to stay as positive as you can! Do your best to love and appreciate everybody. Let everyone around you know how grateful you are for them. I want each of you to know that I love you, and I hope to meet you one day. Thank you for reading my story!

God bless you!

JEFF CALENBERG

Jeff is most grateful for the amount of quality time he has been able to invest in his family and the fruit in others that God has used him to produce (John 15:5).

Living in Manhattan for 25 years and working in the fashion industry, Jeff has appeared in print and TV ads for a wide variety of clients, including *Vogue, Vanity Fair, GQ,* Christian Dior, Ralph Lauren/ Polo, Peugeot, Acura, Sony, Bloomingdales, Brooks Brothers, Neiman Marcus, LL Bean, Lands' End, etc.

Jeff is also an accomplished fashion photographer who has created images for many clients, including international ad campaigns for Burberry Children's wear.

Jeff enjoys connecting people to each other and to Jesus and has started several outreach groups for young professionals, such as Models for Christ.com, Impact NY. Living in the Palm Beach area since 2010, Jeff currently leads the ministry Palm Beach for Christ and the dynamic Palm Beach Men's Group. PB4Christ.org

Jeff is currently writing a book that shares his journey around the globe and into the world of fashion. The book highlights radical stories of life-saving transformation within the fashion industry. More is available at JeffC.com

Jeff is an avid mariner who enjoys sailing, surfing, and all other water sports.

Navigating Storms from Yacht to Runway: The Strength of the Cord

by Jeff Calenberg

A person standing alone can be attacked and defeated, but two can stand back-to-back and conquer. Three are even better, for a triple-braided cord is not easily broken (Ecclesiastes 4:12 NLT).

It was 4 o'clock in the morning, and I was awakened abruptly as our sailboat was thrown sideways by a giant wave. Dishes, pots and pans, and anything not tied down were tossed about our 50-foot aluminum sailing yacht. The cockpit was filled with water, which was flowing down to the main cabin.

We were deep into our journey of sailing across the South Pacific—the adventure I had dreamed of since graduating from college two years earlier. But this part was more like a nightmare. For the next three days, we were battered by a storm that delivered heavy 15-foot seas and steady winds of 30 knots.

During one of my predawn watches at the helm, the waves were like large black shadows rising up behind the boat. It was a challenge to safely steer our tiny vessel under sail down each wave as it crested. As we ran downwind, the mainsail and boom would skim on the water, with the boat rolling to the side when we reached the bottom of a wave. It was like steering my surfboard down a wave.

We were navigating with a sextant, which depends on accurate sun and star sites. But, the magnitude of this storm blocked any opportunity to gather those measurements.

With no GPS, we were now using "dead reckoning"—estimating our position by carefully recording compass heading and speed and factoring in nautical chart information such as currents and depths.

After three days of weathering the storm, our estimated position told us we would see our first island of Fiji sometime the following day. At midnight on September 18th, I had just finished my 2-hour shift at the helm when we glanced at the depth sounder out of curiosity.

A depth of 2000 feet would be typical well off the coast of Fiji, but to our surprise, we were getting a reading of 60 feet. Suddenly, it was clear that we were much closer to the islands than calculated. Immediately, we turned the boat 180°, steering away from whatever might be in front of us.

Over the next four hours, all five of us worked together as a team, zig-zagging our yacht back and forth through the darkness, searching for deeper waters.

The situation worsened as the readings reached dangerous levels again. We turned in another direction, but soon, we hit a depth of only 12 feet. We could not see or hear breaking white water, but the imminent danger of shipwreck was gripping each of us with fear.

Then, the depth sounder began reading five feet, inches away from the depth of our hull. We immediately threw the engine in reverse at full speed, causing a wave to crash over the transom and flood into the main cabin. The depth increased for a few minutes. But then it happened. The depth sounder registered 0.0 feet for 30 seconds. We braced for impact with the reef, knowing that gashes in our hull would fill the boat with water and pin us to the reef within seconds.

But we did not hit anything. Perhaps the keel had slipped through a deeper section of the reef.

This was clearly a miracle. My three fellow crew members and the boat owner could not acknowledge that. But they all knew of my faith.

The best part of this story was yet to come.

As daylight filled the sky, giving us clarity that several towering islands of Fiji were surrounding us, we estimated our position on the chart. Physically and emotionally exhausted, we took turns resting below deck.

In the early afternoon, we spotted a huge white cross on the hillside of the island to our left. After some research, I found that our nautical chart noted a 60-foot tall white cross on the side of an island 30 miles to the north of our estimated position.

Yes, it was that cross that gave us our exact position. The amazing and obvious hand of God had saved us from that reef and then used the cross to keep us from being lost.

I will never forget the storm that so nearly shipwrecked us. Sailing over 5,000 miles of open ocean taught me a lot about the importance of teamwork. With God's help, we eventually sailed the boat safely to its home in Sydney Harbor.

Over the next three years, my quest to explore the world after graduating from college continued. With my trusty backpack and hard-earned personal savings, I embarked on unforgettable adventures through Australia, New Zealand, Japan, Korea, Taiwan, China, Thailand, Malaysia, Singapore, India, Egypt, Israel, Greece and Italy.

I faced many physical, financial, and emotional challenges and was stretched to adapt to a wide assortment of diverse cultures. This variety of experiences became a valuable well of life lessons that would help guide me in the challenges ahead.

When I landed in Italy, I spent my first night in my sleeping bag in a cornfield on the side of a highway. Little did I know that the comfort of my travel would soon change dramatically.

After making my way to Milan, Italy, I sensed a change coming. I planned to stop there on my way into Europe and explore the potential to earn some extra cash through modeling. God began stirring something in me, and I felt a mix of excitement and uncertainty.

Sixteen days later, after knocking on several agencies' doors with beginner photos I carried in my backpack, I found myself represented by a top modeling agency in Milan and attending castings at Armani, Versace, and other famous design houses. The one agency gave me a short two-week window to prove my value in this renowned market for men's fashion. Just one day before that time was up, I was booked to do two high-paying TV commercials—this was a huge confirmation that God was opening this new door for me.

That's when I entered a new storm with extremely challenging sea conditions: I was soon surrounded by others following their lusts and passions without boundaries.

Was God really calling me into this industry? How could I maintain my faith and values in this environment?

After visiting the typical "Pensione" hotel where most models would rent a room, I could see that this communal living with 25 other women models would not be a wise decision. I prayed for help, and God soon provided a fully furnished, inexpensive, shared apartment with a private bedroom and no doors of temptation.

Still, I realized I could not stand alone in this new atmosphere filled with enticement. So, I prayed for others who would encourage, challenge, and even hold me accountable. A few weeks later, Rod Caulkins arrived from New York. Luigi, the head of the agency, boasted of Rod's "star" status—working with GQ magazine, top NYC photographers, and having potential movie contracts. In contrast, I was a low-level walk-on addition to the agency's roster of talent.

To my surprise, I soon discovered Rod was a believer. He was the answer to my prayer. We began to meet and pray together daily, discussing our journey and challenges. We needed each other to be strong.

We began to sense the need to reach out to other models who did not have a relationship with Jesus and were struggling as they battled the insecurities that this industry cultivates. As a model, you may go on 25 potential job castings a month and never be confirmed for one job, causing frustration, disappointment, and a hit to your self-esteem. Loneliness can also set in due to the challenges of being in a foreign country. Those unfamiliar with the industry are likely unaware that models on the glossy pages of fashion magazines often struggle this way.

Previously, I had created a small handout leaflet for fellow surfers that explained the gospel message of Jesus' love and salvation in a way that any surfer could relate to. So now I suggested we print something like that for models to give out as we interacted with our peers.

I created the layout for our pamphlets, leaving a blank space at the very end. Then, I designed a logo, printing "Models for Christ" in bold letters underneath. At that time, I had no idea how God would use these steps of faith to touch many lives in the years ahead.

When I was on a photo shoot or at the agency, I would put my little pamphlet down somewhere in the open, and almost every time, struck with curiosity, another model would start to read it. The captivating front photo was a magazine cover featuring a model couple whose faces were blurred out. The inside caption read: "Guess who's on the cover of GQ this month? You are!" Rod also wrote another pamphlet titled "Dear Model." They both spoke of the fulfillment, true peace, and contentment that can only be found through a personal relationship with Jesus. Many opportunities to share our faith were now open to us.

Appearing in a cigarette campaign was perhaps the most lucrative opportunity you could land as a male model. One of my friends had earned well over 1 million dollars through his work on an international cigarette campaign. Rod and I both made it clear to our agent that we would not be available to audition for advertisements promoting cigarettes or alcohol. Perhaps I would have been dropped by the agency for this decision, but since I was standing with Rod, "the star," I was allowed to remain.

Establishing these clear and decisive choices was awkward but helped the agency avoid pressuring us with lucrative jobs in this area. We were determined to live up to what God had called us to. The word of our boundaries spread to other models and opened up many conversations about why we would avoid this gold mine of opportunity.

One evening, Rod insisted that we go to a movie that had just opened in Italy. With Italian subtitles, it told the story of an Olympic athlete who had stood for his convictions under intense pressure from his country leaders and teammates. As we walked out of the movie *Chariots of Fire,* we were filled with a renewed sense of God's call in our lives.

After four months, Rod's agency in New York City summoned him back, but our commitment to shine for Christ in our industry held strong.

God provided in every way during my nearly two years in Milan. I never rose to the status Rod had with our agency, but God supplied a steady stream of bookings. Italian and German magazine tear sheets started to fill my portfolio, and occasionally, I worked with some of the great photographers in the industry. I could see God was using me in this unusual place and allowing me a respectable level of success. I eventually completed my around-the-world dream by traveling through most of Western Europe. When I was on photo shoots, the client paid for first class. But on my own adventures, I returned to my youth hostel and backpack travel style.

I had risen from a walk-in vagabond to a relatively successful model. But I began to think and pray about moving into the ultimate arena of challenge—New York City. NYC is perhaps the most competitive market in the world. It was never my ambition to pursue having my face plastered across magazine pages or TV screens, but I felt God was guiding my path in this direction and showing me a mission of need and opportunity. I now had a great portfolio, but there was no guarantee that any NYC agency would accept me. So, I began praying for God's wisdom, favor, protection, and direction. After interviewing with the top four agencies and receiving a good response, I prayed about and evaluated my options and decided to sign with Elite.

One day, I was in my booking agent's office when I heard a female voice in the hallway saying, "Praise God." I rushed out and introduced myself to Laura Krauss. She was a successful cover model who had worked in Paris for two years and had just moved to NYC. After she realized that I was not just another aggressive admirer, we began to share our journey of faith with each other. She had also told the agency that she would not endorse cigarettes, alcohol, or pose for suggestive images. There had been talk among the agents that we should meet since we were both such an anomaly. God had provided me again with a like-minded friend who also wanted to honor God and was willing to make the tough decisions.

A few weeks later, Laura and I attended a photo exhibit at a nightclub in Manhattan. A top photographer was showcasing his images, of which Laura was one of the featured models. As we exited the club, a young man was face down on the pavement, passed out. While others made a wide path around him, Laura and I stopped and tried to rouse him. His eyelids only fluttered. Then, I recognized he was a model I had briefly met. We found his address on a piece of paper in his pocket. He lived about 40 blocks north of our location. We hailed a cab, and two others helped us hoist him to his feet and into the back seat. The three of us rode uptown, the young man leaning his head heavily on my shoulder. The air was thick with the smell

NAVIGATING YOUR STORMS

of alcohol. Laura and I struggled to get out of the cab with 190 pounds of dead weight. Somehow, we dragged him into his apartment and put him on the bed. And we left a Bible next to him. We both realized this guy was just a small example of how empty many of our peers were without Christ. We decided to do something about it.

Laura had a large living room in her apartment on the Upper West Side. "Let's meet there and invite other people. We can't be the only Christians around," she said.

I showed Laura a tattered copy of the pamphlet I had written in Milan. It was a "no brainer"; we would call ourselves Models for Christ. We would have our first meeting at Laura's apartment in one month. In the meantime, we began to pass the word to those who might be interested. We were thinking mainly of other models, but we also included photographers, agents, makeup artists, designers, buyers, and anyone else who was open. Seven people showed up at the first meeting. A makeup artist named Maria Macheda attended and shared that she had been praying for ten years for this group to exist. We spoke of our challenges, prayed together, and had a short Bible study. Six months later, 30 people attended. And then 40. God was using Models for Christ as a light in the darkness, attracting believers and seekers as well. Young people were hungry to connect with peers who wanted to honor God but were challenged by the pressures and temptations of life in Manhattan.

When attendees began spilling out of Laura's living room into the hallway, we rented a large studio at the Joffrey Ballet. Our mission was to provide a place where people in our industry could gather and feel challenged yet comfortable. There were some skeptics and cynics. Some guys came from Wall Street just to meet girls. Yet some who came to scoff eventually stayed to pray and believe.

Our group grew in numbers, and we sought ways to "do the gospel," not just talk about it. We started a month-long clothing drive. The 10 top modeling agencies allowed us to put collection boxes in their reception areas along with an invitation for others to join our group at the final event.

On Thanksgiving Day at the Bowery Mission, many first-timers came out to help us. We handed out bags of clothing and food that our teams of four delivered to needy families around New York City. One agency booker arrived to help and said, "I was so wrong about you people. I thought you were just Bible Thumpers." That was only the beginning of what God began and what He continues to do today through Models for Christ.

FYI...

Eventually, Laura and I married and now have two wonderful children.

MFC continues to grow and today has satellite groups in Milan, Paris, London, Sydney, and many other locations around the world. I serve on the board. ModelsForChrist.com

MFC gave birth to an additional target ministry reaching all young professionals: Impact. After five years of growth to four other US cities, we renamed it Priority Associates NYC, which was a new division of Campus Crusade/Cru.

As I look back at all God has done in my life, whether I was sailing through the storms of the South Pacific or navigating the dangerous waters of the modeling industry, I have learned one important lesson.

I would have been shipwrecked many times over were it not for others who stood alongside me—encouraging, challenging, and keeping me focused on the path and mission God had for me.

So my question to you is this:

Who is standing with you today in the storms you face?

Ask God to provide the cords of others to strengthen you for your calling. I know that God will answer your prayer.

> *"I say to you: Ask and it will be given to you; seek and you will find; knock and the door will be opened to you"* (Luke 11:9 NIV).

Navigate with God's Word

by Asaad Faraj

> *And the words of the Lord are flawless, like silver purified in a crucible, like gold refined seven times* (Psalm 12:6 NIV).

How many times have you asked yourself that age-old question, "What must I do to know God?" Be encouraged. The answer is not like a Sadie Hawkins dance, where you wait for the invitation. For the believers, God is waiting on us!

Come close to God, and God will come close to you. Wash your hands, you sinners; purify your hearts, for your loyalty is divided between God and the world (James 4:8 NLT).

But how can you know if God and Jesus are for you if you don't know them?

In the beginning the Word already existed. The Word was with God, and the WORD WAS GOD. He existed in the beginning with God. God created everything through him, and nothing was created except through him. The Word gave life to everything that was created, and his life brought light to everyone (John 1:1-4 NLT, emphasis added).

So the WORD BECAME HUMAN and made his home among us. He was full of unfailing love and faithfulness And we have seen his glory, the glory of the Father's one and only Son (John 1:14 NLT, emphasis added).

KNOW GOD'S WORD

God's Word is how we do battle.

Put on salvation as your helmet, and take the sword of the Spirit, which is the word of God (Ephesians 6:17 NLT).

Jesus used the Word of God to fight off the devil in the wilderness. Even Jesus put on the armor of God and used the sword of the Spirit.

> *Jesus answered, "It is written :'Man shall not live by bread alone, but by every word that proceeds from the mouth of God'"* (Matthew 4:4 NIV).

> *Jesus answered him, "It is also written: 'Do not put the Lord your God to the test.'"* (Matthew 4:7 NIV)

> *Jesus said to him, "...it is written, 'Worship the Lord your God, and serve Him only'"* (Matthew 4:10 NLT).

> *Then the devil left him, and angels came and attended Him.* (Matthew 4:11 NIV).

Notice the keywords "It is written." Stay in the Word and practice it each day.

God's Word is a double-edged sword used for correction and teaching.

For the word of God is alive and powerful. It is sharper than the sharpest two-edged sword, cutting between soul and spirit, between joint and marrow. It exposes our innermost thoughts and desires (Hebrews 4:12 NLT).

MEDITATING ON GOD'S WORD CAUSES US TO PROSPER

Oh, the joys of those who do not
follow the advice of the wicked,
or stand around with sinners,
or join in with mockers.
But they delight in the law of the LORD,
meditating on it day and night.
They are like trees planted along the riverbank,
bearing fruit each season.
Their leaves never wither,
and they prosper in all they do.
(Psalm 1:1-3 NLT)

GOD'S WORD HEALS PEOPLE

I've been blessed to travel the world and do evangelical mission outreaches. I had the honor of visiting Haiti after the worst earthquake struck in 2010. I remember looking at the Haitian neighborhoods—the houses were nothing more than four sticks and a tarp with no floors or walls. The people were hungry and thirsty, seemingly hopeless and overwhelmed with despair.

However, I witnessed a powerful contrast between those who went to the churches for worship and sermons and those who didn't. Both lived in the same conditions. However, the believers looked alive and healthy—because God's Word heals!

> *My child, pay attention to what I say.*
> *Listen carefully to my words.*
> *Don't lose sight of them.*
> *Let them penetrate deep into your heart,*
> *for they bring life to those who find them,*
> *and healing to their whole body.*
> *Guard your heart above all else,*
> *for it determines the course of your life.*
> (Proverbs 4:20-23 NLT).

God's Word helps us navigate life. As we come to know God's Word, we will come to know God and be poised to receive all He has prepared for us.

. . . .

TYLER GRAEFF

Tyler Graeff was born and raised in Lancaster, Pennsylvania, and currently lives in Davie, Florida. Tyler has been married to his wife Lauren for three years; they both serve in full-time addictions ministry at the Teen Challenge Southeast Region Davie Women's Home. Both Tyler and Lauren are passionate about seeing those trapped in the clutches of addiction or other life-controlling issues come into a relationship with God. Having graduated from the program of Teen Challenge themselves, they know firsthand the pain and devastation a lifestyle of addiction produces.

Outside of serving in Teen Challenge, Tyler has a passion for evangelism and street ministry. He is a credentialed minister with the Assemblies of God. Through partnerships with other ministries or organizing local outreaches, he loves sharing the gospel on the streets in some of the neediest neighborhoods. On their off time, you may find Tyler and Lauren at the beach, going on adventures, or spending time with their friends and family. Through the years, Tyler has been blessed to share his story and the hope that's found in Jesus!

For more information about the Teen Challenge program, please visit www.teenchallenge.cc

Trusting God's Presence Through the Storm

by Tyler Graeff

I woke up kneeling on a dirty motel room floor, my head nearly buried in a worn-out mattress. My glasses were creating a barrier between my face and the musty fabric—the only thing keeping me from suffocating. I took a deep gasp of breath as I lifted my head.

Two weeks earlier, I had been evicted from an apartment and was forced to move into the motel where I could pay by the week.

As I came to my senses, I began to look around the room. Surrounding me were empty drug baggies, liquor bottles, and other trash. Fortunately, I was able to find my phone under the bed. It was almost dead. After seeing the date on the screen, I was shocked to learn that I had blacked out for an entire week on Xanax. My wallet had been stolen along with a few possessions that were of minimal value. The people I was partying with and buying drugs from had robbed me and left me for dead. As the reality of my situation began to set in, so did opiate withdrawal. *When the sun rose, God provided a scorching east wind, and the sun blazed on Jonah's head so that he grew faint. He wanted to die, and said, "It would be better for me to die than to live"* (Jonah 4:8 NIV).

This defining moment of my life in 2012 was my wake-up call. I finally accepted that I had a drug and alcohol problem. A few hours later, I made it to detox and entered a 30-day program to get sober. I wish I could tell you that, from that point, I was able to maintain lasting sobriety and never looked back. But that was far from the case.

A vicious cycle of relapse, mental health struggles, and brokenness consumed my life for an additional three years.

Although my situation seemed bleak and hopeless, I was not alone. God was with me in the midst of my storm and was waiting for me to call upon His name. *"When you pass through the waters, I will be with you; and when you pass through the rivers, they will not sweep over you. When you walk through the fire, you will not be burned; the flames will not set you ablaze"* (Isaiah 43:2 NIV).

When I was growing up, I didn't plan on becoming an alcoholic or drug addict. On the contrary, I made promises to myself as a little boy never to use drugs or alcohol because of what they had done to my family. There was an understanding that if I decided to drink or use drugs, I would inevitably become hooked. I grew up in a dysfunctional home; my father was an alcoholic. The condition of our home was that of violence; my mother eventually had to divorce my father when I was in the 4th grade for our safety. I had experienced the abuse and trauma that alcohol could inflict on a family and home firsthand. I made promises to myself to never become like my dad. Yet, that little boy who resolved never to do these things eventually started to grow up and made choices that led down the one path he promised never to go down. *"Though the Lord is exalted, he looks kindly on the lowly; though lofty, he sees them from afar. Though I walk in the midst of trouble, you preserve my life. You stretch out your hand against the anger of my foes; with your right hand you save me"* (Psalm 138:6-7 NIV).

By the time I was a senior in high school, my teenage life had become consumed with partying and experimenting with drugs. That year, I tried every drug I could get my hands on. It was all but a miracle that I graduated from high school and was accepted into a college.

Leaving my hometown and family behind me, I was free to do whatever I wanted. This led to my addiction spiraling out of control in college. I was drinking and getting high almost every day. Rather than attending class, I would party. After my first semester of college, I was placed on academic probation. The following semester, I did not amend my ways, and I failed out of college and lost control of my life. I lost jobs, failed out of summer college classes and community colleges, and lost more jobs. I no longer had a sense of stability. My life was consumed with drugs and alcohol. I was in a full-blown addiction by the age of 20.

For several years, I attempted to start a career or go back to school, but I was met with failure after failure. I went from moving back home to trying to live on my own and everything in between. When I woke up on that motel floor, I finally decided that I had to get help.

I started to pursue recovery, but that familiar friend, failure, met me. I was unable to put together honest sobriety. The flood of addiction surrounded me. I was reaching for anything to hold on to, anything to save me. When I reached out to the things of the world, I was met with nothing but a slippery slope. Nothing would stick. In a period of three years, I tried so many different ways of getting sober and finding freedom in my life: AA, NA, psychiatrists, counselors, and short-term rehab programs.

I was looking for freedom in all the wrong places. But while going through the worst storm of my life, Jesus was on a rescue mission for my soul.

How do I know that Jesus was after my heart and life during this time? Because I recall the countless times I should have overdosed and died, my constant choice to recklessly get behind the wheel of a vehicle while blacked out on drugs and alcohol, the numerous sketchy situations I found myself in, and all the failed suicide attempts. His grace and mercy surrounded me. As much as addiction sought to take me out, Christ's presence was in my midst, overcoming all that was coming against me. *The Lord is not slow in keeping his promise, as some understand slowness. Instead he is patient with you, not wanting anyone to perish, but everyone to come to repentance* (2 Peter 3:9 NIV).

That first time I went to a rehab facility after waking up on the motel floor, a life-changing seed was planted. While I was in a broken place, not even entirely sure I wanted to live a sober life, God was with me. He was trying to turn my attention toward Him so He could rescue me. I was outside of the program facility smoking a cigarette when I walked by two guys sitting on a bench. One said to the other, "They are trying to send me to Teen Challenge, a year-long program." There was no reason for me to listen or take note of the conversation; it was random and no different than overhearing any other conversation in public. In one ear and out the other, or so I thought. He answered, *"The one who sowed the good seed is the Son of Man"* (Matthew 13:37 NIV).

My options were running out as I continued the cycle of relapse and mental health struggles, and I was quickly losing my ability to fight. I was one decision away from giving up and drowning in my storm. In 2015, I found myself checked into yet another rehab in South Florida. While lying in bed, I remember thinking how sick I was of getting arrested and going into programs, only to encounter continuous relapses. At that moment, the words "Teen Challenge" came to my mind as I was reminded of that conversation I had walked by several years earlier. The only explanation for remembering it had to be God!

After those words came into my mind, I told the counselors I wanted to go to Teen Challenge. I was met with, "You don't want to go there. That's a Christian program. You won't be able to smoke cigarettes or be on all your medication."

I responded, "I am willing to give all of that up in order to go to Teen Challenge. I'll do whatever it takes."

I was desperate, and this was my last hope for sobriety. A hope had been ignited deep within me, and I could not afford to let this flame be quenched.

After being accepted by phone interview and application, I hopped on a Greyhound bus and made my way to Sanford, Florida, to enroll in the Teen Challenge program. Everything I owned at that point fit in two suitcases. Upon entry into the program, my life would never be the same.

Having experienced multiple programs up until that point, I quickly realized that something was different at Teen Challenge. The men in the program testified about what Jesus was doing in their lives, and I was encouraged to give everything a chance and fight for a better life. During my second week in the program, I met Jesus at the altar and encountered the love of God. After surrendering to Christ in that moment, things in my life began to change. *For it is by grace you have been saved, through faith—*

and this is not from yourselves, it is the gift of God— not by works, so that no one can boast (Ephesians 2:8 NIV).

Now, as I reflect back to that time of my life, I am grateful God met me with such love and compassion. I certainly would be dead from an overdose or suicide if Christ had never intervened in my situation.

Teen Challenge was a year-long program; five months in, I received a call from God to "lead others to Christ." Upon surrendering to that call, doors began to open up in my life. I was commissioned as a witness and trusted with more responsibility. Just as I was encouraged at the beginning of the program, I encouraged others by sharing my testimony and story with new guys coming into the program who were in a state of hopelessness, just like I was before Christ. My life had finally found purpose! Sharing the gospel and testifying of all God brought me through gave me such deep joy.

I graduated from Teen Challenge in January of 2017, and God has been faithful to allow me to serve Him through various ministry assignments since. I am now happily married to my best friend, and we serve the Lord side by side in full-time ministry. Together, we lead a Teen Challenge program, offering the same hope to others that was so freely offered to me those years ago. Above all else, the Lord has called me to preach the gospel and evangelize to the lost. Furthermore, due to the type of ministry I serve in, I have been able to be up close and hands-on in the discipleship process of many men and women who have chosen to lay down addiction and embrace Jesus. *"Therefore go and make disciples of all nations, baptizing them in the name of the Father and of the Son and of the Holy Spirit, and teaching them to obey everything I have commanded you. And surely I am with you always, to the very end of the age"* (Matthew 28:19-20 NIV).

It would be unfair of me to say that my life has been perfect or that I haven't encountered storms since I accepted Christ as my Lord and Savior. On the contrary, I have faced many storms since being reborn in Christ. The good news is that through these storms, God has equipped me and given me the tools to navigate them. Holding to my faith in Christ and believing in God's power and grace has carried me through. Now, when faced with difficulties, I am able to look back and recount what God has done in my life and how He has already rescued me. Holding to God's faithfulness and eternal hope and keeping the right mindset helps me continually overcome life's adversities. *For the grace of God has appeared that offers salvation to all people. It teaches us to say "No" to ungodliness and worldly passions, and to live self-controlled, upright and godly lives in this present age, while we wait for the blessed hope—the appearing of the glory of our great God and Savior, Jesus Christ, who gave himself for us to redeem us from all wickedness and to purify for himself a people that are his very own, eager to do what is good* (Titus 2:11-14 NIV).

Life's storms look different for everyone—we all have unique stories and experiences. The major storm in my life looked like addiction and mental health struggles. Yours may be different. But our commonality is that without Christ, life's storms have the potential to take us out, robbing us of the divine opportunity to share our victories with others. God is faithful. When I accepted Jesus, I became a brand new person. *Therefore, if anyone is in Christ, the new creation has come: The old has gone, the new is here!* (2 Corinthians 5:17 NIV). The same can be true for anyone in need of life transformation if they put their faith and trust in Jesus and accept Him as their Lord and Savior. Living for Christ is worth it. And living for Him in the midst of the storm is the key to coming out on the other side of it. If you are in the roaring wind and the stinging rain, please know that this, too, shall pass. God's mercies are new every morning! When you feel distant from God, you can trust that He is much closer than you think. *The one who calls you is faithful, and he will do it* (1 Thessalonians 5:24 NIV).

> *"Therefore everyone who hears these words of mine and puts them into practice is like a wise man who built his house on the rock. The rain came down, the streams rose, and the winds blew and beat against that house; yet it did not fall, because it had its foundation on the rock. But everyone who hears these words of mine and does not put them into practice is like a foolish man who built his house on sand. The rain came down, the streams rose, and the winds blew and beat against that house, and it fell with a great crash"* (Matthew 7:24-27 NIV).

JOSHUA D. HORWITZ

Josh Horwitz, a proud Florida native, epitomizes a life rich in diverse experiences. As an Eagle Scout, he demonstrated his commitment to values and leadership early on. Growing up, real estate was more than a profession; it was a way of life, with his family owning their brokerage.

Today, Josh, alongside his wife Maria, leads the "Best Home Ever" real estate team, where they turn dreams into reality for clients. Simultaneously, they own "Village Management Services," a property management company committed to caring for their clients' properties.

Beyond his professional endeavors, Josh's spiritual journey has led him to embrace his Jewish heritage and follow the teachings of Yehoshua Hamashiach. In Palm Beach Gardens, he finds solace and joy with his growing family, proudly parenting a beautiful baby girl with another bundle of joy on the way.

Josh and Maria's commitment to faith extends to their monthly "Home Church" gatherings, a heartfelt blend of food, fellowship, worship music, a powerful word, and prayer, offering a nurturing space for their community to come together.

Josh can be reached at:
BestHomeEverTeam@gmail.com
BestHomeEver.com
VillageMaint.com

How Yehoshua Sought and Found Me

by Joshua D. Horwitz

All things considered, I was born into a very loving family. My mother is a Christian, and my father is a conservative Jew. My mother converted to Judaism right around the time I was born because she was committed to my father and our family to raise us in G-D's Word. As a child, I went to Hebrew school twice a week, kicking and screaming. We occasionally went to Shabbat, did all the high holy days, and labeled ourselves "good Jews." I didn't quite grasp what that meant. Even after I was Bar Mitzvahed, I didn't connect to the Word.

Growing up as a Jew, I've been called a "Jesus killer," "dirty Jew," and "cheap." I even tip more to this day because I don't want to be thought of as a "cheap Jew." Silly, right?

As a Jewish teen, I went on a trip called Gesher Hai, which is where we spent five weeks in Israel, exploring almost every square inch of what the Holy Land had to offer. I also did March of the Living, which consisted of 20,000 Jewish teens, resembling the 20,000 Jews that died per day at Auschwitz. We went to the concentration camps and learned the deep history of the holocaust and the horrific events that took place against my people.

Let's rewind a little and do a scenic flashback.

Growing up, my father battled many addictions. The one I remember the most was alcoholism. He would hide bottles all over the house. I would catch him in the middle of the night drinking from the bottles if I were to use the bathroom or come home late from my sinful activities. But I wasn't aware of how his addictions were affecting our family or myself.

When I was 21, my father shared a three-page letter he had written me the day I was born. The history behind it was that my father had been dealing with a cocaine addiction and my mother had given him an ultimatum: us or the cocaine. Praise G-D he chose us! The letter was about his love for me. I couldn't get through one sentence without crying my eyes out. It was one of the deepest, most emotional cries of my life.

We were always close as a family. We had family dinners, friends often came over, and we would drink heavily together almost every weekend—even when I was a teenager. My parents felt that if I was going to drink, it should be at home where I was safe and couldn't get into much trouble. Many nights, we would get drunk and get in fights with other people, or my brothers and I would fight. Once, three Horwitz's went to the emergency room at different times. But we always made up and stuck by each other no matter what! Family was everything. No matter what happened, we would always be by each other's side.

My parents were more like friends than leaders and parental units. I didn't quite know what I wanted to do with my life, and I tried many different careers and attempted to find love in all the wrong places with many different women. My first serious girlfriend became my fiancé. I didn't realize it then, but looking back now, I was still a boy. I had no business being in a relationship, let alone committing myself for eternity with anyone. She loved me and wanted to spend her life with me; I was selfish and only cared about myself. Two years into the relationship, she got pregnant and had a miscarriage. While she was dealing with her physical pain and suffering, I was selfishly in the other room, looking at pornography, trying to soothe my pain.

Unbeknownst to me, I had a pornography addiction that started when I was only eight years old and grew worse and worse as time went on. I'll never forget the day my fiancé walked in while I was looking at pornography. She was heartbroken and claimed I was cheating on her. I felt ashamed and guilty! I didn't understand. I "loved her," and in my mind, I never cheated once on her. We had broken up and gotten back together time and time again.

My brother, who was living with me at the time, was also going through an unhealthy relationship. When I came home one day, I found that he had moved out, and I couldn't make the mortgage payments by myself. I was so devastated that I didn't speak to him for eight months. When I was invited to dinner at Mom and Dad's house, I would ask if he would be there. But to tell you what type of bond we had, when his relationship ran into serious trouble and his girlfriend cheated on him. I was by his side immediately and was there for him.

I eventually moved to Las Vegas, Nevada, where I worked for a commodity brokerage firm dealing in precious metals—like a stock broker but for metals like gold, silver, and palladium. My parents, after being married for 32 years and separated twice, divorced. I was devastated. Even at 31, it hurt. My father eventually found somebody else and got remarried. I started to distract myself, finding love online through dating apps. I had many relationships, but I had no idea why each one kept failing.

I eventually met a girl on Instagram who was married. She and her husband were separated but not divorced. It was a fun and exciting relationship at first, until she got pregnant. Then everything changed. I didn't want her to have an abortion, but she didn't see any other way. She was still living with her husband, and I was naive to the fact that she was most likely having an affair. She was pregnant with twins. She told me that when she was eight years old, she had a drawing of two boys, her sons named Joshua and David—my first and middle name. I was so blind to what was happening and thought I could make it work. But she had an abortion, saying I was not fit to be a father. I felt so inadequate! Eventually, our relationship turned very toxic. She was emotionally and physically abusive. I still stuck by her side and allowed this abuse to continue, making excuses because of the effects the abortion had on her.

While I was seeing this woman, I was also seeing another woman who lived in Vegas. She had gotten a divorce, which I encouraged. I was becoming quite the player. She wanted to be with me, but she couldn't bear children, so I never attached myself to her.

Then, along came another woman from the Philippines. She was engaged to another woman. You can really start to see how lost I truly was. I was able to get this woman to cheat on her fiancé and leave her for me. While at the same time having another girlfriend back in Florida. A few months in, the woman from the Philippines got pregnant. I told her that from my experience, it would be okay if she wanted to have an abortion because there wasn't a heartbeat, so it wasn't yet a baby. So I took her to Planned Parenthood. I was by her side and allowed her to stay at my house until she recovered from the procedure.

Throughout this time, I had no connection to our heavenly Father. I did not understand His love for us! I even identified as an atheist, saying religion was all made up and was just for the weak-minded. And now that shame was really starting to build up, I was plunging head-first into a downward spiral. I was without G-D and completely lost touch with who He created me to be.

Fast forwarding past even more failed relationships, I finally met my wife as a broken 35-year-old man who could barely afford to pay his rent. I had no business being in a relationship, yet part of me was still fighting for true love, as funny as that sounds.

I'll never forget the day that I saw Maria walk by. I was captivated by her essence, her power, her confidence, and her beauty. I was now back in real estate, running a team for the owner of the office, and Maria was curious about joining our team. We had an interview, and she invited me to meet her and her friends after work. I was reluctant, having just been out the night before, but the Holy Spirit was screaming inside me, "Go! Go!" So I went.

On the way there, Maria called me, saying, "There's a bunch of lights on my dash. I'm not sure what's going on with my car. I might be out of gas. Can you help me?"

So I said, "Not to worry. I'm 30 seconds behind you, and I have a gas can in the back of my truck. What side of the road are you on?"

She replied, "The only logical side I would be on."

I replied, "You are the one that ran out of gas after all."

So I came and got her. By the time we circled back around to her car with gas, we were already naming our children. As our relationship progressed, becoming deeper and deeper, I questioned how such a beautiful woman was so interested in me. I discovered I had a tendency to think I wasn't good enough—believing that women would always leave me, just like they always had.

Three years into our relationship, Maria and I chose to get married. It was very important to her that her father walk her down the aisle. For that to happen, we needed his approval. My journey to Jesus, or as I lovingly call Him, Yahoshua, began. In Hebrew, my name is Yahoshua, also.

Maria's father would repeatedly ask to speak to his daughter in private—I had no idea why. Later, I would find out that in those conversations, he told her I was not good enough for his daughter because I did not believe in Jesus.

One night, like many nights before, Maria's father asked to speak to his daughter for 15 minutes. Those 15 minutes ended up lasting for 2 1/2 hours. I was waiting in the driveway for her to come out so we could go home. After multiple calls and texts and no word from Maria, I threw my hands up in the air and said, "I'm done. F this. I'm out!"

I then drove home, and as I was pulling into the driveway after a 30-minute drive, Maria finally called me, crying her eyes out, barely able to speak a word.

I asked her, "What happened? What's going on?"

She said, "My father doesn't want me to marry you because you don't believe in Jesus."

I immediately got even more upset and started cursing and saying, "Who is he to judge?!"

Reluctantly, I turned around and drove another 30 minutes back to pick up Maria. We got home, parked in the driveway, and started to have a lengthy conversation.

"Well, I don't even know what your father believes or anything, really, about Christianity. I'm willing to go on this journey and investigate, but I can't make any promises!"

Maria, being a devout Catholic at the time, said, "So am I. There are things my father has been trying to tell me, things that I haven't been open to yet. But I'm willing to go on this journey with you."

So, little by little, I started reading books like *The Hebrew Gospel of Matthew, The Case for Christ,* and the Bible to learn more about the prophetic words spoken about the Jewish Messiah. In the middle of this journey, my pornography addiction lingered in the background. Something I still didn't quite grasp had such a strong hold on me. Maria caught me one day in the shower, looking at pornography, about to masturbate. There's that heartbreaking look again. Something I had done to my previous fiancé was now repeating itself.

I felt even more shame, judgment, and guilt than ever before.

Except this time, I also heard G-D's Word and felt His love. Maria was strong enough to listen to me, stand by my side, and help me research this terrible addiction sweeping across the nation and the world. She was able to speak to my heart in a way that no one else ever could. She was able to get me to see that I had a problem with pornography. We read scripture, watched documentaries, and fought this demon together as one flesh.

I was finally able to see the grip the devil had on me, and I was done. It was time to break myself free. I then proceeded to share my trials and tribulations with others, shining light on the darkness of my soul. To see the effects this addiction had on others and, most importantly, the effect it had on me and loving another person made me feel lifeless and dead inside. I was blinded, believing it was just a victimless act. In reality, my addiction was keeping me from being connected with my true love, the person G-D wanted me to be with.

Maria and I took a trip to Israel. G-D had put it on my heart that during the trip, I would read the letter my father wrote to me aloud in front of the Wailing Wall. After I read the letter, I walked up to the wall and proceeded to read from Genesis 1:1. I don't remember what verse I stopped at, but I folded up the letter, put it into the wall, and began to pray over my father— praying all his sins would be forgotten, he would forgive himself, and live a blessed life. As my eyes were closed, a face spoke to me in the darkness. It was unmistakably the face of Jesus, Yehoshua Hamashiach. Even after that, however, I didn't want to admit that Jesus visited with me. I made jokes with Maria that it was either Moses or Abraham or even G-D himself.

Previously, Maria had asked me what it would take for me to believe in Jesus. I said, "He would have to come down here and slap me upside the head and say, 'Hey it's Me!'" It still didn't dawn on me that He had done just that. It's funny how G-D can give us exactly what we say and pray for and be right in front of us, and we are still completely oblivious!

We then had an amazing trip visiting all the Christian sites, all the stations of the cross, and being so connected to the Holy Land that we never wanted to leave.

Seven or eight months went by; we had begun attending church. It was the beginning of the service, and while I was worshiping and crying, I got a tap and a message that completed the whole thing. Jesus told me my mission and purpose is to connect Jew and Gentile as one tribe and follow the words of Jesus to go back to our Hebraic roots.

For a while, I was still very private about what had transpired; I was afraid people would judge me and laugh, either to my face or behind my back. I didn't want to be portrayed as some weirdo or something to that effect. So, I was tight-lipped with my newfound faith. I was also afraid to upset my father and to leave my Jewish heritage. But more than ever, I was connected with G-D even as we kept Kosher and lit the Shabbos candles every Shabbat.

After this, Maria and I got married and began a beautiful life together as one flesh. Our goal was to have a child immediately. After months and months of trying to conceive, we were unsuccessful, and in the back of my mind, I wondered if G-D was punishing me for all the things I had done since I had easily gotten women pregnant before.

After five months into our marriage, we attended a faith-based marriage retreat in Colorado. There was a portion in which we had to forgive ourselves and write about our sins. I started to write about the two abortions and the miscarriage, forgiving myself, crying and praying to G-D. I remember feeling so free. After we left the retreat, we drove through a mountain called Genesee Mountain. I remember it like it was yesterday. Maria said, "If I'm pregnant with a baby girl, I want her name to be called Genesee"—which is Native American with Hebraic roots and means "a beautiful, pleasant valley."

A month later, we found we had conceived our beautiful baby girl, Genesee Marie Horwitz, that very weekend! A year later, I proclaimed my faith and got baptized in the Jordan River in Israel—with Maria and our beautiful baby girl!

We now have another baby on the way!

I am living proof that even a lost soul like me can be found! G-D is good!

NAVIGATING ADDICTIONS

by Ken A. Hobbs II

God is still here for you during addiction. Psalm 50:15 reminds us that God asks us to call on Him in our times of trouble. God is our shelter and strength and is always there to help in times of trouble.

Our ability to enjoy life the way God designed us is due to His goodness. Therefore, despite any storm that rises, we cannot take our eyes off Him if we wish to maintain a fully secure life.

Addiction is like the eye inside the hurricane. The whirlwind pulls you into the center, surrounds you in self-destructive behavior, and only leaves the feelings of hopelessness and loneliness inside as you battle alone. You are sucked in and pulled about; the struggle of overcoming the disorder can feel like an impossible battering experience you cannot exit. The only thing that can pull you out of the middle of it is the fulfillment that God has to offer.

Becoming addicted can stem from a lack of satisfaction in life because we feel that a needed component is missing for our completion. A person with addiction looks for comfort from the world instead of from God. They seek advice to help them deal with stress or escape situations beyond their control.

Addictions cause us to think we need something to satisfy us, leading us to wander as we seek ways to meet our increased temptations and desires as we are sucked into the center tornado of desperation and despair. Before long, we realize all complete satisfaction is gone. The entangled winds of darkness caused by addictive behaviors grow, swirling around our minds as our eyes are fixed on themselves, not God.

The world is full of trials and temptations, with funnel clouds popping up everywhere. The extensive list of potential addictions includes drugs, alcohol, and lustful pursuits. Any of these can become full-blown, deadly tornadoes. Yielding to the destructive behavior of these deadly tornados brings misery. The moment we grasp our desire, we may feel good or even great, but the longing is never truly fulfilled, and the pain and struggles return, often bringing a feeling like the end of the world is upon us. Then, we repeatedly give in to the temptation, which pulls us to the center of the tornado with no way out.

As the walls of water and wind close in around you, you may think there is no option to perpetuate the vicious, addictive cycle except to scream your way out. You might think God has forsaken you, withdrawn all His support, and left you to gasp for air by yourself. But this could not be further from the truth.

God reminds us to call on Him in our times of trouble.

> *"Call on me in the day of trouble; I will deliver you, and you will honor me"* (Psalm 50:15 NIV).

It is vital to know that love, forgiveness, and redemption are core values, and no matter which path you followed in the past or are on now, there is hope for you to release any addiction in the name of Jesus. The Bible clearly talks about self-discipline and how important it is to focus and stay on the right path.

> *No temptation has overtaken you except what is common to mankind. And God is faithful; he will not let you be tempted beyond what you can bear. But when you are tempted, he will also provide a way out so that you can endure it* (1 Corinthians 10:13 NIV).

While your addiction has made you feel worthless at times, you must remember that God sees through your faults and loves the person you are. Submit your addiction to God. Be prayerful and heartfelt with the surrender of your addiction, and you can be assured that God will step in. When you allow Him the ability to take over what you can no longer control, the tornado of addiction, He intervenes. It is important to immerse yourself in God's Word and communicate with Him continuously. The tornado of addiction may cause you to think it has a stronghold over you, and it should not be fought without the power of the Living God.

> *The Lord is my rock and my fortress and my deliverer; my God is my rock, in whom I take refuge, my shield and the horn of my salvation, my stronghold* (Psalm 18:2 NIV).

To take shelter from the tornado, stop self-medicating. Surrender your heart to God. Arm yourself with God's provisions. Take shelter in the bunker of God's Word, clothing yourself with the full armor of God. It is only with Him that all things are possible, even withstanding the storm of addiction (Ephesians 6:10-17).

A Band of Brothers will hold you accountable and keep you from the forceful winds and pounding a tornado brings. Stay away from what you so desperately are trying to quit. You are not alone; God never leaves you, and only He can bring you peace and stability from the funnel clouds that loom and try to take you out. And be aware, keeping yourself in good company.

> *Do not be misled: "Bad company corrupts good character"* (1 Corinthians 15:33 NIV).

Jesus is the rock to build your peace on, so keep your eyes and mind on Him when the winds are swirling around you. Start a "positive spiral" out of the funnel and into the light of Jesus' love, grace, and freedom.

. . . .

Michael C. Hopkins

Michael Hopkins was born in Brooklyn, NY, and currently resides in sunny South Florida. He is blessed with an immeasurably supportive, dynamic, and loving wife and daughter. He credits his victories to faith in God, from which he extracts the drive and willingness to be available to impact others.

Michael has an insatiable passion for travel, cultivated by his father. His hobbies include cycling, birding, horticulture, photography, and digital creation. He's in his element in nature, and the waterfront is his happy place.

With a passion for the well-being of others, Michael often shares his journey of healing and redemption. His inspiration and encouragement to write come from God and his wife, with confirmation from Kenny Hobbs, a colleague and dear friend.

Caregiving for aging parents and involvement on the Leadership Team of Band of Brothers FL have instilled in him a special level of compassion and empowered him to be a positive change agent in the lives of others.

He and his wife are in business together and consider themselves financial freedom fighters, assisting others with education and strategies for achieving their particular goals as they pursue their life dreams.

https://livemore.net/johnson-hopkins-teamcompassion

You may connect directly with him at Michael.hopkins1@outlook.com

GOD-DIRECTED HEALING

by Michael C. Hopkins

"We want Christ to hurry and calm the storm. He wants us to find him in the midst of it first."
– Beth Moore[1]

My storm has been contending with the overarching effects of hidden and unrecognized trauma. This has been compounded by memory challenges and overcoming the related negative voices conspiring to deter me from what God has for me and convince me to believe that I am neither worthy nor valued.

> *When you pass through the waters, I will be with you;*
> *and when you pass through the rivers, they will not sweep over you.*
> *When you walk through the fire, you will not be burned;*
> *the flames will not set you ablaze.*
> *For I am the Lord your God, the Holy One of Israel, your Savior;*
> *I give Egypt for your ransom, Cush and Seba in your stead.*
> *(Isaiah 43:2-3 NIV)*

For me, Navigating the Storm has been about self-care. It has meant choosing to value myself and putting a plan in place to direct my path towards life-giving and life-changing decisions. First, I needed to recognize there was a problem and then fine-tune my willingness to put in the work necessary to achieve my desired level of healing. Throughout, many scripture verses have encouraged and strengthened me. God's truths have also come to me through God-inspired music. During this process, God has drawn me closer, even when I resisted Him.

When seeking healing, whether medically, spiritually, or otherwise, questions are asked by others about your past in order to craft a plan of care unique to your circumstances and situation. Certainly, reflecting on where you've been is helpful in charting a course forward. However, what do you do when you feel like your memory has been erased? How do you respond when you feel like you have nothing to offer that can tangibly help your situation? When I am asked what may seem to most to be simple questions about my childhood or any time since then, I usually don't have an immediate response because I simply do not recall those things that impacted me. Sometimes, something comes. But most of the time, I go vacant. When clear, distinct memories do come through, I am reminded that so much of what I experienced in childhood and adolescence has helped form many negative patterns that I am still overcoming. Growing up, I was never aware of the concept of trauma and the grip that developed.

According to verywellhealth.com, trauma is an emotional response caused by experiencing a single incident, a series of distressing or traumatic emotional or psychological events, or both.

I have some glimpses of events, occurrences, and interactions—but never the full story. Although most of the precise details have not been revealed, they have clearly been contributing factors to my experience and have resulted in behavior that leads me to remain silent, not join in a group conversation, and simply be an observer rather than a participant. Consultation and treatment with various therapeutic modalities have yielded a consensus of diagnosis that my impaired memory was born out of trauma. Uncovering and addressing the combination was my challenge.

Proceeding through this uncovering, I often found myself angry, bitter, and unsatisfied. My words and thoughts were planted in dark places as the fog of never being good enough engulfed me. However, as I began embracing the idea that "I need help" and "Healing is possible and available," the walls started to come down. Although my faith journey has often been a roller-coaster ride, I have repeatedly been drawn back to what I know to be true: God loves me, and He always has my best in mind.

> *"For I know the plans I have for you," says the LORD. "They are plans for good and not for disaster, to give you a future and a hope"* (Jeremiah 29:11 NLT).

It has been disturbing to realize that, as men, we are often resistant or reluctant to request or receive assistance. For many, we have accepted and internalized the idea that weakness is implied when help is made available. An example that comes to mind concerns a time when my dad was hospitalized while straddled with incontinence. Incontinence is the involuntary loss of bladder or bowel control. Not unexpectedly, he soiled himself. Rather than allowing the nurse to tidy him, he told her he would wait for my mom to return to the room, and she would handle that task instead.

Additionally, I find that we, as men, are not particularly diligent with our self-care. I am referencing the total package: diet, exercise, nutrition, grooming, medical and dental checkups, and follow-ups with specialists as needed. All too often, we choose to wait to see if the symptom goes away on its own rather than taking proactive steps when it presents itself. I feel it is necessary to highlight this point, as many of our readers may be men who are earnestly seeking healing from something.

On my trek, the trauma I experienced paved my path. Early on, I remember being distracted, disillusioned, prone to wandering, isolated, unattended, depressed, and disconnected. I also remember that I learned isolation from my parents. We were taught that you do not associate with or talk to "those people," as Dad described family. This was because of the splintered family relationships of *his* childhood. The cycle continued with us, as my parents' families did not get along either. I also recall being ridiculed often for un-satisfactory performance and simply being a disappointment. Here, I was unknowingly introduced to the concept of generational trauma.

"Sometimes, trauma gets passed down through families. You might not have experienced a traumatic event yourself, but you may still be dealing with the consequences, including 'adverse emotional and behavioral reac-tions,' according to the American Psychological Association (APA). This is known as generational trauma, or intergenerational trauma."[2]

In response to this, let me state that "therapy" is not a bad word. Therapy is a means by which one may choose to engage the services of a professional to help pursue a level of heightened wellness.

My pathway to healing employed counseling in different styles and various modalities. Each individual must find what resonates with them to increase the propensity for success. It was of utmost importance to me that all my therapy practitioners approach my healing from a Christian perspective. This is a map of some of what I undertook.

• EMDR Therapy. Eye movement desensitization and reprocessing therapy is a mental health treatment technique. This method involves moving your eyes a specific way while you process traumatic memories.[3]

- Narrative Therapy. "Narrative therapy is a style of therapy that helps people become—and embrace being—an expert in their own lives. In narrative therapy, there is an emphasis on the stories that you develop and carry with you through your life."[4]

- Pastoral Counseling. "A clinical practice that integrates both psychological and theological concepts into its framework, is not unlike other modes of therapy when it comes to the therapeutic process. What sets it apart is the way faith, spirituality, and theology are incorporated into the model."[5]

- Traditional Christian Counseling. "Draws on the principles of Christianity to help clients cope with challenges. Because religious faith can play a significant role in an individual's life, many prospective therapy clients who identify as Christian feel more comfortable seeing a counselor who shares their beliefs."[6]

I also engaged in group dialog, social gatherings, and networking settings. All of these also played a role in reorienting my life with purpose and confidence. One group in particular has a focus on trauma-informed care and the advocacy of mentorship, networking, and education. When the facilitator made the simple statement, "It's okay to say, 'I need a friend,'" a domino effect of freedom ensued! The overflow of these social outlets has been an amazingly authentic, life-affirming birthing of relationships—I no longer feel isolated!

With each experience, another layer of the onion was exposed. There were exercises and assignments that helped me rediscover so much of what had been apparently lost. Certainly, I recovered memories of things I had not thought of in years, and I have been able to utilize them in my growth.

In order to present an accurate picture of where this all originated, I should go back to what I do recall from my childhood. My story started in Brooklyn, New York, in the sixties. Our family attended church on a regular basis. I was the middle child between two sisters. Dad was born in North Carolina, and Mom was from Jamaica, West Indies. Dad was a pharmacist, and Mom was a registered nurse.

When I was in first grade, Dad accepted a position at a pharmacy in Rockford, Illinois. This was the mid-sixties, with all the racial tension and discrimination that is our history, and Dad was a strong-willed, outspoken black man. I don't know the intricate details, but in a few short months, as a result of an explosive exchange in the workplace, abruptly and suddenly, it was time to get back to Brooklyn. Immediately. Knowing the forthright nature of Dad, I imagine someone probably spoke inappropriate, condescending, derogatory remark(s) one time too many, Dad responded in his signature manner, and then it was not physically safe for us as a family to remain because of the threat of retaliation. There had been a similar confrontation at the place of worship we attended before we left, with someone expressing how we did not belong there. Let's add that to the trauma bucket.

We returned to our local church. However, I can't say that the plan of salvation was ever shared. One day in the midst of the busyness that is New York City, I encountered God and His plan. A nameless, faceless person (I don't remember if it was a man or woman) got my attention, and there, at the bottom of a landing in the middle of the stairs in a NY subway station, I accepted Christ as my personal savior. However, because of the climate at home (discouraging my interests), this was my secret, and I never shared it. Although I found great interest in being involved in the youth choir, Dad made it clear that we were spending too much time in rehearsals leading up to a special event. So that was shut down. I'm guessing I was in high school at the time. I continued with business as usual, and as I became an adult, I drifted away—literally. Yet, God's seed had been planted in my life.

Another event that comes to mind is related to discouraging growth and advancement and concerns high school choice. I was on track to pursue a science career, as that was where my interests were. At that time, any serious NYC science student knew enrollment in one of three top science high schools was the goal for success in post-secondary studies. Although I was accepted to one of these highly rated institutions, Dad discouraged me from going, maintaining I would be better served in a smaller, locally zoned high school, away from the crowds. The effects of what I later learned to be the father-wound (emotional and psychological wounds passed on by my father's own trauma) took control.

Years later, I had three major life changes. My wife and I got married, our daughter was born, and we moved to the United States Virgin Islands. As time passed, I was far from home and far from God. My closest connections were not living God-honoring lives, and I was a sponge—just soaking up destructive behaviors. Our marriage was on the verge of collapse. Alcoholic beverages became my addiction of choice. After a near-death accident resulting from a self-imposed protracted season of premeditated drunk driving, my vehicle was damaged beyond repair. I finally agreed to pastoral counseling. The trauma continued to mount. But, God! Seeing my life spiraling, I recognized I was ready to hear, know, and embrace God. Our sessions led me back. I rededicated my life to Christ and began seeking Him and His ways. Following this, we returned as a family to the States to make ourselves available to care for our aging parents.

Subsequently, all our family was in Florida. Although I felt I did not have any support to call on from my own family, my wife's family embraced me as their own—to the point that I was, and still am, closer to them than any of my natural family. The bonds were so different. So now I had a wife who loved, respected, and supported me and an equally supportive, attentive family with reciprocal love.

Fast forward to seven years ago. Dad was gravely ill. But, of course, he had perpetuated the isolation that he taught me despite his compromised health. Long story short, by the time I knew the extent of his condition, his remaining time was short. I got to him at a hospital in Orlando, Florida, had him transferred to a nursing home in West Palm Beach, then to a hospital in Palm Beach County, and ultimately, to hospice (an end-of-term care facility). This all happened in the space of less than a week. Just like that, he was gone. I felt like I had never truly known him. Following Dad's demise, Mom lived with us for six years until she passed away in April of 2022 at the age of 99. That was also a part of our COVID-19 experience. Throughout that time, we followed lockdown procedures out of an abundance of caution to keep mom safe with her health challenges. This period during the global pandemic became the deepest, darkest, loneliest time I can remember. But God.

You see, despite physical restrictions, I connected with my God-ordained family—Band of Brothers, Florida. I also found community and daily support from my church family through our online marriage life group, affirming that online communities of faith can absolutely be authentic, empowering lifelines. Although I was physically distanced on lockdown and a 24/7 caregiver, I was connected. Special shout out to my brother, Miguel Lewis. He is a true hermano/brother, confidante, and friend. He never gave up reaching out to me; we talked often. So many brothers stood with me even while I stepped away from the Leadership Team of BOB to care for my family. Of course, Guy Shashatay, who heads the organization, has been a constant source of support and encouragement; he is a dedicated mentor and friend.

I also completed a 20-week discipleship experience, where I found freedom, direction, and purpose. This program emphasized spiritual growth while teaching the Word and disciplines and doctrines of the Christian faith.

What does Navigating My Storm look like now? One day on the beach, as I was reflecting on all God was showing and imparting to me, I received this revelation –

God is telling me that it's okay not to have a more complete memory of where I've been. He is telling me that I have used my memory loss as an excuse not to move forward for too long. It is now time to embrace and collaborate with Him in crafting new, positive, productive, life-giving experiences, thus formulating bold, new, audacious memories. Rather than stumbling through the process of recovering and processing what the past has been, it is time to look to what is and can be—if only I will allow myself to dream.

I have forgiven my father, breaking the bondage of the wounding. Additionally, I have taken steps to improve my overall well-being. I have committed to a vegan diet, am attending worship service in person again, and am embracing outreach opportunities to serve. I also cycle daily and have been alcohol-free since January 2023. I embrace my calling as an encourager, holding fast to one of my life verses: *Trust in the LORD with all your heart and lean not on your own understanding; in all your ways submit to him, and he will make your paths straight* (Proverbs 3:5-6 NKJV).

My wife and I are now on the other side of a long season of caregiving and bereavement. We are intentional about self-care as we spend time together and are deliberate about who we allow into our space. Although we are through the storm, we know that our strength lies in following God's guidance, who wants us to care for others but also to care for ourselves and value who He made us to be. Honing that strength will allow us to navigate any storms that may be headed our way. We are committed to each other and God's leading in a new, revitalizing journey. We are keenly sensitive to where He is directing us as we are called to serve His people.

Together, we have embraced the importance of being obedient to God's direction. And we continue to focus on what He is doing in our lives and join Him in His work. I encourage you to do the same. When we commit to God and focus on His leading, He will always direct our paths—through sunny and stormy days.

Let us think of ways to motivate one another to acts of love and good works. And let us not neglect our meeting together, as some people do, but encourage one another, especially now that the day of his return is drawing near (Hebrews 10:24-25 NLT).

[1]Moore, Beth, *Whispers of Hope: 10 Weeks of Devotional Prayer* (ed. 2013).

[2]Sweeney, "17 Signs of Generational Trauma, According to Therapists" March 23, 2023, menshealth.com

[3]"EMDR Therapy: What It Is, Procedure & Effectiveness," https://my.clevelandclinic.org/health/treatments/22641-emdr-therapy

[4]Clarke, "How Narrative Therapy Works" May 5, 2023, https://www.verywellmind.com/narrative-therapy-4172956#:~:text=Narrative%20therapy%20is%20a%20style,with%20you%20through%20your%20life.

[5]"Pastoral Counseling" https://www.goodtherapy.org/learn-about-therapy/modes/pastoral-counseling

[6]"Christian Counseling" *Psychology Today,* https://www.psychologytoday.com/us/therapy-types/christian-counseling

JONATHAN RIOS

Jonathan Rios is a father of four, a former Division 1 athlete, and a Military Academy graduate. He holds a Bachelor of Science in Psychology and a Master's in Counseling Psychology.

For the past 21 years, Jonathan has worked in the mental health space. His private practice is located in Jupiter, Florida. He facilitates a 3-day men's training in the Blue Ridge mountains as well as an 8-week Rite of Passage experience for men.

Visit www.thriiv.co or follow him on instagram @primalvirtues

BAD DRIVING AND ANGRY NEIGHBORS

By Jonathan Rios

"If you forgive other people when they sin against you, your heavenly Father will also forgive you" (Matthew 6:14 NIV).

"You have heard the law that says, 'Love your neighbor' and hate your enemy. But I say, love your enemies! Pray for those that persecute you!" (Matthew 5:43-44 NLT).

The moments that mark us are often the ones we don't see coming.

The accident happened suddenly. One moment, we were joking around. The next moment, we were flying through the air at 50 miles per hour. As a teenage driver, I lost control of our borrowed red Honda Accord, slid into a ditch, and successfully flipped the car five times. Neighbors reported a tree eventually stopped us. Although my life didn't flash before my eyes, I can tell you this: time really did slow down. I remember the intense force of gravity as I smashed my head repeatedly against the roof of the car. I remember dirt in my eyes and mouth. I remember extreme pain in my legs and arms. I remember coming to consciousness with glass lodged in my scalp. Turning to my right, I realized neither of my friends (Mike Donehey and Sam Deihl) was in the vehicle with me. They had been ejected.

We were on our way to school, ready to continue our dominance as a top-ranked high school soccer team. We never made it.

I took my first conscious breath as panic began to set in. My body was shaking uncontrollably, and my leg was throbbing. With great effort, I crawled out of the driver-side window. I scanned the area. No bodies in sight. I low-crawled through the grass, holding back tears, desperate to find my friends. Praying to God they were alive.

I found a mangled body lying stationary in the grass. It was Mike. I screamed. I grabbed his hand, thinking he was dead. Blood was pouring from his skull. Not just trickling but gushing. The pool of blood around his head was roughly two feet in diameter. His ear was dangling by a thread. Bubbles came from his mouth as he made an eerie death gurgle.

In that moment, you have no choice but to pray. I was completely powerless. As they say, "There are no atheists in foxholes." I begged God out loud, "Take my life and spare his...let him live. Please, God!"

It's embarrassing to admit it, but even during a traumatic moment like this, my selfish persona was present. I thought to myself, *Oh my God, I just killed my best friend. I'm going to prison. My life is over. I want it to be over. How can I blame this on someone or something else?*

I was jolted out of my analytical mind by the realization that I hadn't found Sam yet. I scanned the grass and found him lying face up with his eyes wide open. He was in complete shock.

I screamed, "Sam!!!! Wake up!!!! Mike needs help!!!!"

He sat up with force. Confused and disoriented, I led him back to Mike. We both panicked, praying gibberish between desperate tears. We made no sense.

A neighbor yelled from her porch, "The ambulance is on its way!"

It felt like two hours before they arrived. They didn't talk much. They simply loaded us onto stretchers. They strapped us down, careful to keep our necks from moving. The worst part was their silence. They gave us no updates. Mike was taken in one ambulance while Sam and I were placed side by side in another. We held hands, begging them to tell us if Mike was alive.

The memories of our hospital arrival are hazy. I had trouble thinking. All I knew was that my head was throbbing. It turns out there was glass stuck in my scalp, and because I was strapped down, my head was pressing the glass further in, causing more and more pressure. None of the doctors were willing to give me an update. They placed us all in separate rooms. Mike was sent to surgery immediately, but I knew nothing about this until much later. All I knew for sure was that he was dead, and I was responsible.

The emergency medical technicians later revealed Mike had flatlined five times on the way to the hospital. After his immediate injuries were addressed, I was afforded the opportunity to hold his hand during surgery as they sowed his ear back on. Mike's dad, Mr. Donehey, embraced me gently with only grace in his eyes, and although his authentic gesture felt good inside, I couldn't see past the damage I had done. I distinctly remember catching a reflection of myself in a hospital gown. I couldn't stand to look at my own reflection. I was racked with guilt.

Miraculously, Mike survived. It was hard to believe, considering what he had been through. He spent months in rehabilitation. While I healed quickly, he was bedridden—uncertain if he'd ever run or be active again. I avoided school like the plague. I felt such shame I couldn't even leave my room. I received cards in the mail, but I refused to read most of them. They meant nothing to me. I felt like a murderer. I felt like an irresponsible piece of trash.

As the days and weeks went by, things began to return to normal. I healed up nicely and began playing soccer again. I attended school. I worked my shifts at Papa John's. The one thing I didn't do was talk about the accident. I tried my best to distract myself. I didn't want anyone to bring it up. I felt like someone was going to find out the truth of the matter. The truth was that I had played with the wheel. I was showing off for my friends, testing my limits. I had successfully taken some turns with speed, and I had effectively learned how to "drift" or fishtail the vehicle. No one knew about this except for those of us in the vehicle. I was terrified I would be found out.

I didn't know who to talk to. I didn't know what to say. I just knew in my heart that everyone hated me for what I had done to my friends.

But, as it turns out, I was about to experience my first real glimpse of grace and forgiveness. As the school year moved forward, I spent less and less time with Mike and the rest of my friends. Shame will do that. It'll keep you isolated. I reached a point where I couldn't take the guilt any longer. I decided to craft a letter confessing my sorrow and remorse. My plan was to give it to Mike in the hopes he could find it in his heart to forgive me. I spent days crafting that thing. I finally grew the nerve to give him the letter in the hallway at school. I said something to the effect of, "Read this when you get a chance."

I walked away thinking, *At least he knows I tried.*

About an hour later, Mike found me in the hallway, looked me in the eye, pulled the letter out of his pocket, and ripped it in two. "You didn't even need to write this. There's nothing to forgive".

I didn't know what to say. I was just a shaggy-haired high school kid with limited emotional intelligence. All I knew was that I was experiencing something powerful, something I desperately needed.

God has a funny way of growing you. It never happens how you think it's going to happen. The forging process is rarely something we enjoy. Mike taught me how to receive grace and forgiveness from others. He taught me how to forgive myself. Once I realized he wasn't holding a record of wrongs against me, I was free to let go of the shame and self-loathing I had for myself. It marked me forever. To this day, we are best friends. We both have four daughters. Our wives love each other. When men spill blood together, they are bonded forever.

One other detail worth mentioning: After the accident, Mike learned how to play the guitar while he was bedridden. He carried that passion with him to college at Palm Beach Atlantic University, where he majored in theatre. He went on to become a successful musician, winning national awards, traveling the world, playing in stadiums, and successfully leading the band "10th Avenue North". His music has touched millions of listeners around the world.

I thank God for Mike. He is the closest thing I have to a biological brother. He taught me how to forgive myself.

Let's change gears now and look at forgiveness from a different angle. What is a man to do when someone is *purposefully* seeking your downfall? How does this forgiveness thing work when your "enemy" actively wants to see you destroyed?

It had already been a long day as I picked up the urgent phone call from my wife. "I can't take it anymore. The hostility is getting out of control. He verbally berated me. He slammed the door in my face!"

Rage came over me like a wet blanket. I wanted to rush home and strangle the man. I wanted to see him squirm like a coward at the wrath he was about to endure.

This was now a daily occurrence. Our neighbor "Jim" was making our lives a living hell. Jim was a hardened Vietnam vet who walked with a limp and cursed like a sailor. The type of man who smoked three packs of cigarettes a day—so much so that the smoke permeated the trees and plants and drifted all the way to our front porch. The smoke ultimately traveled through our front door and windows—for five years. It was a common occurrence to see Jim cleaning his guns and drinking vodka on his front porch.

Jim called the cops on us so many times I lost count, all because he hated our dog. He made it his mission to make our lives miserable until the dog was eliminated. He hated our babysitters and would berate them until they never returned. He attempted lawsuits, creating lie after lie, threatening legal action just to let us know we were hated. He sat on our neighborhood homeowners association board and slandered us in a public setting. He fined us multiple times. He frequently took pictures of my property, noting if the garbage can or a bicycle was left outside for longer than a few hours. He was entirely unapproachable. Any time I attempted a civilized conversation to address our issues, he would slam his door in my face and cuss me out.

To add icing to the cake, he would offer my four daughters popsicles and money when I wasn't around so as to win their affection and convince himself he wasn't entirely rotten.

After five years of this, I had finally hit my limit. I felt powerless. I woke up early one morning totally distraught under the threat of a lawsuit. After all, we were living next to an unstable man. I began weeping with rage. I was at a loss for words. I couldn't even go on my front porch without being triggered by the residual smoke layers caked all over my property. Everything in me wanted to get revenge, put him in his place, and let the world know just how dysfunctional he was.

I began to pray.

My eyes fell upon these words, and I spoke them out loud, *"I come to you for protection, O Lord my God. Save me from my persecutors—rescue me! If you don't they will maul me like a lion, tearing me to pieces with no one to rescue me... Arise, O Lord, in anger! Stand up against the fury of my enemies! Wake up, my God, and bring justice!"* (Psalm 7:1-4, 6 NLT).

In my spirit, I heard a subtle voice say the word *"Sosthenes."* I wrote the word down flippantly in my journal. It didn't make any sense. It sounded like the name of a famous Greek philosopher. I decided to google it. It turns out Sosthenes is a man in the Bible. I quickly turned to the passage in 1 Corinthians. In the story, the Apostle Paul is taken before a tribunal. He was being persecuted for his faith. A Roman official named Gallio refused to allow the case to continue and demanded that the Jews handle the issues amongst themselves. In a fit of rage, the people seized their Jewish leader, "Sosthenes" (the man likely spearheading the persecution), and beat him in front of the tribunal.

I read that and sensed God was telling me, "What happened to Sosthenes will happen to Jim. He will be removed from his position of power and will be dethroned. Just be patient. Do not curse him. Forgive him."

I wrote all this in my journal and set my mind to forgive Jim for all the times he had threatened or dishonored my family. I began to write out, in detail, each event, how I felt about it, and then a declaration whereby I forgave each offense.

Example

EVENT: Jim berated my wife, cussed at her, belittled her, and slammed the door in her face.

FEELING: I felt blind rage, disgust, fear, sadness.

DECLARATION: Of my own free will, I choose to forgive Jim for disrespecting my wife, belittling her, and causing so much heartache in our lives. I release my need for vengeance. I refuse to hate him or wish him ill. I release him into God's hands. It's not my job to judge another man. That's God's job.

Example

EVENT: Jim smoked cigarettes in front of my children while drinking vodka and cussing profusely, knowing that Logan wrestles with asthma. I opened my front door, and the cigarette smoke came into my living room.

FEELING: Anger, disgust, powerless, irritable, sad

DECLARATION: Of my own free will, I choose to forgive Jim for smoking around my children, drinking vodka in proximity to them, and making our home environment feel so unwelcoming. I forgive him for disregarding my child's medical condition. I release my desire for vengeance. I extend grace to him. He is God's job, not mine.

It wasn't more than two weeks later when I heard the news. Jim had been removed from the HOA board. We were so relieved. More than that, I remember walking onto my front porch one day after work, seeing Jim smoking from a distance, entering my front door through the smog, kissing my children, hugging my wife, and feeling no sense of resentment or anger. As if Jim no longer occupied mental real estate in my psyche.

Three months after that, Jim died of a heart attack in his home. We were invited to his funeral by his wife and met many of his extended family members. We were afforded the opportunity to buy his wife dinner. I was so glad I had actively forgiven Jim and worked through my resentment. I felt no joy at his passing and only wished the best for him.

I have since learned to apply this method whenever someone offends me or slanders me. It continues to serve me well. We live in an era of "outrage," but I refuse to participate. Moderns are so easily offended and enslaved by the hooks of resentment, but we can choose a different path.

I choose to be a forgiver because I refuse to allow the offenses of another man or woman to govern my life. As a Christian, I don't have a leg to stand on. Christ has forgiven me. It is my duty to repay the favor. More than that, I truly believe our destiny and potential hang in the balance.

The man who cannot forgive is a man who cannot move forward into the strategic plans of God. He will remain stuck while others continue to ascend the mountain.

NAVIGATE YOUR THOUGHTS

by Asaad Faraj

In God's Holy Word, many things are said about how important our thought life is, and even though we may not act on each thought, the Lord hears them.

A tremendous amount of coaching exists in business and sports about the battle being in the mind. When we pray, we must ask the Lord to sanctify our minds and let us see things as He does. Scripture instructs in 2 Corinthians 10:5 *to take captive every thought to make it obedient to Christ* (NIV). When you begin to do this, you can stop a multitude of sins before they take residence in your mind and manifest in your actions. When I see the words "take captive," that indicates a fight. When a thought pops into your head that's not pleasing to God, visualize literally putting that thought into a headlock. Punch it in the stomach. Force it down to the ground, tie it up, and lay it defeated at the feet of Jesus. The battlefield is truly in the mind.

We should also be praying for God to reveal blindspots in the way we think. King David, the writer of many Psalms, prayed this in Psalm 139:23-24: *Search me, God, and know my heart; test me and know my anxious thoughts. See if there is any offensive way in me, and lead me in the way everlasting* (NIV).

Have you ever heard that whatever we focus on grows? Or that our life will follow our most dominant thoughts? The Bible teaches about this.

Summing it all up, friends, I'd say you'll do best by filling your minds and meditating on things true, noble, reputable, authentic, compelling, gracious— the best, not the worst; the beautiful, not the ugly; things to praise, not things to curse (Philippians 4:8 MSG).

We need to think bigger! After all, we serve a God who is bigger than we can imagine.

Years ago, I heard a preacher tell a story of an American who visited a wealthy family in an Arab nation to play at a golf tournament. Having enjoyed golfing and feasting together, the Sheik was grateful to the American for visiting. He said to him, "It is our custom to give you a gift. What may I give to you?"

The American, trying to think of a simple and inexpensive gift, said, "A golf club would be nice."

A few weeks later, the American received word that his golf club had arrived. He was shocked when a car picked him up and took him to his very own golf club, complete with a clubhouse, 18 holes, and a driving range. The Sheik's thoughts were obviously higher than the American's. And so are God's thoughts higher than ours.

> *"My thoughts are nothing like your thoughts," says the LORD." And my ways are far beyond anything you could imagine. For just as the heavens are higher than the earth, so my ways are higher than your ways and my thoughts higher than your thoughts"* (Isaiah 55:8-9 NLT).

When we pray to hear God's thoughts for each area of our lives, we will be astounded by the miraculous!

Izzy Pichardo

Izzy Pichardo, aka Isramil Pichardo, is Dominican-American, born and raised in Massachusetts with one brother and one sister by great nurturing parents who are still married today. His passion for basketball and academics got him accepted to attend Williston Northampton prep school.

After losing interest in basketball, he dropped out of Manhattan College and began working as a merchandiser for Pepsi.

In 2005, he was introduced to the financial services business. He worked the business part-time for four years before going full-time in 2009.

Izzy has spent the last 10-plus years recruiting, training, and developing agents to become successful in business. He now has three regional vice presidents who run their own offices, and agents in over 20 states.

Izzy married his wife Jeidy in 2019. He has two sons—the late Cayden and Xander—and two daughters—Ava, and Avah. If you would like to know more, you can schedule a time to meet Izzy at calendly.izzypichardo or email him at izzypfs@gmail.com.

GOD IS ALWAYS THE CENTER

by Izzy Pichardo

> *"If a man has a hundred sheep and one of them gets lost, what will he do? Won't he leave the ninety-nine others in the wilderness and go to search for the one that is lost until he finds it? And when he has found it, he will joyfully carry it home on his shoulders."* (Luke 15:4-7 NLT).

When a hurricane is grabbing up everything in its path, it is well-known that the eye of the storm is actually the calmest section of the hurricane. Hopefully, by the time you finish reading, you'll have a better understanding and sense of peace that God is at the center of every storm you have been through or will go through. He is the everlasting Prince of Peace. So what's it like to be the one God left the 99 for? Feelings of unworthiness and doubts of having no bearing on what He can do filled my thoughts in my storm. The Bible has numerous stories of God pursuing the ones who ignored Him. Here is another to add to His countless reputation. You may find yourselves in the heavy violent outskirts of the storm, but I challenge you to keep your eyes on the center, where God is. He will extend His hand into the swirling winds and bring you to Him.

In my early years, I went to a Catholic school from kindergarten through 8th grade. Besides loving the sports of basketball and baseball, I was also an altar boy. Though I didn't understand the significance of serving in that position, I did appreciate the days I was called out of class to serve at someone's funeral. And I enjoyed them slipping me $10 as I held the cross at the end of the mass. Going back to school with money in my hands and knowing that I had missed a test was exciting to me. These acts down the road would play a huge part in shaping who I am today.

When I went away to prep school to play basketball, I stopped going to church. My mother would call me and ask me if I had found a church to attend yet, and each time I brushed it off. I thought I didn't need church; I didn't even understand what was said at mass. I figured if I never went back to church, I wouldn't be missing anything.

I went to college but dropped out and started hanging with the wrong crowd, and life sort of lost meaning.

Then, one day, I walked into an office to get a part-time job in addition to my full-time job. I thought I was going to learn about mortgages, but they sat me in a back room by myself and in front of a video of a guy named John Maxwell. The video had to do with leadership; all I thought to myself was, *What does this have to do with mortgages?* I found out over the years it was a pursuit jab that God was throwing at me as John Maxwell used to be a pastor and is now a great author who has led many people to Christ. There I was, pursuing money, and He met me where I was and spoke to me in a language I could understand.

They say most people will never step foot in a church. As believers of Christ, we work daily either for God's kingdom or for His adversary. I liked the fact that the company I was working with was okay with God's name being mentioned in the workplace. But don't think for a second that I was a full-blown missionary. In fact, I still have work to do today.

I continued working full-time in addition to beginning that part-time job in financial services as I tried to transition it to a full-time career. But they say if you want to make God laugh, tell Him your plans.

The day a male finds out he's having his first child is a proud moment. I say "male" because I wasn't yet a man, and any adult male can conceive a child. I was having my first kid! That feat was minimal compared to the work that was to follow to care for this true masterpiece of God. The moment of realization had great hope and promise of being a part of something bigger than myself. The news was thrilling. The next few months were a time of excitement, nervousness, and anticipation as we got close to finding out the gender. Then, the news of learning I was to have a son was something that, like most men, made me feel proud and caused me to walk with a pep in my step. But my news was accompanied by something else. Something I didn't understand but would soon find out was coming to my door, whether I liked it or not. That devastating news was that my son would be born with what the doctors considered a terminal illness.

For the last few months of the pregnancy, we needed to go into Boston every Monday for a check-up. At work, I requested Mondays off, which I didn't think I would be granted but surprisingly was. However, my extra day off caused a cut in my income. Luckily, I had already started working in financial services part-time, so I was able to quit that full-time job, allowing me to make my own schedule and be there for every appointment. My income suffered for a while, but it was worth it to be able to be there as a father.

It was confirmed that my son suffered from Trisomy 18, which is like Down syndrome or Trisomy 13, but much worse. Trisomy 18 children are 80% likely to die within the first year of life. Out of 100 children diagnosed, only 20% make it to their first year. Of those 20, 99% are female. My small mustard seed of faith at the time allowed me to handle the odds that my son would live past the first year. Remember, by the time I was a young adult, I had strayed away from the church for over ten years. but the seed of faith was there deep inside me, waiting to germinate.

The odds were against him, but when I was asked if I had made my son's funeral arrangements, I told the doctor that he would make them himself. However, I also remember thinking to myself, *What is wrong with me that my first child wouldn't be born normal?*

In a counseling session with one of the medical staff, the counselor put things in perspective. She told us there was nothing different we could have done. She asked, "Do you know how many things have to go right for a baby to be born what's considered normal by society's standards? From the act of conceiving, all the way to childbirth, is such a meticulous process with so many moving parts. To only have one issue, which is just one of you giving one extra chromosome, is a miracle in itself."

She definitely put my mind at ease with her words. We ended up finding out that most children with Trisomy 18 have congenital disabilities in their lungs, brain, feet, hands, and especially their hearts. He had all of those minus the heart defect. As I looked for what to name my son in a children's book of names, I stopped on the letter C and saw the the name Cayden. Its meaning was Spirit of the Battle. I knew I didn't have to look any further as he was going to be a warrior, and we were in for a battle along with him.

Cayden Isramil Pichardo was born 4 pounds five ounces, and by the time we left the hospital, he was 4 pounds and one ounce. Somehow, we were able to leave within a few days as he was pretty stable. I remember putting him in the car seat—he sunk right in and was swallowed by it. The straps and constraints were too big for him; we swaddled him with extra blankets so he could be snug in the seat. It had just started. And my life would never be the same again.

It was a miracle that Cayden made it past his first year; however, it wasn't without stress, anxiety, and doubt. As the years continued, there were countless hospital visits, overnight and weekly stays, ambulance rides, and even a few med flights. The weight of those tough times heavily impacted our finances and contributed to relationship issues, resulting in divorce.

Once, while on an appointment with a client, I got a phone call that Cayden had pulled out his G-tube, which had been surgically inserted into his stomach for feeding purposes. There was blood everywhere, and the ambulance was on its way. I had to remain calm as I finished my appointment, knowing we needed the money and I was not a doctor and couldn't do anything from where I was. At the time, I was struggling in business; I had actually walked to that appointment because my car was at the mechanic shop. So after, I had to walk for over 30 minutes in the cold, thinking about what I would find when I got to the hospital. Luckily, I learned that the situation wasn't that serious. Cayden wasn't in pain and was laughing throughout the whole ordeal. The nurse and his mother had been able to get the G-tube back in without any serious complications. Looking back now, I can tell that Matthew 6:26 (NLT) rang true, even though I didn't know that scripture like I do today. It says, *Look at the birds. They don't plant or harvest or store food in barns, for your heavenly Father feeds them. And aren't you far more valuable to him than they are?* God was pursuing and taking care of me, all at the same time and without my knowledge.

By the time Cayden was 11 years old, I had gotten used to the close calls: the school nurse calling to say that he had no heart rate or pulse or had pulled his G-tube out or a plethora of other things.

> *"I have told you all this so that you may have peace in me. Here on earth you will have many trials and sorrows. But take heart because I have overcome the world"* (John 16:33 NLT).

February 12, 2018, was a normal day as I sat with a client. My phone rang numerous times, but I didn't hear it. As I walked out of the client's house, I called my mother because of her three missed calls, and she related to me that Cayden was headed to the hospital. I'm originally from Massachusetts, so I've seen my fair share of thunderstorms, but this storm came in its own category.

When I arrived at the hospital, I heard the same story I had become accustomed to hearing, and I prepared myself to be ready to be in the hospital with my son for a few days or maybe a week. The initial hospital decided to have him medflighted to a Boston hospital. Helicoptor rides are usually a great sight-seeing experience, but this one had no thrill. Those few days turned into three weeks. All of a sudden, the things the doctors were saying started to sink in as a real possibility. They told us there was a high chance Cayden wouldn't bounce back from this one. We played Christian songs by his ear to try and breathe life into him—songs like "Tell Your Heart to Beat Again" and "Hope in Front of Me" by Danny Gokey. Hundreds of people started to follow his condition on social media. It was tough to give updates, but the prayers were definitely felt from far away.

More time passed, and there was no improvement. We started to prepare to let Cayden go. On 3/3/2018, we all stepped out as my mother stayed behind with him. The medical staff had told us his respiratory levels were high, so we would have some time to say our goodbyes. I left to get a priest who was a family friend so he could pray over Cayden and read him his last rites. As we pulled up to the hospital, my wife said she wanted to use the valet, which I hadn't done in our three-week stay. When we got up to the front desk of the ICU, I was told to wait for the doctor, which was unusual since previously I had just been able to check in and walk back to his room.

The doctor arrived and asked me, "Are you ready?"

I answered very quickly, "Yes. Let's go." I wasn't sure why I was ready, but I knew I was.

We got into the room, and Cayden's oxygen levels were below 50%. It was happening. The priest prayed over him as I laid my hand and head on his chest. I felt and saw him take his last breath. It wasn't a floating body you hear about in the movies, but I felt as though his spirit had just left his body.

As I write this, it's still hard to describe the event. Even though it was peaceful, it was still difficult. One extra red light. One stop sign. If I hadn't valeted. I would've missed it. Cayden went on to be with the Lord on 3/3/2018 at 11 years old.

As my new earthly reality set in, the next few days were filled with late nights of drinking and oceans of tears. Telling his two sisters he was gone was not an easy task. I knew I couldn't remain in that condition. A couple of days before the funeral, I woke up at 3:00 a.m. still hungover. I looked at my phone to read a message on social media. A woman I did not know personally had reached out to give me her condolences and share something that has impacted me to this day. She told me she, too, had a son born on 2/2/07, the same day as Cayden. Although he was born across the country, her son suffered from the exact same illness. However, the huge difference was that her son did not make it through that first day.

Something in that message sobered me up, and I turned on the lights and started writing Cayden's eulogy. In it, I said, "Thank you, God, for the 4047 days I had with my son, when not one day was promised."

A week later, my pastor gave a sermon about how we don't hear much about Mary after Christ was crucified, but it is known that she continued to spread the gospel. Right there, I knew he was talking to me (like everyone feels on a Sunday), and I knew that I couldn't sink into depression and drinking as I still had a family to raise and take care of. I had to continue to talk about God's grace and my son on pretty much every appointment, even though I was there to talk about finances. The work was not done.

It's not ironic that my income got cut back in my previous job, positioning me to start a business that would give me the freedom to be there with my son during the times he needed and not have to worry about money. Nope. Not ironic at all. It was in God's promise to give me a hope and a future.

Hopefully, throughout my story, you can see the seeds that were planted and even the situations that, at the time, I thought were irrelevant. Like the fact that being an altar boy made me a man of faith and someone who understands God's grace. And that I went from getting money at funerals to having a business that helps provide people money for funerals and more through life insurance. But most importantly, I have the privilege of being able to talk to my clients and agents about the goodness of God.

Most people have a GPS, a Global Positioning System, but the best Global Positioning System is a different three letters: GOD. He placed us here, He loves mankind, and He will never abandon us. Even when we can't see Him, He is there. Sometimes, He is quiet, and we can't hear Him. But remember when you were taking a test in school? The teachers were always quiet. You will finish the test you have been given, and you will have a testimony to tell of God's great grace.

Remain faithful even in sorrows and expect God's relentless, reckless pursuit of your heart.

A month after losing my son, I found out I was having another kid with my new wife—another miracle. See, we had been trying for over a year, and all of a sudden, we found out we were pregnant a month later. It was tough to celebrate it because I was still mourning my son, but at the same time, I had to appreciate the gift of life that I was receiving once again.

When we did the gender reveal, we found out our child was another boy. Many people told me they knew it would be a boy because God wanted to bless me with another son as I had done so well with the first one He entrusted in my care. We decided to give him "Cayden" as a middle name since he never got a chance to meet his brother but would carry part of his spirit with him.

I now reside in Florida, so I've traded thunderstorms for hurricanes. But one thing remains true—God is at the center of every storm, holding our hand and testing our faith to step out and walk to Him. I'm so glad He pursued me and that He is pursuing you as you read this book!

And since we are his children, we are his heirs. In fact, together with Christ we are heirs of God's glory. But if we are to share his glory we must also share his suffering. Yet what we suffer now is nothing compared to the glory he will reveal to us later (Romans 8:17-18 NLT).

Pray with me.

Dear heavenly Father,

I want to thank you for the circumstances that come into my life—whether they seem negative or positive. Remind me that you will always walk beside me. Even when times are tough, you will never let go of my hand and heart. And remind me to appreciate you when times are good. We know that you can take the most difficult, treacherous, sad event and work it for your good and something that can last for generations. So help us to navigate the next storm so we can hand over and share our original GPS with others. Thank you.

In Jesus' name. Amen

MAX GOLD

Max Gold is a native New Yorker and a graduate of Boston University. After living through 9/11, he and his family moved to Orlando to start a fresh life. It was there where Max started his financial service agency. The firm grew, and after living in Florida for 20 years, Max (becoming an empty nester) decided to start a new episode in life.

Max now resides in Santa Monica, California, where he is expanding his business.

Recently, Max released a Christian self-improvement book titled *Planestorming!* (available on Amazon). Stay connected to see what the next chapter brings... @maximilianr717

THE FUJIWHARA EFFECT

by Max Gold

The National Hurricane Center defines the Fujiwhara Effect as this: "The tendency of two nearby tropical cyclones to rotate cyclonically about each other." This phenomenon occurs when two cyclones come together and merge as one. The end result is a massive, devastating storm. An example is Typhoon Hinnamnor, which took place in September 2022, affecting Taiwan, Japan, South Korea, The Phillippines, and Russia. This powerful storm created over 1 billion dollars in damage and took a dozen lives.

In my life, I have also experienced the Fujiwhara Effect. But through it, God never left my side, and I continue to praise His name.

I was born in New York City in 1973 and raised in the Lower East Side of Manhattan. My childhood was chaotic due to my parents' separation, which led to a fair amount of instability. Although painful, I was blessed to have love from my parents and attend good schools where my education (but mostly my friends) helped me always stay focused on the next levels of life.

I attended college in Boston and returned to New York to start my career in the music industry. Unfortunately, I did have a secret, which was my alcoholism. As it became more intense, I knew I had a problem but didn't know where to turn. My drinking was part of the culture I was in; still, it led me to become aggressive, have blackout moments, and treat women with disrespect. But I was stuck and didn't know how to get out.

By the grace of God, I had a near-death experience (sounds funny, right?), which led me to stop drinking cold turkey. I have now not had a drink in over 25 years. As part of my transition to sobriety, I knew I needed a change. So I opted to move out of Manhattan to Astoria, Queens. Although it was only three stops away from midtown on the N train, it might have been a move to another part of the world.

Astoria has long, tree-covered streets, large apartments, and fantastic eateries producing lovely cuisine from all over the world. There, I felt inner peace for the first time in my life. Prior to moving, I said to myself, "This is it! I'm done being a jerk to women. I'm done with alcohol. It's time to change, and I'm ready to be alone."

We all know that if you want to make God laugh, tell Him your plans.

The first night in my new location—August 1, 1999—while moving my stereo equipment into my beautiful and spacious apartment, this beautiful woman with the most amazing eyes came out of her apartment with a pack of girls. All I could say as she locked her door was, "I assume you live here." OMG, the guy with "the game" had none at that moment.

She looked at me and said yes as her girlfriends chuckled. Then they got in the antiquated pre-war elevator and disappeared.

"Oh man," I thought to myself. "I can't believe this."

It turns out that on the ride down, Christine told her friends, "I'm gonna marry that man."

Three years later, we wed in St. Augustine, Florida. I married the girl next door!

Our passion and love for each other grew stronger and stronger. I adopted her son Jonathan, whom I met when he was two. And we had our daughter Maxine in 2005. Of course, life always has its challenges. I was laid off from my "amazing job," and after a deep depression that lasted for one year, we opted to move to Orlando and start a new life.

Now that you know a little about my history and baggage, let me share a little about Christine. She grew up as a NewYoRican (New York Puerto Rican) in the South Bronx (need I say more?) and did not have the opportunities I was given. Even though she was born as a preemie (premature), her heart was massive. Christine had her own battles, including alcoholism and experiencing physical and sexual abuse as an adolescent. After we dated for a year, she decided to move to Tampa with her son and find a career and, more importantly, herself.

The day after she moved, she called me and said, "Guess what? I enrolled in The Manhattan Beauty School." She completed the 1200-hour state requirements in what felt like 900 hours (lol) so she could get back to New York and start her career as a stylist (and, of course, be closer to her man). Upon moving back, we decided to take separate apartments because I had rubber legs and was afraid to commit. I bought an electric scooter, which allowed me to zip back and forth in Astoria.

On September 11, 2001, I was en route to work on the N train and getting ready to switch to the 7 Train at Queensboro Plaza when all our lives changed. A stranger said to me, "Big fire. Trains delayed!" As I crossed the platform, I received a text on my 2-way pager from my boss, which read, "Stay home today." Simultaneously, I looked down the Manhattan skyline and saw a massive cloud surrounding the North Tower. 9/11 was in full effect.

Christine and I decided to accelerate our lives and move in together. There was no more time to take life for granted. Ironically, I had proposed to her three weeks earlier at Windows on the World, the rooftop restaurant at the World Trade Center.

One year later, I was laid off, and New York City had a massive blackout that led many to believe it was under another terrorist attack. After Christine walked home over the Queensboro Bridge because the trains were down, we knew our time in New York had come to an end. I was done fighting God and trying to do life how I wanted.

We moved to Orlando, halfway between where our mothers lived. After we signed a lease, the job Christine had lined up fell through. "Oh boy, now what?" I went to a career fair and was able to join a company right across the street from where we moved. I started my business, and Christine eventually found another salon and built a great client base.

Our beautiful Maxine was born in Orlando, and Jonathan grew up with us and spent summers with his biological father in New Jersey. We joined a large church, then opted to move to another that was more intimate with a powerful Bible study. Of course, I only attended on Sundays because I was "busy." After struggling, I opted to join Christine on a Wednesday night. My pastor finished his teaching by stepping his 350-pound body and size 14 feet on the Holy Bible and screaming, "Stand on the Word!"

"Is that ok, God?" I asked myself.

Still, week after week, we attended church as a family. Eventually, I was ready to fully commit and live all the Christian principles to the best of my ability.

Our businesses grew, and our finances increased. We bought our first family home, and I opened my first office. Christine opened her sole proprietorship salon, and by the grace of God, we were up and running!

In June 2017, Christine and I attended my business convention in Indianapolis, Indiana. We had rallied our team to travel by bus from Orlando; it was the first time my company hosted in Indy instead of Atlanta. It was hot, and we didn't know our way around. Think of it as the times when people walked around Jerusalem before Jesus came—lots of chaos and no leadership! We had a spousal disagreement on the last evening of the convention. Thank God for double beds!

The next day, we were still on non-speaking terms. I left the room early in frustration. "It's Father's Day, and I'm getting no love!" I said to myself as I wandered the empty Sunday morning urban streets. I looked about 150 feet down the road and saw Christine coming out of a convenience store. I ignored her, and we reconvened at the hotel only to bring our bags to the lobby and take the rideshare to the airport. We were early for our flight and found a quieter section of the airport to sit and wait. After a few minutes, Christine sat on the floor. She emptied her large purse and started organizing the contents unnecessarily and meticulously on the floor. It looked like a live version of Tetris. Something was wrong. I finally spoke after more than 12 hours of silence.

"Is something wrong? This is weird." I asked, "Did you take something?"

She replied, "Yes," and pulled out a bottle of nighttime over-the-counter sleeping pills.

I asked how many she took, and she presented about half the bottle. Thus, the beginning of the first storm...

Christine had developed a habit of taking over-the-counter pills to numb her pain. I have learned that, particularly with women, if they don't deal with serious childhood and teen trauma, it exacerbates and eventually leads to a nervous breakdown in their 40s. Christine was 41.

"What happened next?" I'm sure you are wondering.

Christine begged me to still get on the plane because of the kids. I researched on my phone and told her that if she drank as much water as possible, we would board and deal with the problem upon returning home. We arrived safely. Thank the Lord.

The next day, she shared with me her addiction and the euphoric feeling she desired. I found bottles and baggies everywhere in places I would never go in the house. We discussed it, and she promised to confront this challenge. I went back to work; it was business as usual until the following Sunday.

We were at church. I was in the back participating in my role with the finance team when I heard screaming during the homily. They brought Christine back to me, and all she could say repeatedly was, "It doesn't matter...nothing matters."

Her breakdown was beginning. We took her to the hospital. Now, we were in the eye wall of the first storm. I brought my wife to eight hospitals in 40+ days, trying to find the right treatment and guidance. At one point, she called me and said she had an incident in which she wrapped a sheet around her neck, put it over the door, and fell. "I'm such a loser I can't even kill myself." I will never forget these words as long as I live. Eventually, we found a good program and the right medication for Christine. I drove her to daily treatment and cared for our kids as best as I could. My business sustained itself because God was on our side.

Christine got better. She was healing and going to therapy. Her medication was regulated, and she returned to working with a few clients a week at her salon. One evening, she took Jonathan to the movies. They had a blast. My daughter came into the room to talk to her mom, and then the second and bigger storm caught ahold of the first as it was leaving. Thus, the beginning of The Fujiwhara Effect...

My daughter came running out to me. I was on our first Band of Brothers Squad meeting via video. What a great time for the enemy to attack.

"Dad, something's wrong with Mom," she said in a panic.

I ran into the room and found Christine slurring, "Caaalllll Mmmmom."

I said, "Ok, honey, but first I will call 911."

I heard the fire trucks while I was still on the phone because the firehouse was across the street from our home. Upon arrival, they asked me a bunch of questions about Christine's medical history. One fireman said we must take her to the mental hospital again, but the Lord sent a raven to my home.

"No," another said adamantly. "She's having a stroke." They followed his lead and took her via ambulance to the right hospital. Yes, it was a stroke.

We spent ten days in the hospital—lots and lots of tests. Christine was so strong. I slept in the recliner next to her every night. Visitors came, including our kids, who would come every day after school. It was determined that my wife's stroke was caused by fully blocked carotid arteries (100% and 90%), and that the best solution was to insert a stint in her neck. We agreed after much discussion with doctors and family. The doctor conducted the surgery and assured me she would heal in the intensive care unit. I went down to the cafeteria, grabbed some hospital food, and began to pray.

I had never before heard God speak directly to me, but He did then. He told me to go upstairs. I threw out my food and anxiously made my way upstairs. Sure enough, Christine was moving speechlessly and uncomfortably in the bed. I knew something was wrong. I told the nurse, but she disregarded this as part of the first-day post-op.

"Something is wrong with my wife," I insisted.

The hospital agreed to conduct a CAT scan. This time, I met a different doctor who was peaceful and compassionate. "Your wife is having a brain hemorrhage." As he explained the options, I noticed a wedding ring on his finger.

"What would you do if this were your wife?" I asked.

He said he would do the craniectomy, a surgery designed to relieve pressure on the brain.

I told him to do it. The estimated time of the procedure would be 2-3 hours.

I stood in the large, empty hospital waiting room all night. I was soon joined by my pastor. All I could do was play the gospel songs Christine had shared with me when we were seeking salvation; holding my hands up, I prayed with my pastor and surrendered to God. Six hours later, the gentle doctor appeared. Fighting back tears, he disclosed, "I'm sorry. Your wife is really, really sick".

Christine passed away on April 19, 2018. The love of my life was gone. The second storm had engulfed the first, and that was it...

As tears roll down my face while I write this over five years later, I leave you with this: my son left for the Navy that year and now is an E-5 living in

San Diego overseeing a team that will go on their third deployment in the Pacific Ocean on the USS Theodore Roosevelt. My daughter graduated high school and is starting college to pursue a degree in Psychology. My business, along with my faith, is stronger than ever. I have chosen to live in Santa Monica, California, where I run my business (and take time to heal), but frequently travel to New York, Chicago, and Orlando for business, family, and pleasure.

Although we were hit by a pair of devastating storms that merged and became one, the Lord has not and will not forsake us. And He will always be present for you if you allow him to be. I will leave you with some passages that have been a blessing to me. May God bless you and your family. Thank you...

I can do all things through Christ who strengthens me (Philippians 4:13 NASB).

Yea, though I walk through the valley of the shadow of death, I will fear no evil (Psalm 23:4 KJV).

"Behold, God is mighty, and does not despise any; he is mighty in strength of understanding" (Job 36:5 ESV).

NAVIGATING HURT

by Ken A. Hobbs II

Many men have abandoned their relationship with God. Others have been called to serve Him but refused because they have been hurt. And in many instances, wayward individuals have allowed pain to crush their lives.

There is a large spectrum of hurts—emotional, physical, and circumstantial—which includes things like dealing with people or losing a friend or relationship. Hurt can stem from changes in our lives, broken hearts, lost hope, aging, death, sickness, and other events that can encompass our minds.

It takes a radical step of faith to overcome hurt before it consumes you altogether. Many Christians have been conquered by hurt when they have let their flesh get in the way. This one powerful word can quickly overcome us. So, we must be on guard to war against fret, envy, anger, wrath, and evil. Hurt can cause us to fall prey to these actions and more. So, what is the solution to a man's hurting heart? As men, we are often so protective and guarded against allowing ourselves to be vulnerable when dealing with past hurts. Do you think you could trust your hurting heart to someone who can help you?

God is your perfect solution—He never makes a mistake.

Someone who makes no mistakes and loves and cares about you IS always with you. Only God can oversee every heart supernaturally. God provides truth in His Word for you to hear. One of those truths is that God loves His children. His perfect love Is all-encompassing. When one of His sons is hurting, He knows it. When one of His sons is feeling pain, He feels it. And He cares. God is a God of wisdom; He is also just and will always take action to protect His children.

> *If any of you lack wisdom, let Him ask God, who gives generously to all without reproach, and it will be given him* (James 1:5 ESV).

The first step in allowing God to humble your heart is to trust Him and His wisdom, knowing He will guide you. The more you know Him, the more you will be open to trusting Him.

Keep trusting in the Lord and do what is right in his eyes. Fix your heart on the promises of God and you will be secure, feasting on his faithfulness (Psalm 37:3 TPT).

Please give your heart and all that comes with it to God. All your past sins will be covered with the healing power He so generously bestows on His children. If you are dealing with pain as a victim, recognize that the pain you experience from your past is not sinful. To blame victims for their pain is a sin against the wounded, the brokenhearted, and the oppressed. It is a sin against God Himself, whose heart is with those who are hurt. Hurt hurts God, and He comes close to those who are brokenhearted; He confirms that in His Word in Psalm 34:18. Please hold the following scripture close if you are dealing with tremendous hurt.

> *Even when bad things happen to the good and godly ones, the Lord will save them and not let them be defeated by what they face* (Psalm 34:19 TPT).

Leo Hinkley III

Leo Hinkley III was born in Miami and now resides in Fort Myers, Florida. Growing up in a Christian household, he attended Christian schools and graduated from Southwest Florida Christian Academy in 2008. He attended Palm Beach Atlantic University and Florida Gulf Coast University with a major in business.

Leo is presently a Regional Vice President with a large financial services company. The family brokerage began in 1995 when he was six years old, and he often jokes that he became a financial coach at the ripe old age of six! Leo's primary duties are the training and development of new agents, product development, and marketing for the brokerage.

His passion is serving his community through several non-profits. He is also dedicated to his church, with the mission of spreading the Word. He is the Co-Founder of Church for the Rest of Us, a grassroots church in Cape Coral, Florida, designed for people with a desire to learn the scripture in an open and safe environment where ideas can be freely expressed with no judgment.

Leo would like to dedicate his chapter to his dad, Leo Hinkley Jr.

For more information or to connect with Leo, visit www.thechurchfortherestofus.com

Faith from a Bathtub

by Leo Hinkley III

Have you ever looked back on your life and wondered where it all went wrong? I thought I had it all. I had the beautiful wife, the house, the car, and a growing business. I felt indestructible. My life felt perfect. Who knew that there was a literal storm brewing on the horizon?

My prayer is that as you read my story, you will see that you can gather hope and strength as you go through the trials and storms of life. My literal storm taught me that, in all circumstances, anything is possible with God.

But in your hearts honor Christ the Lord as holy, always being prepared to make a defense to anyone who asks you for a reason for the hope that is in you; yet do it with gentleness and respect (1 Peter 3:15 ESV).

When I was 14, my mom enrolled me in a Christian school with a class of 32 people. I was shy and nervous about the coming four years, but I met my future wife on our first day of class. Sitting next to each other, we quickly hit it off as our personalities were similar. She was incredibly kind with a genuine spirit. I knew we were going to be great friends. She had other intentions; we started dating during our freshman year.

We dated off and on during high school, finishing off our senior year apart. We stayed in touch while I attended Palm Beach Atlantic University. During my second year there, I realized college was just not for me. I wanted to move back home, but my mom encouraged me to get established, buy a house, and start my career.

So, I began to search for a home and soon made an offer on a house. What a thrilling experience! I mean, how many 20-year-olds do you know who have the opportunity to purchase a house? It was such a huge milestone that I had to tell everyone I knew. In my excitement, the first person I called was my soon-to-be wife to tell her I was moving back home. After I moved into the house, we began dating again. We were not the perfect couple, with several previous breakups, but we actively worked on our relationship.

In June of 2012, I asked her to be my wife—in Disney World, of all places. From that moment, I thought I would spend the rest of my life with her. We complimented each other so well. Because we met in a Christian school, I felt our relationship was a "God thing." We were both believers but never attended church regularly. We became holiday Christians, only showing up to service on important dates to appease the families.

Not everyone was as enthusiastic about our engagement as I was. Many people, including my parents, advised me not to marry this person. Certain people told me, "Love is blind, but the neighbors ain't," implying that they could see her true colors and I could not. I had heard stories of couples who had married young and, even though their parents and friends had objected, they lasted for 20, 30, or even 40 years. Everything turned out perfectly. Why couldn't that happen to me?

The week before my wedding, I was approached by some family members and offered a significant sum of money to cancel the wedding. I did not take it as an insult but more of a loving gesture to try and protect me from whatever they thought my marriage would become. I remember saying to my family, "I know her more than any other person. She is going to be my wife; she is my best friend. How can anybody guess how my marriage will turn out?" I made a conscious decision to move forward and make her my wife.

We married in September 2013; it was one of the happiest moments in my life. I felt like I had everything. I had a beautiful wife, a house, a paid-off car, and a growing career. I felt like I was on top of the world. Nothing could take this away.

The week after we got back from our honeymoon, a friend of ours, who was in our wedding party, had a birthday party. Because I had taken so many days off work and could not take any more, I had to skip his party. My wife, on the other hand, was close friends with this guy and decided to go to the party without me. While I was at work, she had too much to drink and made some bad decisions. I didn't think much of it; he was a friend from our wedding party. Why should I be concerned?

A few days passed, and the guy came to me and told me what happened. He asked for forgiveness and was deeply apologetic. I loosely forgave him, but our friendship was over. For the first time ever, I had a major blow to my self-esteem. I felt like the entire world had collapsed around me. I kept thinking, *Why would she do this? Why would she do this to me? Why would she do this to our brand-new marriage?*

I asked God, "Why would you allow this to happen? What did I do to deserve this?"

I placed the blame on God instead of asking for His guidance. I let my anger get the best of me and went to her without a plan to work through it. I didn't want to leave her. I thought we could resolve our issues and come to some understanding. She swore up and down that it meant nothing. It was the alcohol making the decision. She had too much to drink, and things got out of hand. She never once apologized or asked for forgiveness. Instead, she blamed me because I was not there to protect her from her mistakes. I remember her saying, "Why weren't you there? You are supposed to be my knight in shining armor. Instead, you failed because you were too busy working."

Deep down, I knew I was right. But I recalled thinking, *She's not wrong; I wasn't there to protect her. I wasn't there to stop her.* I felt emasculated and started to believe her. Looking back, I know it was the worst reaction I could have had. I felt that everything was my fault. I never saw myself as a man. Instead, I became an empty shell. I lost faith in our marriage. From that moment on, in my mind, our marriage only lasted two months. But I stuck around because, according to her friends, "it was the right thing to do."

I felt completely useless. Her family became the priority, and I was not allowed to see my family for holidays. We stopped attending church and church functions because she decided she no longer believed in God. I followed her, trying to salvage what little marriage we had left. I gave up on my dreams for my business and felt like a second-class citizen in my own home. I lost my own identity; I couldn't look in a mirror and recognize who I was.

After four years of marriage, I could not stand the pain any longer and filed for divorce. After all the court paperwork was signed, I fell into a deep depression for three months. I stopped eating properly and lost almost 40 pounds. I didn't have the strength to get up to go to work. I knew deep down that I needed to change. My close friends were saying, "You need to get over it." "There are other fish in the sea." "Go out and start dating again." But I couldn't. I had lost something so precious. I had given up so early in our relationship and lost the battle.

My literal storm was soon approaching; hurricane season had arrived. In the days leading up to September 10, 2017, Florida was preparing for a massive storm coming our way. We were told that Hurricane Irma was coming right for Fort Myers and to secure our valuables and evacuate. However, being native Floridians, we decided to stay and make a party of it. My mom and I invited 12 other people to her condo to watch the storm and just have a good time. We had been through three major hurricanes and thought we would ride this one out.

I gathered up all the supplies needed from my house, including some clothes, food, water, and my two dogs. As I was finishing packing, I felt something I hadn't ever felt before. I sensed that was the last time I would be coming back to my home. I felt that everything I was looking at around me was gone. It was such a strange feeling; I was looking at the things around me, and I couldn't shake that I was never coming back to it.

When the hurricane made landfall, it was devastating. It had wind gusts in excess of 160 miles per hour with torrential rain. As it was bearing down on the condo, we took shelter in a small room where we could hear the wind ripping through the door frames. We lost power, and all the 14 of us could do was wait in the dark. I prayed for God to let the storm pass and for us to come out without any damage.

The next morning, Mom and I decided to check my house. When we arrived, portions of my neighborhood were underwater, trees had fallen, and debris from people's roofs was blocking the roads. When I arrived at my house, I saw my mailbox was ripped from its foundation, and my home was without a roof. My heart sank. Everything I owned was inside. My worst fears had come true. Clothes, furniture, pictures, and priceless family tapes were soaking wet and destroyed.

However, my bedroom looked as though it did not have damage. I quickly ran to my neighbor to ask if they had a tarp so I could cover the one part of the house that was undamaged. Mom went into action, gathering some items that weren't ruined and putting them into the car. My next-door neighbor, Mathew, kindly gave me his only tarp and offered to help nail it down before the next wave of rain fell.

When we got off the roof, I heard a loud crash from inside and a blood-curdling scream from my mom. I had no idea what had happened and rushed inside. The ceiling had collapsed, and she was standing two feet from where it fell. She was visibly shaken, but thank God, she didn't have a scratch. I could have lost her that day, but God was really looking after her. It was too dangerous to be in the house, but we packed what we could. As we were leaving, my car broke down in my driveway, and we were stuck. As if it couldn't get any worse.

I remember standing in my driveway, feeling so helpless, scared, and alone. I started to tear up; I thought to myself, *God, why would you do this to me? What did I do to deserve this?*

That night, Mom felt sorry for me and found the only restaurant with power in town and brought back Chinese food. She thought a hot meal would help me feel better. She also wanted to wish me a happy birthday. I had completely forgotten that it was my birthday. But what did I have to celebrate? I lost my home, my car broke down, all my personal possessions were destroyed, and my marriage failed.

That night, since there were 14 people still staying at Mom's condo, the only place I had to sleep was in the bathtub. Laying there with two dogs and a dimming flashlight, I started to pray in total silence, asking God, "What is it that you have in store for me? Why would everything be coming down on me this hard?"

I felt God reach out to me and say, "You must make a decision. You have two choices. You can become a victim of everything that has happened to you and stay a victim for the rest of your life. Or, through My strength, you can see that I have given you a fresh start on the path I have for you."

I had a decision to make: become a victim or, through Christ, take strength in Him.

> *"The LORD will fight for you, and you have only to be silent"* (Exodus 14:14 ESV).

The next morning, I got up from the bathtub and began putting the pieces back together. I wasn't going to let anything stop me from what God called me to do. I was to clean up the pieces of my home and clean the doubt in my head. I felt powerful again and ready for the next chapter in my life. I was going on faith; I had no idea who or what was coming, but I was ready.

> *"You will seek me and find me when you seek me with all your heart"* (Jeremiah 29:13 NIV).

The following month, a mentor helped me with a plan to refocus my business. The next January, I earned our company's highest contract—Regional Vice President.

After my promotion, I asked my family to recommend some churches. My Aunt Christine mentioned that I should start with her church and see if I could meet some new people. After a few Sunday services, I started wanting to do more. I felt the Spirit leading me to join a weekly Bible Study. There were several ministries available to join. I sent a message to each one

I found interesting, and only one contacted me. Matt Podrasky sent me a text inviting me to his "Lifegroup" (yes, that's exactly how he spelled it). At first, I was nervous, thinking I had to speak in front of strangers, but what I found was a group of people who wanted to find God and be closer to Him and His Word. They were real with each other and found strength through adversity. For the first time, I felt comfortable and started attending every group function.

While going to the Lifegroup, I never had a full night's sleep. I kept dreaming of my ex-wife and our fights. Most nights, I would wake up drenched in sweat and panicking. I couldn't shake this deep weight on my heart. Then I talked with a friend, Jan Scher, who told me I needed to attend the Band of Brothers. He told me they focus on the hearts of men through the Word of Jesus and overcoming the enemy. Being at the Boot Camp allowed me to find what I was looking for—peace through forgiveness.

During one of the sessions, the speaker quoted the book *Forgiving Forward*. Reading, "bitterness is the poison we drink hoping someone else will die."1 Bitterness is what I was feeling—I was still hurting and reeling from my marriage. My heart was bitter from the divorce. I had to ask for and show forgiveness to my ex-wife. It was because of the Band of Brothers that I finally gained the courage to ask her to have a real conversation. This time, it came from the strength of God and His teachings. It was a tough moment for us, but it was extremely healing. Tears were shed, but we finally forgave each other and had our closure. After that, I finally got a full night's rest.

Therefore confess your sins to each other and pray for each other so that you may be healed. The prayer of a righteous person is powerful and effective (James 5:16 NIV).

O Lord my God, I cried to you for help, and you have healed me (Psalm 30:2 ESV).

While searching for a church home, Matt, my Lifegroup leader, had a brilliant idea of starting our own church—one for people who have never had a relationship with God, who have been alienated or felt unwelcome by the conventional church. He said, "What if we created a place for people who have been othered? More like a *'Church for the Rest of Us?'"* And we had a name.

To us, a church isn't a building. It's anywhere where two or more believers can come together, lift each other up, and experience God together. On our first day, seven people were in attendance, including four organizers. Today, I am proud to say we have built a family from all walks of life and are going through the wonders God has in store for us. Almost every week, we have someone give their heartfelt story of adversity and the incredible power we find in Christ. We all have a story, and we all face adversity, but through Christ, we find His mercy and healing.

So do not fear, for I am with you; do not be dismayed, for I am your God. I will strengthen you and help you; I will uphold you with my righteous right hand (Isaiah 41:10 NIV).

Not only so, but we also glory in our sufferings, because we know that suffering produces perseverance; perseverance, character; and character, hope. And hope does not put us to shame, because God's love has been poured out into our hearts through the Holy Spirit, who has been given to us (Romans 5:3-5 NIV).

The storm I went through wasn't a bit pleasant at the time, but God used it to shape me into the person I am today. If you've ever asked, "Why would God allow these terrible things to happen to me?" the simple answer is growth. Just as a caterpillar grows in a cocoon to break free as a butterfly, we weather the storms of life to come out stronger on the other end. God doesn't permit our storms because He enjoys our suffering; He allows them so we can be shaped into the people He made us to be. Struggle can be necessary for growth. Blessed are those who trust God in the valley after they've seen Him move mountains.

Everyone has a different storm. Mine was a literal one.

God always has a plan. Only you can decide whether to be a victim or get back up, rebuild, and fight as a victor.

> *The LORD is my strength and my shield; my heart trusts in him, and he helps me. My heart leaps for joy, and with my song I praise him. The LORD is the strength of his people, a fortress of salvation for his anointed one* (Psalm 28:7-8 NIV).

[1]Hebel, Bruce Wayne and Toni Lynn, *Forgiving Forward: Unleashing the Forgiveness Revolution.* Bruce and Toni Hebel, 2011

FC CLARK

FC Clark is a dynamic and accomplished individual with a background in finance and business administration. As an entrepreneur, investor, and philanthropist, Clark has made significant contributions across various fields. He has successfully established and led multiple startups in technology, real estate, and renewable energy, driving economic growth and creating employment opportunities.

Clark's expertise in business development has made him a sought-after as an advisor. Additionally, he is deeply committed to philanthropy, supporting initiatives in education, healthcare, environmental conservation, and social welfare. Clark has funded educational resources, built schools, and advocated for quality education. He has contributed to healthcare initiatives and promoted accessible healthcare. Clark has also been involved in environmental conservation, supporting organizations focused on protecting natural resources and promoting renewable energy. Furthermore, he has contributed to social welfare programs, including poverty alleviation and support for marginalized communities.

Through his multifaceted achievements, FC Clark continues to inspire others with his unwavering determination, versatility, and dedication to excellence.

A Journey to Faith

by FC Clark

In the depths of my childhood, darkness seemed to prevail. At the tender age of six, I endured a harrowing experience that forever changed my life. It was a tragic betrayal that unfolded behind closed doors, as I became a victim of molestation by my sister and neighbor boy. The weight of this unspeakable act burdened my young heart, casting a shadow over my innocence.

Sadly, the horrors did not end there. I witnessed my father's gradual descent into madness, a transformation that unleashed a storm of abuse upon my older sister. The once-loving and caring father became a tormentor, inflicting physical and emotional pain upon the child he was meant to protect. Faced with such unbearable circumstances, my sister and I made a desperate decision—we ran away, seeking refuge from the torment that had consumed our lives.

Our escape led us to separate guardian homes, providing a temporary respite from the chaos that had defined our existence. For years, we endured separation, each carrying the burden of our shared past. Then, at twelve, I longed to be reunited with my sister, my anchor in a world that seemed intent on tearing me apart.

It was in the year 1989 when hope, in the form of a church camp, came into my life. Seeking solace and guidance, I stepped foot into the sanctuary, unaware of the profound impact it would have on my journey of healing. I grew stronger as I listened to the words of compassion and redemption. In that moment, I discovered a refuge in God, a source of unwavering support that would carry me through when humans would fail me, even in the darkest times.

As for my mother, she battled with drug addiction, dragging me and my brother into a world of despair. I clung to my newfound faith for protection and guidance. In the face of my mother's self-destructive habits and the harrowing reality of her engaging in dangerous activities to sustain her addiction, I found the strength to endure. God's loving arms became my sanctuary, a place where I could seek solace, understand, and draw inspiration from the stories of others who had overcome their trials.

Let my story testify to the transformative power of faith and resilience. Throughout my tumultuous journey, the scriptures served as beacons of hope, reminding me that I was not alone. Psalm 34:18 whispered to my wounded heart, assuring me that God would be close, providing comfort and deliverance. In Philippians 4:13, I found the strength to believe in my capacity to overcome obstacles in my path. Jeremiah 29:11 became a guiding light, promising that God had a purpose for my life, a future filled with hope and prosperity. With these scriptures etched deep within my soul, I embarked on a path of healing, forgiveness, and redemption. I broke free from the cycle of violence and addiction, emerging as a beacon of hope for others trapped in similar circumstances.

At the age of 16, a significant encounter took place amidst the tumultuous cycle of my life. I met a girl who had recently lost her father and felt an inexplicable connection to me. Our bond grew more robust, and unfortunately, she became pregnant at a young age.

However, my challenges intensified as I entered the age of 17. I strayed from what I knew was right, losing touch with my connection to God. I became involved in selling drugs and engaging in exploitative behavior, taking advantage of vulnerable women involved in prostitution.

At 18, I eagerly embraced a new challenge when I stumbled upon an advertisement in the newspaper. Little did I know that this sales job would become a stepping stone towards owning my own business. By the time I turned 20, I had successfully established four distribution centers across three states, with over 4,000 independent representatives selling our products.

However, as my business prospered, I faced a personal crossroads. Before opening the fourth location, I made a fateful encounter with a woman of deep faith who would forever change my life. She became my first wife, and her presence brought a sense of purpose and direction that I had never experienced before. But tragically, I made a series of terrible mistakes that would ultimately lead to the downfall of our marriage.

I committed adultery, lied, and let my destructive behavior consume me, causing us to divorce and me to lose everything I had built. Not only did I lose my business, but I also lost custody of our two children. The weight of these failures and the consequences of my actions left me with nothing, and I found myself spiraling into a life of homelessness and drug addiction once again.

My journey into destruction was a painful and arduous one. During this dark period of my life, I truly hit rock bottom. The drugs became my only solace, numbing the pain and masking the remorse I felt for the destruction I had caused. I was lost, broken, and desperate for a way out.

Little did I know that this rock bottom would become the foundation for my redemption. It was here, in the depths of despair, that I was forced to confront my demons and face the consequences of my actions. It was a long and grueling journey, but with the support of loved ones and the strength I found within myself, I gradually began to rebuild my life.

I sought help for my drug addiction, entering rehabilitation programs and surrounding myself with positive influences. I worked tirelessly to rebuild my relationships with my family, seeking forgiveness and making amends for the pain I had caused. Slowly but surely, I started to regain control over my life and rebuild the trust I had lost.

Through determination, perseverance, and the guidance of a higher power, I managed to turn my life around. I started a new business, this time with a renewed sense of purpose and integrity. I vowed never to repeat the mistakes of my past and to use my experiences to help others who were facing similar struggles.

While the scars of my past will always be a part of me, I have emerged from the darkness stronger and more resilient than ever before. I have learned the value of honesty and forgiveness and the importance of cherishing the relationships that truly matter. My journey serves as a reminder that even in our darkest moments, there is always hope for redemption and a chance to rebuild a better future.

Yet, God had a different plan for FC Clark during my wayward journey. He orchestrated a series of bold encounters designed to redirect my life unbeknownst to me; He approached and boldly proclaimed that I was called to be a pastor.

Encounters with strangers who proclaimed my calling as a pastor profoundly impacted my decision to change. I was deeply lost and engaged in destructive behaviors at that point in my life. I had strayed from my faith and lost sight of my purpose.

When these strangers approached me and boldly declared that I was meant to be a pastor, it was a jarring wake-up call. It felt as though God was speaking directly to me through these people. Their words resonated deep within my soul and ignited a spark of hope and possibility.

These encounters were powerful reminders of God's presence in my life and His unwavering love. They provided a glimpse of a different path that aligned with my true purpose and allowed me to impact others positively. The strangers' conviction and the divine timing of their messages made me realize that I could no longer ignore this calling.

Their words planted a seed of transformation within me. They reminded me of the person I was meant to be and inspired me to seek forgiveness, redemption, and a renewed relationship with God. I recognized that I had strayed far from the path of righteousness, and it was time to turn my life around.

So, I decided to leave behind my involvement in drugs, exploitation, and the destructive cycle I had created. I embraced the calling to become a pastor and committed myself to a life of service—spreading hope, guidance, and the message of God's love to others.

The encounters with these strangers catalyzed change. They provided the clarity and conviction I needed to break free from my destructive patterns and embrace a new direction. I am eternally grateful for their intervention, as they played a pivotal role in redirecting my life and setting me on the path of healing, redemption, and purpose. These divine interventions prompted me to reevaluate my choices and seek a different direction. I recognized the need for a profound change, embracing the calling I knew and believed God had placed upon me. With newfound determination, I set forth on a path of redemption and transformation, leaving behind my involvement in drugs and exploitation. I also left behind my little brother, who rejected God and is now serving a 30-year sentence.

I pray that you find my journey a testament to the transformative power of divine intervention and the ability to find purpose even in the midst of darkness. From my troubled past, I emerged with a renewed sense of faith and a calling to serve as a pastor, spreading hope and guidance to others who may have lost themselves.

This unexpected turn of events became a pivotal moment in my life, igniting a passion to share my story and offer hope to those who have experienced similar pain and struggles. Through my ministry, I strive to create a safe space for individuals to heal, find redemption, and discover their own divine purpose.

And while my journey has been marked by darkness and adversity, it has also been shaped by resilience, faith, and the transformative power of love. Today, I stand as a living testament that no matter how broken or lost one may feel, there is always hope for a brighter future.

This unexpected turn of events became a pivotal moment, inspiring me to become FC Clark— dedicating my life to God's work, making amends for my past actions, and embracing a higher purpose. Through my own story of redemption, I now offer others a message of hope, forgiveness, and the capacity for change, demonstrating that even in the darkest times, God's plan can unveil itself in the most unexpected ways. Drawing from my own experiences, I offer the following advice to others who have experienced similar traumatic events in their childhood:

- Seek professional support: let me emphasize the importance of seeking help from mental health professionals who can provide guidance and assistance in processing traumatic experiences. Therapy, counseling, and support groups can offer a safe space to explore emotions, heal, and develop coping strategies.

- Embrace faith or spirituality: I found solace and strength in my faith. I encourage others to explore their spirituality and find a source of support and comfort that resonates with them. Whether through religion, meditation, or personal beliefs, connecting with a higher power or inner strength can be a source of healing.

- Prioritize self-care: Taking care of oneself is crucial after experiencing trauma. I suggest engaging in activities that promote physical and emotional well-being. This can include exercise, healthy eating, practicing mindfulness or relaxation techniques, and engaging in hobbies or activities that bring joy and fulfillment.

- Connect with supportive communities: Surrounding oneself with understanding and compassionate individuals can be immensely helpful. Seek out support groups, communities, or organizations where individuals with similar experiences can share their stories, offer support, and provide a sense of belonging.

- Practice forgiveness and healing: The importance of forgiveness, not only for others but also for oneself, cannot be overstated. Forgiveness can be a powerful tool in healing, allowing individuals to let go of anger, resentment, and pain. Forgiveness is a personal journey that may take time.

- Share your story: This gives us power by sharing personal experiences to inspire and support others. By speaking out and sharing our stories, individuals can raise awareness, break the stigma surrounding trauma, and offer hope to those struggling.

- Focus on building a positive future: Our past does not define our future. I encourage individuals to set goals, pursue education or career opportunities, and surround themselves with positive influences that can help shape a brighter future. Personally, my determination to pursue a higher calling significantly impacted my relationships. As I embraced the calling God had placed upon my life, I underwent a transformation that influenced how I interacted with others and the nature of my relationships.

- Reevaluate romantic relationship: My commitment to my higher calling also affected my romantic relationship with the girl I had bonded with and who had become pregnant. My dedication to the spiritual journey and the responsibilities that came with it necessitated a reevaluation of our relationship. I needed to prioritize personal growth and commitment to my calling, which could have led to changes or even the end of our romantic involvement.

- Be aware of and remove relationships with exploited women: Before my transformation, I was involved in exploitative behavior, taking advantage of vulnerable women in prostitution. As I embarked on my path of redemption and left behind my involvement in drugs and exploitation, my relationships with these women changed significantly. I sought to make amends, offer support, or distance myself from those harmful connections.

- Develop relationships within the faith community: My commitment to my higher calling caused me to cultivate relationships within the faith community. As I pursued becoming a pastor, I connected with fellow believers, mentors, and leaders who shared my passion for spiritual growth and service. These relationships provide me with guidance, support, and opportunities to learn and develop in my chosen path.

- Lean into relationships with family and friends: My transformation influenced my relationships with family and friends. My newfound determination and commitment to a higher calling inspired and impacted those around me. Some family members and friends did not support my journey or encourage my pursuit of becoming a pastor and struggled to understand and accept the changes I was undergoing. My determination to pursue a higher calling influenced the dynamics of my relationships and, at times, required me to make difficult choices as I sought forgiveness and made amends, established new connections within the faith community, and navigated the support and understanding of my loved ones.

You may stray, as I have many times, from God's calling in your heart and soul, but like me, God will never leave you.

I leave you with further encouragement. As you grow, develop a limitless mindset through faith and a knowledge of your true power. We all have that power given to us when we accept God into our hearts and lives.

My faith In Christ influenced new knowledge in me. Yet I emphasize my own tendency to deviate from God's calling, acknowledging that I myself experienced moments of straying. However, know that God remains steadfast and does not abandon us.

To conclude my message, I encourage individuals to cultivate a mindset transcending limitations by anchoring it in faith and acknowledging the true power of accepting God into their hearts and lives. This mindset, rooted in a deep connection with God, allows individuals to tap into their inherent potential, embracing the limitless possibilities that lie within them.

Today, I am FC Clark—a living testament to the indomitable human spirit. My unwavering faith and resilience propel me to overcome the unimaginable. Through my story, I seek to offer solace, inspiration, and practical advice to those who find themselves facing similar challenges. Let my journey remind you that no matter how dark the past may be, there is always hope for a brighter future.

NAVIGATE TOWARD RESTORATION

by Asaad Faraj

Loss is devastating. As we journey through the hourglass of time, we all experience loss. However, loss does not have to be permanent! Restoration literally means "the action of returning something to a former owner, place, position, or condition."

Let us all take heart in the fact that because the concept of restoration is mentioned 66 times in the Bible, we can trust that we serve a God who is able and loves to restore. One of the most famous yet tragic stories in the Bible is the life of Job. He lost his family, his health, and his wealth! However, at the end of the story, God showed up mightily and bestowed restoration onto each area of his life.

> *When Job prayed for his friends, the LORD restored his fortunes. In fact, the LORD gave him twice as much as before!...So the LORD blessed Job in the second half of his life even more than in the beginning. For now he had 14,000 sheep, 6,000 camels, 1,000 teams of oxen, and 1,000 female donkeys. He also gave Job seven more sons and three more daughters...Job lived 140 years after that, living to see four generations of his children and grandchildren. Then he died, an old man who had lived a long, full life. (Job 42:10, 12-13, 16-17 NLT).*

The New Testament is commonly referred to as the Good News, as God sent his Son on a mission to save humanity. When Jesus described His purpose in Luke 19:10, he chose words to provide hope for our lives. He said: *"For the Son of Man has come to save that which was lost"* (NKJV). *God confirms Jesus' purpose of restoration by turning it into a promise! In his kindness God called you to share in his eternal glory by means of Christ Jesus. So after you have suffered a little while, he will restore, support, and strengthen you, and he will place you on a firm foundation* (1 Peter 5:10 NLT).

Does anybody besides me enjoy a Fourth of July fireworks celebration? My favorite part is the grand finale. God's design for the end of times is the ultimate grand finale!

> *And I saw the holy city, the new Jerusalem, coming down from God out of heaven like a bride beautifully dressed for her husband.*
>
> *I heard a loud shout from the throne, saying, "Look, God's home is now among his people! He will live with them, and they will be his people. God himself will be with them. He will wipe every tear from their eyes, and there will be no more death or sorrow or crying or pain. All these things are gone forever."*
>
> *And the one sitting on the throne said, "Look, I am making everything new!" And then he said to me, "Write this down, for what I tell you is trustworthy and true."*
>
> (Revelation 21:2-5 NLT)

Because we serve a God of restoration, we can navigate through loss knowing that God promises a glorious future.

THOMAS J. STEWART

Thomas Joseph Stewart is a passionate pursuer of God and has been born again for 30 years. He currently lives in Chesterland, a suburb of Cleveland, Ohio, and has lived in Ohio all his life. Tom is a husband to his wife, Shirley, of almost 35 years and has three grown children and two grandchildren, with a third on the way.

Tom enjoys the outdoors because that is where he connects to God easily and hears the Father's voice. He accredits everything he has and has done in life to the grace and gifting of his heavenly Father's love.

Tom has served in men's ministries for over twenty years and walks in the office of evangelist, spreading the Good News of Jesus Christ wherever he goes. He is a God-made entrepreneur and stewards a small and prosperous business for the Lord. Tom loves people and carries the Father's heart towards them.

FROM THERE TO HERE

by Thomas J. Stewart

Within your heart you can make plans for your future, but the Lord chooses the steps you take to get there (Proverbs 16:9 TPT).

Have you ever been tired of being who you are? I sure have. I was born the youngest of four children in a family of six, yet I always felt alone. And as far as my identity, I had no clue who I was. It was like I just didn't fit in. But at the same time, I had a thought inside, way down deep, that constantly eluded me: I was meant for something or someone.

Just as He chose us in Him before the foundation of the world, that we should be holy and without blame before Him in love (Ephesians 1:4 NKJV).

Getting right to the point, let me share with you what put me off course to start with. When I was eight or nine, I was sexually molested, which was very confusing for me. I was afraid to go to my mom or dad with it because of the shame attached to it. Fear has always been the biggest obstacle in my life. I could not overcome it, and it paralyzed me.

For God has not given us a spirit of fear, but of power and of love and of a sound mind (2 Timothy 1:7 NKJV).

Furthermore, my dad was not a very relational father at that point in his life. In fact, his nickname for me was "Dummy." You see, he tried to use a form of reverse psychology by telling me I was dumb or I couldn't do it. He thought I would try and prove him wrong. Only it had the opposite effect—I actually believed him. After all, he was my dad, the most significant male figure in the eyes of an eight-year-old. All of these things had a very negative impact on my life, especially in school. Don't get me wrong—it is never really about what has been done to us but what we do with it. And what I did was make bad decision after bad decision.

In school, I was constantly rejected and teased, but I was never bullied because I grew very fast for my age and was rather tall. I was a gentle giant, you could say, but wow, did I have a temper. You see, I could not control all the bad stuff going on inside of me. So, when I hit that certain limit, I blew up. Mainly, I would release my anger on bullies. I didn't like being picked on, and when I saw other people being picked on, I had a sense of compassion for them. So, I became the protector of the ones who could not protect themselves. Yet I had no one to protect me from the horrible things that can happen to a child.

To get away from my perceived identity, I chose to follow others I thought were cool. This only led me into a deeper, more messed-up life filled with cigarettes, alcohol, and drugs of various forms, which only made matters worse. Those things lied to me and said they would make my life better. But they didn't.

At fifteen years old, I met a girl who I became attracted to in a meaningful way. She was a "good girl." Honestly, I thought she might be able to save me. Not a chance. Our connection just complicated things even more. My understanding of things such as love, sex, and relationships was very much skewed.

Trust in the Lord with all your heart, and lean not on your own understanding (Proverbs 3:5 NKJV).

I brought a lot of baggage into the relationship, like lying about doing drugs, smoking, and looking at other girls in a sexual manner. She stayed with me through all this, and we eventually got married and had our first child, although my decisions weren't getting any better. My problems actually got worse, and I got better at hiding them. Looking back, I can see that my opinion of myself was really bad. I had low self-esteem, I didn't believe I fit in, and I believed I was not good enough. Actually, I thought I was just an all-around waste product of society. So, guess what comes next? Yep—suicide. Or a botched attempt at it, thank God. I tried several times in several ways, but I was unsuccessful again and again. I could go on and on, telling you about the "off course" portion of my life, but that is not my good news. So, I'm going to change gears and tell you how I went from there to here, which is where I am today.

In all your ways acknowledge Him, and He shall direct your paths (Proverbs 3:6 NKJV).

Eventually, everything came to a head. My wife asked me to move out of our home until I got help and changed. So, I did. I went to stay with my brother, and as I did, I was singing song lyrics from Lynard Skynyrd's "Free Bird." The first day I thought I was going to rape the world of all that was in it. The second day, I started to hear a little Voice inside me saying things like, "Are you sure this is what you want?" I contemplated that Voice and came to the conclusion that I had never wanted to be in this situation in the first place—I had just somehow ended up there (actually by a chain of events brought on by my bad choices). So, I decided to make one "good" choice. And that choice was that I didn't want to be here in life. But I did not know how to maneuver out of it.

Then, on March 18th, 1994, I was on my way to work when I saw the sunrise in such a way I had not seen since I was a young child—before all the bad stuff happened in my life. At that point, I decided I didn't want to lose my wife and daughter, whom I love. I didn't want my daughter to grow up in two different homes. I didn't want her to go through all the crap. I knew I needed help—because I had no strength. I just wanted someone to rescue me.

In my distress I cried to the Lord, and He heard me (Psalm 120:1 NKVJ).

I then decided to meet with a friend of mine who had offered to talk with me. I thought to myself, *I'll take any help I can get at this point.* His name was Gene; I went to his house to talk.

Without good direction, people lose their way; the more wise counsel you follow, the better your chances (Proverbs 11:14 MSG).

Gene had to make some deliveries to his pizza shops and asked me if I would come along. His wife had made cookies for us for the ride. That act of kindness touched my heart in a way that hadn't happened before.

> *Don't you see how wonderfully kind, tolerant, and patient God is with you? Does this mean nothing to you? Can't you see that His kindness is intended to turn you from your sin?* (Romans 2:4 NLT).

During the drive, I told him my story. He was not shaken in the least, and he told me that his story was similar. I was blown away. This was a man, in my opinion, who had it all together. He asked me if I thought that maybe Jesus Christ could help me. I blew a gasket. In anger, I said, "My problems are real, and you want to give me this Jesus crap?"

Again, He didn't flinch. He told me his story and how Jesus helped him.

By the end of it, I couldn't help but think that Gene had been where I was; and where he had arrived was where I wanted to be. So, I chose to listen.

> *They conquered him completely through the blood of the Lamb and the powerful word of his testimony. They triumphed because they did not love and cling to their own lives, even when faced with death* (Revelation 12:11 TPT).

Gene told me all about what Jesus did, using the Bible to support his story. Seeing the evidence in his life, I said I wanted Jesus in my life, too. So, we prayed together. And I prayed out loud, meaning every word, with every ounce of my whole being, "Jesus, if You are real, I really need You in my life. Please forgive me for all the bad things that I have done. Please help me."

> *For God so loved the world that he gave his one and only Son,*
> *that whoever believes in him shall not perish but have eternal*
> *life. For God did not send his Son into the world to condemn*
> *the world, but to save the world through him* (John 3:16-17
> NIV).

What happened next was absolutely incredible. I felt a presence enter my body through my abdomen. It moved up through my arms and head. It went down and into my legs and feet. It was almost like in the movie *"Beauty and the Beast"* when the Beast turned back into a human being.

Jesus replied, "Loving me empowers you to obey my word. And my Father will love you so deeply that we will come to you and make you our dwelling place" (John 14:23 TPT).

Instantly, I felt free, and I had a clean conscience. I immediately knew the Bible was the Word of God. I was immediately cleansed from a ten-year drug addiction. I never touched or even wanted to touch drugs again. It was like God reached inside me, ripped out all of my hard wiring, and then proceeded to rewire me.

> *Therefore if the Son makes you free, you shall be free indeed*
> (John 8:36 NKJV).

I had such a desire to go to church and learn more about God. And I heard Him speak to me through His Word, His people, and even through His creation. His Voice was addictive. I just couldn't get enough, so I fervently continued to seek after Him everywhere.

"My own sheep will hear my voice and I know each one, and they will follow me" (John 10:27 TPT).

God began to change me from the inside out by renewing my mind – exposing the lies I believed and helping me to replace them with the truth.

> *Stop imitating the ideals and opinions of the culture around you, but be inwardly transformed by the Holy Spirit through a total reformation of how you think. This will empower you to discern God's will as you live a beautiful life, satisfying and perfect in His eyes* (Romans 12:2 TPT).

One day, the Lord said to me, "Tom, who created you?"

I answered, "You did."

And He responded, "The One who created you is the only One who can define you. You cannot be defined by others or even by yourself. Only I have the authority to define you."

That day, I laid down my false opinion of myself and decided to let only the Lord define who I am.

You formed my innermost being, shaping my delicate inside and my intricate outside, and wove them all together in my mother's womb (Psalm 139:13 TPT).

For some people, their experience with God might not happen as it happened for me, but that's not the point. The point is that my choices steered me away from God, and then my choices steered me toward God.

So, today, if you hear His still, small Voice trying to guide you toward Himself, what choice will you make?

> *So God set another time for entering His rest, and that time is today. God announced this through David much later in the words already quoted: "Today when you hear his voice, don't harden your hearts"* (Hebrews 4:7 NLT).

If you let Him, God will transform your life. He will show you the lies you believe and help you replace them with the truth. He will show you your value and what you mean to Him. He will open your eyes so you can see things that most people will never see or understand. His ways are incredible. His mercies are new every day. His grace and compassion are all around you. He is slow to anger and quick in love and forgiveness. He is the master planner who holds the blueprints to everything living, that is, that was, and is yet to be. Don't try to define your own life. Let Him define your life for you. From the day of my salvation on, I am His, He is mine, and my life is interwoven with Him. It cannot be unwoven.

> *I am fully devoted to my beloved, and my beloved is fully devoted to me* (Song of Songs 6:3 TPT).

By the way, today I am still married to that same beautiful woman with whom I fell in love so many years ago, and we have three amazing children and two incredible grandchildren. God has also blessed me with a prosperous small business that not only supports my family but also supports the families of my employees. God has also given me a circle of influence and the opportunity to help people who are where I once was come to know the One who has me where I am today. And where I am today is in a wonderful relationship with God, who speaks and guides my life with His love and understanding, knowing me better than I even know myself. Truthfully, I didn't navigate my story. He did. I just surrendered to Him and His process.

> *Truth's shining light guides me in my choices and decisions; the revelation of your word makes my pathway clear* (Psalm 119:105 TPT).

The Lord created all things, including you. It is His desire for you to know Him personally and intimately. He wants to direct you from where you are and take you where He wants you to be. He wants you to live the way He intended life to be lived—in Him, and with Him, and through Him. If you want to get away from where you are or what you have become, recognize you have a choice today whom you will serve: God or yourself. If you want to live freely and purposefully, choose God. Ask Him to forgive you and cleanse you from all your bad decisions and mistakes. Believe that Jesus paid a price for you. Receive His love, mercy, grace, and acceptance. Allow Him to teach you through His Word. Ask Him to show you where He is all the time. You will find out that He is right there beside you and inside you, enjoying your love for Him and washing you with His love as well.

If you want Jesus to navigate your storm, bow your head right where you are at this very moment. Pray the following to God from your heart, meaning every word. "Lord, I know I have made a mess out of life, and I don't want to continue this way anymore. Jesus, thank You for Your sacrifice on the cross that takes away all my sins and connects me to Your Father. Please come into my life with Your Holy Spirit and show me how You want me to live. I want to love You and be loved by You. Thank You, Lord. Amen."

For by grace you have been saved by faith. Nothing you did could ever earn this salvation, for it was the love gift from God that brought us to Christ! (Ephesians 2:8 TPT).

Remember, God is a rewarder of those who diligently seek Him. When you pray, do so believing He will come to you and make His home inside of you. Then, rejoice and celebrate the newness He is going to do through and in you!

And without faith living within us it would be impossible to please God. For we come to God in faith knowing that He is real and that He rewards the faith of those who passionately seek Him (Hebrews 11:6 TPT).

Therefore, if anyone is in Christ, he is a new creation; old things have passed away; behold, all things have become new (2 Corinthians 5:17 NKJV).

DAVID RODRIGUEZ

David Rodríguez is an entrepreneur, family man, and passionate follower of Jesus Christ. He has been married to his wife, Hady, for 32 years, has a financial services business, three wonderful sons, and two amazing daughters-in-law.

David and his sons have been leaders of Band of Brothers ministry, dedicated to empowering men to be leaders for God. His wife is also a leader in Hearts of Beauty ministry, dedicated to restoring the hearts of women through a relationship with Jesus Christ. As a family, they are involved in many service projects designed to bless the community and are intent on leaving a godly legacy everywhere they go.

David would like to send his heartfelt thanks to a few men God has and continues to use in his life, including Alex Azpiri, Guz Gonzalez, Joe Ortiz, Guy Shashaty, Rodmey Perez, Nelson Guerra, and Art Williams.

From atheist to passionate about Christ, David is committed to living for God. His prayer is that you seek God, knock at His door, let Him answer, and allow yourself to be transformed by His love.

Seeing Beyond the Eye of the Storm

by David Rodriguez

Everyone in this life has had or will go through a storm. Some through many. I am not different! I want to share with you my biggest storm—one that I believe we will all have to deal with at some point in our lives. The challenge is that many, like me, will be in a storm without even realizing it. Often, for many years. The storm I found myself in can be compared to being in the eye of a hurricane. The storm was destroying everything in its path, but in the eye, all was calm and peaceful.

I was born in Cuba and lived there for 12 years before coming to the United States. Cuba is a communist country where the government seeks total control, and they do not embrace a relationship with God. As a result, I was an atheist, completely clueless about God. I was lost. My mom and dad got divorced when I was two years old, and my mother was left to raise me by herself. Not only was she a single mom, but my maternal grandparents were in the United States, and my paternal grandparents were never part of my life. So, for me, my mother was everything. You could say my mother was my "god."

After moving to the United States, I lived my life like a robot for 16 more years. I did everything I thought I was supposed to do the best way I knew how. Even so, I felt empty, lost, and, without a doubt, spiritually dead. The most important part of my life was missing; the scary thing is that I was not even aware of it!

My dad used to travel a lot for work in Cuba, so I did not have the chance to see him often. When I was young, he would visit me once a month, but as I grew, I saw him less and less. I always felt the need for the love of a father. Although I never had a bad relationship with him, it was always a poor one. For many years, I felt an emptiness or void, a sensation that something was missing. I attributed those feelings to my poor relationship with my dad.

I reconnected with my maternal grandfather when I arrived in the United States. He became my father figure. We loved each other and had a great relationship, but our time together was short—he died soon after we reentered each other's lives. My mother then married my stepdad, Julio, whom I love like a dad. We have a great relationship.

I believe a father-son relationship is crucial. I, for certain, felt an emptiness and the need for a father. Yet, little did I know that a different Father was pulling me towards Him!

When I was 15, I met my future wife Hady. She was 14 at the time. Four years later, I made the second-best decision of my life by marrying her. We were just 19 and 18 years old! Hady came from a broken family. Her mother left Cuba and came to the US when she was three years old, was raised by her grandmother and great-grandmother, and didn't meet her father until she was 28. We both decided never to make the same mistakes our families did. We committed to each other and agreed to always fight for our marriage and our family. Divorce was not an option, as we wanted to provide the best possible example for our children. When I was 22, our son David was born. I became a father and made the third-best decision of my life: to become the best father possible. Soon after, at 24, our second son,

Danny, was born.

I was constantly seeking truth—looking to become a better person—so I could be a good dad. I worked full-time and was going to college to become an engineer. In 2002, at the age of 26, I made the fourth-best decision of my life. I stopped studying and started to work part-time with a financial services company that offered great potential to become my own boss and have my own business. Little did I know the kind of people I would meet there! People who are now my brothers and mentors. These people paved the way so I could make the BEST decision of my life.

Remember, I was an atheist. I didn't believe in God. To make matters worse, my wife thought God was bad, so we were not interested in anything that had to do with Him. Yet these great people I was around, whom I admired and looked up to, were always putting God first. I can't explain why, but I thought of Christians as weak and poor because they always prayed and asked God for help. In this case, these people were clearly not poor or weak, and they were investing time to help me grow a business and as a person. They were the opposite of what I thought Christians would be. They were strong leaders, tough but kind, and very wealthy, yet they were so humble and always put God first in their lives.

Art Williams, the founder of the company and someone I admire and look up to, said in one of his speeches, "This is easy to say but difficult to do; if you want to be successful in every area of your life, you have to put God first, family second, and business third." A seed was planted when I heard this. From the eye of the storm, where I felt comfortable, I started to realize maybe a storm was coming. A storm that would make me understand that perhaps I was missing something.

I remember thinking, *These people have what I want. I want to be like them. They are great husbands, great fathers, great friends, great businessmen, and they all put God first in their lives. Not only that, but they also don't keep quiet; they want everyone to know Him. Why?*

That is when everything started changing for me. I thought, *I am following these people. I am coachable to them. I am accountable to them. I want to achieve the success I see they have—not just their financial success, but ultimate success. They are living with purpose, achieving personal growth, and making an impact in the world while having financial success.*

Then I noticed I was not coachable to the number 1 priority in their life: a relationship with God, our creator.

In fact, I was destined for hell and running happily towards it. I didn't even notice it! But these people cared more about my eternal life than anything else. At some point, I had to be humble enough to ask myself, Could it be that I am missing something? *Could it be that I am not seeing something they see? Should I pay attention to this?* If what they were saying was true, this was a big deal—not only for me, but also for my wife, children, and family.

Two years later, when I was 28 years old, a great friend, Alex, invited me to Gus and Johana's home for a Bible study to help couples improve their marriage. That interested me, but I didn't even realize God was in it! Guess what I learned there? I learned about the most important relationship in the world: the Father-son relationship. I learned that God had a plan to save me and the world! God the Father sent His Son Jesus Christ to give His life to save mine—and yours.

> *For God so loved the world that he gave his one and only Son, that whoever believes in him shall not perish but have eternal life* (John 3:16 NIV).

In Romans 3:23, the Bible says, *we all have sinned* (NIV), and Romans 6:23 says that the payment for sin is death. This death is not physical but spiritual. We will all live eternally somewhere, either in heaven or hell. Romans 6:23 also states that God is giving us the best and most important gift we could ever receive: eternal life in Jesus Christ, our Lord.

In that Bible study for couples, I made the BEST decision of my life: I accepted Jesus Christ as my Lord and Savior. The most important part of my life, the spiritual, was awakened, and I was born again.

> *Jesus replied, "Very truly I tell you, no one can see the kingdom of God unless they are born again"* (John 3:3 NIV)

This was just the beginning. The sky did not suddenly open. I didn't see God. I didn't see nor feel a miracle happen. Keep in mind that before that, I didn't believe in God, so all I did was "knock on the door," and the door was opened. I still didn't want to enter, but the door was open.

> *"Ask and it will be given to you; seek and you will find; knock and the door will be opened to you"* (Matthew 7:7 NIV).

Although I didn't see or feel a miracle, the miracle started to happen. The Holy Spirit, now living in me, began to work in my heart. I started going to church to learn more about God. I was serious about this because if this was truth, I should not take it lightly. After all, we are talking about the creator of the Universe wanting to have a relationship with me. I needed to know more!

I had one challenge: my wife! She had a very hard life, and she blamed God for it. Although she is also Cuban, she was raised in Venezuela and had believed in God at one point. But because of the harsh situations in her life, she felt that God was not a good God. She questioned Him, wondering how a good God could allow such tragedies to happen to her.

> *And we know that in all things God works for the good of those who love him, who have been called according to his purpose* (Romans 8:28 NIV).

Nonetheless, I started going to church by myself. I studied His Word, and Christ began to rescue my heart. I started to see life differently and wanted to be and behave more like Christ. And my wife started to notice. As God was transforming my life, my wife benefitted from it. The change she saw in me humbled her heart, and she wanted to know more.

I was lost, but God's plan was to rescue me as He rescued my wife. Together, we started to build a relationship with Christ. As I learned more about Christ and who He is, why He came, and what He came to do, the most important relationship in my life started to grow. I discovered who my true Father is, how much He loves me, how much He cares for me, and who He really is. The emptiness and void I used to feel and the feelings I suppressed, thinking I could do nothing about them, were gone.

The Father-son relationship that was so important to me was God pulling my heart towards Him. Now I know why it was never about my earthly father and me, or even my sons and me, but about God the Father and me.

For he has rescued us from the dominion of darkness and brought us into the kingdom of the Son he loves (Colossians 1:13 NIV).

Devin, my third son, was born when I was 30 years old. As my three children were growing, my relationship and understanding of God was also growing. The more I knew about God and His Word, the more I wanted to know about Christ, and the more I wanted to be like Him. The more I understood the price He paid for me, the more grateful I felt. The more I understood the love He has for me, the more I was able to love Him.

I was lost, but He came to rescue me and give me a new heart. Not only me but also my wife and our three sons, and I know this will be the case for my future grandchildren. Nineteen years after the beginning of my new life, I am now 47 years old, my wife is 46, David is 25, Danny is 23, and Devin is 17. Words cannot describe how blessed I am—not because of me, but because of the love God has for me.

My wife, Hady, is a beautiful woman inside and out. How great is my God who protected our relationship through the years? She was my first and last girlfriend. David and Danny married amazing women, Jarling and Angie, who also love and serve the Lord, and we love them as our daughters. All of this is because God's hand is over us.

My wife, children, and their wives embody the teachings of Christ in their actions, thoughts, and interactions. They demonstrate tremendous love, compassion, forgiveness, and humility while living a life aligned with God's Word.

My wife serves in Hearts of Beauty, a ministry that benefits women, helping them restore their hearts and bringing them closer to the Lord. For years, my sons and I have been part of the leadership team of Band of Brothers, a bootcamp designed to empower men to be the servant leaders God created them to be. Looking back, I can see God's love and protection over my life. Have I had a perfect life? Of course not! Have I had many storms? Yes, I have! But now I can see God's hand in all of them.

What I wanted the most in my life was to be a great father and husband, providing the best possible life for my family. Being financially successful and providing material things like houses, cars, toys, and big bank accounts is great. But having all these things without God is meaningless when you are lost and destined for hell. The best years on this earth will be nothing compared to eternity in heaven.

I went to God's house and knocked. He opened the door and came into my heart, transforming my life. Not only my life but the lives of the people I love the most: my wife and sons, my mom, my stepdad Julio, my father, and many others.

I wanted to be the best father in the world, but I couldn't be. I wanted to be perfect, but I couldn't be. I wanted to be loving all the time, but I couldn't be. I wanted to be the perfect example, but I couldn't be. I did many things wrong, but I did one thing right. Not just any "one thing," but the "one thing" I needed to do right for my ultimate desires to be fulfilled: I invited all my sons to have the most important relationship in the world, which is the relationship between them and the true and perfect Father—the One who will never fail them; the One who is perfect; the One who loved them with His life. Now that they know about Him and have a personal relationship with Him, I have the satisfaction of knowing they are on the right path and well taken care of.

I was lost, but now I am found.

I was lost in a country where God was not embraced or talked about. I was running in a race without knowing where the finish line was. It's scary to look back and see that everything looked okay when I was in the eye of the storm, but I was blinded and without divine purpose. I thank God for letting the storm keep moving so I could see Him in it.

My father did the best he could with the limitations he had. I felt a need and a longing for a better relationship with my dad, but God was pulling and redirecting me to Him. My desires were selfish. I wanted to be the best father, to be the one my sons would look up to. I wanted to be their god, just like my mom was for me, but Christ opened my eyes and showed me who the best Dad is so I could point my children to Him.

I can now see God's hand always with me. Looking back at my life, I can connect the dots and see His direction to the door of life! I found the door and knocked. The Lord opened it and came into my life to open my eyes and heart, and I was able to make the BEST decision of my life: receiving the gift of eternal life through Jesus Christ.

As a father, I can understand how much and how big the love for our children is. I love mine with all my heart, but can you imagine how much more love God has for us? I understand God's message of love for us is the ultimate example. He gave His only Son for us!

I was lost, but He rescued my heart. I was blind, but God opened my eyes. He gave me a vision and a purpose that now runs my life, and I know my role in His plans. I thank God for who He is and for His love, grace, mercy, and for always being there for me. And I thank Him for all His blessings and the opportunity He gave me to be found.

If God has rescued you from the worst storm of your life, I want to challenge you to help others who are lost, like I was. Help others find the way, the truth, and the life, just like this group of godly people did for me. And if you are still in the eye of the storm, I will pray for you to go and knock. As you do, the door will open for you, your life will be transformed, and you will find the divine purpose God has prepared for you.

NAVIGATING YOUR INSECURITIES

by Ken A. Hobbs II

Do not carry the weight of insecurity!

The weight of insecurity comes in many forms. Most of the time, it is something that was drilled into us in our youth. As we grow up, so do our insecurities. So, how do we navigate insecurity and find confidence and hope in our everyday lives?

First, we must understand how our insecurities can destroy who we are and how we see ourselves. The enemy will use our insecurities as his biggest weapon against us. Satan loves us to question who we are and how we measure up to others. His favorite words are, "YOU ARE NOT ENOUGH."

Second, we must fight against insecurity. The devil wants us to feel insecure over the meaning and purpose of our lives. If we find the root of our insecurity, we can use truth (and love) to fight against it.

Insecurity is not a stranger to most people, but we all deal with it differently. We can travel through the Bible to see examples of others who dealt with insecurity. God spoke to each one in different ways, and He used them greatly in different ways.

We are not alone!

Insecurity presents itself through fear, worry, doubt, and so much uncertainty about tomorrow!

For example:

- The disciples were afraid in the boat in the storm.

- Jonah was worried about going to Nineveh.

- Thomas doubted that Jesus rose from the dead.

- Moses was apprehensive to deliver Israel from Egypt.

- Gideon was uncertain about the entire situation of God using him to deliver Israel from the Midianites.

We grow through our relationship with God. We mature our faith by going through trials with God. Hard things! Our character develops and we mature through our suffering. We can trust God to hold us tight and give us refuge and strength while going through these trials.

> *You are my hiding place; you will protect me from trouble and surround me with songs of deliverance* (Psalm 32:7 NIV).

It is easy to become distracted with trying to build up our own self-confidence. Instead, turn your heart (and all the junk in the trunk) completely over to our loving Father. Then you will grow and mature with confidence that will not fade away in the wind, and you will gain a confidence that cannot be shaken.

We can use LOVE as a tool to navigate our insecurities. Jesus left us the number one command and answer for everything that life will toss at us. LOVE. Love in response to EVERYTHING! Jesus instructs us to *"Love the Lord your God with all your heart and with all your soul and with all your mind"* and *"Love your neighbor as yourself"* (Matthew 22:37, Matthew 22:39 NIV). In other words, love God and love others. Insecurity must be countered with love. At its core, insecurity causes us to question our significance.

If we take the focus off ourselves and put it on others, we can battle the inner war inside us. Because, with our focus on the unhealthy view we may hold of ourselves, we are putting ourselves, instead of others, first. Constantly thinking of our perceived inadequacies causes us to stay focused inward rather than outward.

The more we remain focused on ourselves, the more we get pulled into the tunnel of insecurity. Focus on God, His truth, and service to His people through LOVE.

Again, the best remedy for insecurity is God—who He is and who He says we are. Do not listen to the lies of the enemy. God will never leave us or forsake us.

You can trust Him.

> *"But blessed is the one who trusts in the LORD, whose confidence is in him. They will be like a tree planted by the water that sends out its roots by the stream. It does not fear when heat comes; its leaves are always green. It has no worries in a year of drought and never fails to bear fruit"* (Jeremiah 17:7-8 NIV).

DANIEL SEPULVADO

Daniel Sepulvado grew up in small-town Mississippi, the oldest of six kids. His mom is Jennifer, his dad is Jimmy, and his siblings are Jacob, Cole, Matthew, Gracie, and Ava. He grew up the son of a catfish farm manager, so he worked out on the farm during the summer from the time he was fourteen until he was twenty-one. He did not grow up in church consistently and came to know the Lord in college.

Daniel attended Mississippi State University, majoring in biomedical engineering. He was the first generation on his father's side of the family to go to college. After getting connected to Pinelake Church, he was invited to step into leadership roles within the college ministry while in college. After his first mission trip, he felt God leading him toward full-time vocational ministry. Since graduating from college, he has worked for Pinelake Church in Brandon at the Reservoir campus in a ministry residency program in student ministry.

Even with the big shift in his career from engineering to ministry, his parents have been loving and supportive.

Today, he enjoys spending time outdoors with friends and family, fishing, reading, and playing sports. Feel free to reach out to him at danielsepulvado06@gmail.com.

THE BEST ADVENTURE

by Daniel Sepulvado

My sophomore year of college was about to begin. I had worked another long summer on the catfish farm so I would not have to work a job during the school year. My parents were able to help me with finances for school as well, so my deepest desire and pursuit at this point in my life was to meet a girl. Above everything else, I just wanted a girlfriend. The priorities of my mind and heart were bent completely out of shape. I looked to girls, the party scene, and finances to fulfill me. My pursuit of satisfaction in these things would leave me alone and completely broken over my choices. But in time, I would learn that not only are God's ways better than our ways, but the adventures He has prepared when we submit to Him will far exceed our own longings and desires.

In March 2020, the whole world was crumbling; I felt like my own world was falling apart, too, as I sat alone in my apartment. I had sought fulfillment in girls, but the financial stability I depended on was quickly fading, and the relationships I thought I could rely on were shaken.

It had all begun at the beginning of the school year. My first weekend back in Starkville, I got invited to this rush party that a fraternity was throwing because I was planning to join a fraternity that semester. I went to the house party and met a girl named Emily*. We talked for what seemed like most of the party. I left hopeful that I had finally met the girl who would be my first-ever girlfriend.

Emily and I began to spend more time together, and then we began to date. There was the initial excitement of a new relationship. All my friends thought she was great. There was one problem—she was all my hope for fulfillment. I believed that once I found a girlfriend, I would finally feel fulfilled.

At that point in my life, I did not yet know Jesus. I called myself a Christian, but there was nothing in my life that pointed to that. And the same could be said about Emily. I was a selfish and broken man who could only think about himself. Around mid-November, our relationship ended in a lot of brokenness. From then on, into the beginning of the Spring semester, I made selfish decisions that hurt many friends around me.

Sarah, a good friend of mine, expressed interest in me not long after my relationship with Emily ended. I was not interested in being exclusive with anyone since I had just gotten out of a relationship, and Sarah was about to leave to study abroad the next semester. Her best friend Megan also expressed interest in me, and I started spending time with her. In my mind, I wanted to be with Sarah, but I was not ready to settle down yet because I did not feel like I was good enough to be with her. The logic I clung to still does not make sense to me today.

Megan was fun—not a serious commitment. And at that time, I did not care how this choice affected Sarah, which broke Sarah's heart. It also broke friendships between me and our mutual friends. As I transitioned into the spring semester of 2020, I was still hurting from my relationship with Emily ending, and it was not long before things fizzled out with Megan.

To complicate matters, my dad experienced a pay cut of around 40 percent during this time. So, I was walking through relational brokenness and financial uncertainty. I did not know how I was going to afford to buy food or pay rent the last few months of the semester. I was fearful. I could not see how things were going to end up. I had no control over any of it. I was feeling lost, hopeless, and alone. I was stressed out.

I applied for jobs to no avail. I tried delivering for DoorDash, but my truck burned gas faster than I could make money. Then COVID-19 shut the world down in March. I had no options left to make ends meet.

There was one glimmer of hope in the back of my head. During that school year, I started going back to church. I had searched for hope and fulfillment in the party scene, in girls, and in financial security and found that each place I searched seemed to leave me emptier than before. During the spring semester, it seemed like every Sunday, the Lord would tug on my heart and say, "You cannot keep living this way. It is not going to end well for you."

Each time, I would just brush it off and think, *I can keep living how I want to live and love Jesus.*

Isaiah 55:8-9 says, *"For my thoughts are not your thoughts, neither are your ways my ways," declares the Lord. "As the heavens are higher than the earth, so are my ways higher than your ways and my thoughts than your thoughts"* (NIV).

I looked at the world around me, and it seemed as if it was more fun to live according to the world than to follow Jesus. I genuinely thought that the hard-core Christians were a bunch of losers who were missing out on fun. I thought I was living life to the fullest—having Jesus and doing what I wanted to do. It seemed awesome for a while—until it was not.

Proverbs 14:12 says, *There is a way that appears to be right, but in the end it leads to death* (NIV).

Let me return to when COVID-19 shut down the world and I was reaping the full effects of my selfish choices.

I was in a state of complete brokenness. I could see that doing things the way I wanted led me to complete brokenness, disappointment, destruction, and heartache. I had spun into a depression. I was frustrated. The party scene, drinking, and girls were where I thought I would find satisfaction. But they left me empty. My pursuit of what I thought would bring happiness only brought brokenness to me and those around me.

Sitting in this realization alone in my apartment in March of 2020, it seemed like the world was crashing down around me. I beat myself up daily for the deep hurt I inflicted on people who were close to me. And being short on money was just an added stress. I felt like a spectator in my life with absolutely no control over what would happen next.

One Sunday, the pastor mentioned Matthew 16:24, where it is recorded that Jesus says, *"Whoever wants to be my disciple must deny themselves and take up their cross and follow me"* (NIV). The Lord grabbed my curiosity, and I began to wrestle with this verse. I finally understood what it meant to surrender my life to the Lord. This entire time, I had been giving God my Sundays and parts of my life but never wanting to surrender all of it. Instead, I hung onto dating girls how I wanted to. I clung to drinking and partying. But God wants all of you and me. He wants us to lay our desires, dreams, worries, hopes, wishes, and goals at His feet.

Surrendering to God says, "God, I want this person, thing, or job, but I know it is contrary to what you would call me to do, so please help me not to pursue that relationship, job, money, pleasure, or power."

Surrendering to God allows God's Word to inform me how to conduct myself in all facets of life.

Through those few weeks of wrestling, the Lord taught me I had a skewed view of Him. I grew up viewing the Bible as a list of rules that were there to take away my fun. But what I saw as rules were actually God's kindness and provision. God designed you and me, so He knows how we best function.

As this understanding grew in me, God's commands began to look less like limitations and more like warnings for protection from a loving Father. God, in His kindness, tells us that following our fleshly desires will end in destruction. Galatians 6:8 says, *Whoever sows to please their flesh, from the flesh will reap destruction; whoever sows to please the Spirit, from the Spirit will reap eternal life* (NIV).

When I fully understood what surrender before God meant, I said, through many tears, "God, I'm sorry I have tried things my way and have done nothing but screw it up. I surrender my life to you. I want to do things your way. Your way must be better than my way because my way ended in complete disaster. Here is my life. Have your way."

Now, I have hope because I put my trust in Jesus, knowing He came and lived the perfect life I could never live. Jesus died the death I deserved, taking my sin upon Himself. And He rose again after three days, clothing me in His righteousness. In Romans 10:9, Paul teaches, *If you declare with your mouth, "Jesus is Lord," and believe in your heart that God raised him from the dead, you will be saved* (NIV). And Ephesians 2:8-9 states, *For it is by grace you have been saved, through faith—and this is not from yourselves, it is the gift of God—not by works, so that no one can boast* (NIV).

I must surrender my worries about the things I cannot control daily. The night I surrendered my life to Christ, I gained a peace and confidence in God that I did not have before. And it became a lot easier to surrender my worries to God and say, "I do not know where the money will come from to buy food and pay rent, but I know you will make it happen." I cannot put into words the confidence in the Lord that I gained; it is unexplainable.

I can look back today and say that God met every single one of my needs. He provided just enough for me to have a roof over my head and food on my table. For a while, I held onto the worry of the relational brokenness I had caused; I had to lay that at the Lord's feet daily. I felt horrible about how I had treated people. I wished I could just take it all away. I wondered if those friendships would ever be mended. I clung to the verse Romans 8:28, *And we know that in all things God works for the good of those who love him, who have been called according to his purpose* (NIV).

Understanding that God has your best interest at heart impacts how you view sex, dating, marriage, substances, friendships, your job, and every other aspect of life. Something I see now that I wish I had known at that time is that your view of God determines your response to God.

As you surrender whatever God calls you to lay down, it is essential to continually remind yourself of who God is. Look at His faithfulness in the Bible, remember what He has done in your own personal life, and contemplate the words in this book as you read the many stories that all point to God. God knew that recalling His goodness would sustain us— that is why He told the Israelites right after they left Egypt to put festivals in place, so they would remember that He was who brought them out of Egypt. In Joshua 4, when Joshua led the Israelites across the Jordan into the Promised Land, he set up 12 stones as a reminder of the miracle that God performed—parting the river so they could walk across the Jordan.

So Joshua called together the twelve men he had appointed from the Israelites, one from each tribe, and said to them, "Go over before the ark of the Lord your God into the middle of the Jordan. Each of you is to take up a stone on his shoulder, according to the number of the tribes of the Israelites, to serve as a sign

among you. In the future, when your children ask you, 'What do these mean?'
tell them that the flow of the Jordan was cut off before the ark of the covenant
of the Lord. When it crossed the Jordan, the waters of the Jordan were cut off.
These stones are to be a memorial to the people of Israel forever" (Joshua 4:4-7
NIV).

I found myself in a place where I had come to the end of myself, but I
still had wounds and scars that needed healing. Today, I have the hope of
salvation because I have trusted in Jesus' finished work, but at that moment,
I was still living in the brokenness of my choices and still am to an extent.
Where is the hope? The answer is in James 5:16, *Therefore confess your sins*
to each other and pray for each other so that you may be healed. The prayer of
a righteous person is powerful and effective (NIV).

I remember being anxious and terrified when I first heard that verse. I so
badly wanted to keep what was in the past in the past.

When I began attending church in my junior year in the fall of 2020, I
joined a small group and started making church friends who knew nothing
about my past. I could easily hide in plain sight— being seen but not truly
known. At first, it was very refreshing because it felt like I could make a
new start. I could project the me that I wanted people to see. This quickly
became exhausting and very miserable. Thoughts began to rule in my
mind, such as, *If they really knew me, would they still want me around?* I was
surrounded by people, but I felt isolated.

I lived in that isolation for about six months; then, I slowly began to allow
close friends to see parts of me I had kept hidden. Some pieces of my story
were easier to share than others. My small group was filled with many guys
who were vulnerable and open about their struggles, which made me more
comfortable sharing my past and current struggles.

When I finally began to open up, I felt a freedom I had never felt before and a peace I lacked. I saw a tangible picture of God's grace. Still, there were a couple of pieces of my time before Christ that I held onto for about another year—mainly because I felt a lot of shame and wondered how people would see me if I shared everything. Fear held me back for a while, and I found out the hard way that anything kept in the dark is the enemy's playground.

Because I stayed isolated in my secrets, the enemy was able to use my shame to speak lies to me that kept me from walking in the complete freedom Christ already paid for, the joy that can be found in Him, and the purpose He has for me. Eventually, God convicted me to tell just one close friend; I finally worked up the courage to do so. I worried about how he would react, but he met me gracefully. It felt amazing to share with him as that was the first time I was ever fully loved.

You cannot be fully loved apart from being fully known.

Since then, I have let a couple more friends know me completely and fully. I do not regret it for a second. Being known is scary, but it is one of the most rewarding gifts to experience. I still battle lies from the enemy who tries to tell me that my past defines me, but I now have people in my corner to remind me of the truth about how God sees me, even in the face of the lies I face. And I can receive what they say about me because they know all of me.

Reflecting on my past, I recognize a lot of brokenness. But I can also see the faithfulness of God, even when I was not faithful to Him. Underneath all my broken choices were holy God-given desires; they were just the wrong approaches to meet those desires. Some desires we crave are to be loved, cared for, seen, known, and valued. The truth is, all these desires are good and are met in Christ; He is sufficient. Nothing can make you too far gone to be reached by God. God is a redeeming God. He has redeemed a lot in my life and is still redeeming a lot. He can redeem the broken pieces of your story as well.

It can be costly to follow Jesus, but the reward is so much greater than what you might lose. I challenge you to let go of any fear of what you may lose by following Jesus and focus on all He has in store for you. When you do, you will embark on the best adventure of your life.

All names have been changed.

KYLE FARRAND

Kyle Farrand grew up in a small town in Wisconsin where he enjoyed 4-wheeling, summers boating at the lake, wrestling, playing soccer, and playing in the school band.

After high school, Kyle joined the Navy. During his six years of active duty, he had the opportunity to travel to 30 countries and five continents, only missing Australia and Antarctica.

Traveling around the world gave him the opportunity to meet, talk to, and learn from people of all different cultures. Kyle feels these experiences have helped him to be more open-minded about people and life.

Upon retiring from the military due to a head injury, Kyle worked really hard to teach himself how to relearn. He proceeded to get his bachelor's degree in Neuropsychology with a focus on Traumatic Brain Injuries and Post Traumatic Stress Disorder.

Kyle spends his time helping family and friends and always makes everyone laugh. Kyle never sees anyone as a stranger; he has the gift of being able to connect with everyone he meets. Kyle continues to help so many people due to his experiences and education, including past military people struggling with trauma or PTSD.

WITH GOD, NOTHING IS IMPOSSIBLE

By Kyle Farrand

My relationship with God has been a rocky one. I have questioned a million times if there really is a God. I grew up in a home where God was a part of our life, but as you grow and experience things in life, you can start to question. I have had many of those times. However, when I look back over my times of struggle, God has always been there in my times of need.

In January 2007, my family and I went to Jellystone Resort to celebrate my father's 49th birthday and my 16th birthday. We celebrated my father's birthday first since I had 12 friends coming to the resort the next morning for my birthday. However, things didn't go as planned. I was startled awake that morning by my brother screaming hysterically and my mother yelling for my help. My father would not wake up; he was not responding. I ran downstairs to help my mother with CPR, trying to revive my father. But to no avail.

The next two years were a blur. My mother tried to keep the family together as well as she could, but there was so much pain, anger, and questions— why my father? He was such a good man. Everybody loved him. He was head of the youth wrestling program and my soccer coach.

My grades plummeted, my friendships struggled, and my desire for life waned. In August of 2009, at the age of 18, I joined the Navy to get away from it all.

Bootcamp certainly was not the most fun. However, with my experiences that were to come, it was the most normal part of my entire time and experience in the military. In December 2009, I suffered a head injury while on base that changed my life forever. Instead of getting the medical help that I needed, any and everything that could go wrong did. Have you ever heard of the "snowball effect"? That's what my life became. One small thing grew into another and another until the snowball was too big to stop and went out of control.

My head injury caused damage to the front and back parts of my brain. The injury in the front caused my face to become paralyzed on the right side. Although I regained control of my face after about six months of rehabilitation, severe damage remained. Over my right eye, I developed an AVF, or Arteriovenous Fistula—an irregular connection between an artery and a vein. It's like a group of veins conformed together with blood supplied to them; it looks like a bunch of noodles twisted together. As a result, my eye was constantly swollen and black and purple; it looked like someone had punched me in the eye. I also started having vision problems in my right eye, and when the AVF would act up, I would experience extreme pain and lose most of my vision. The injury to the back of my brain was diagnosed as a Cavernous Malformation, and it was too deep in the brain to do surgery. Instead, it would have to be monitored as we hoped and prayed it would never rupture.

Once my rehab was finished, I was deployed overseas.

While my first deployment overall was not a bad experience, I began struggling to do some of the jobs every sailor could and was expected to do. For example, we were doing a training drill for fire, and I was wearing firefighting gear—including a firefighting mask—to practice for emergencies. I passed out due to the pressure the mask put on the area of my face affected by AVF. Failing that training procedure led to me having issues with the upper chain of command, who felt I was a bad sailor.

Upon returning to land and base, I hoped to see a specialist as my headaches and pain were getting more severe. Receiving medical care would have been the proper protocol, but that did not happen. Even though the ship had records of my injury, the ship's doctor thought I was lying about my symptoms, so he would not issue approval for me to see a specialist.

My headaches increased, and I began suffering from depression, partly because no one believed me. I also started experiencing memory loss and increased anger issues. Feeling lost, I went over the head of the ship's doctor and contacted the specialist myself. Although my symptoms were obviously getting worse, I was reprimanded instead of receiving the medical help I needed because I went above my command. I was not allowed to go to the specialist anymore. If I did, I risked the possibility of getting kicked out of the military.

Then, I was scheduled to be deployed overseas for a 2nd time. I decided to keep my head down and wait until I could get the help I needed.

We were to deploy on my 20th birthday, but right before the ship left port, my mother called and informed me my grandmother had passed away that morning. I tried to get a leave, hoping to fly back home to make sure my family was okay. However, that didn't happen because I was part of the essential crew and did not receive the proper paperwork prior to our departure. As a result, I was not able to attend my grandmother's funeral and could only communicate with my family in a very limited fashion via email.

Those circumstances, combined with my head injury, caused me to fall into a major depression. Knowing I would not get help from the ship doctor, I held everything in and acted like I was fine. But I wasn't sleeping, and when I did return to land, I had even more family loss to deal with. So, I turned to alcohol to help me cope.

How had my life gotten to be this way? My father was gone. I hardly ever saw my family due to deployments. My headaches were constant and severe. And no one believed me, so I couldn't get the help I desperately needed. I was losing hope and didn't even know if continuing to live was even worth it.

Looking back, I can now see that God was watching out for me, even though I didn't understand that then. God puts people in your path when you need them the most. And knowing what I needed, He gave me an unexpected message from an unlikely individual.

While most people try to be nice when someone is struggling, a new friend I encountered took a completely different approach. We were in Boston for Fleet Week, a celebration for the Navy. And I was struggling when I should have been having the time of my life. So this man pulled me aside and chose some very colorful language to tell me I needed to grow up. He told me I may not be able to see it right now, but God had bigger plans for me, and all the struggles I had been going through were happening for a reason.

I'm sure you can imagine what I wanted to say back to him, but in retrospect, what he told me was exactly what I needed to hear, and it helped me somewhat snap back. His words helped me regain both my faith and my focus, and I began believing things would work out even if they took a while longer than I had hoped they would.

> *But as for you, be strong and do not give up, for your work will be rewarded* (2 Chronicles 15:7 NLT).

Shortly after that, I got transferred to another ship. Thankfully, that ship's doctor understood my injury and was willing to help send me to the right specialist. The specialist told me I was one of the luckiest people he had met because the AVF I had in that location could have ruptured if I had taken one hit to my head, and yet I was able to make it through two deployments without incident.

> *Though I walk in the midst of trouble, you preserve my life. You stretch out your hand against the anger of my foes; with your right hand you save me* (Psalm 138:7 NIV).

He set up two surgeries to try to fix some of the damage and offered other treatments to help with my depression and anger. Unfortunately, the relief of finally having things move forward after over three years without treatment was short-lived. The 2nd ship I was on overruled my doctor and made me deploy for a 3rd time. I questioned, *Why, Lord, after all this time, would you get me so close to getting the help I needed just to pull it all away? How could you let this fall apart?*

While that deployment was slightly better than the previous one, with my hope pulled out from under me once again, I spiraled back into a deeper depression and lost my hope and faith. I started to agree with people who had no faith, beginning to believe there really wasn't a God. I would even argue with anyone who would claim there was a God.

Once I returned from the 3rd deployment, I returned to the specialist who set me up with a surgeon. It was agreed that I needed surgery, and the surgery was scheduled. Finally, after nearly five years, maybe I would get some relief from the headaches and pain. However, surgery was not approved by my command.

By this time, it was getting close to the end of my five-year contract with the Navy. Due to all my issues, I could not re-up for another year, which would have allowed me time to have the surgeries. I would have to start over with a different set of doctors. What another letdown and disappointment.

I desperately kept trying to figure out what to do, but I had no luck. Then, one night, while I was in my room looking for a way out, I gave up.

That was when I heard a voice telling me not to give up; I would get the help I needed.

But I was alone in my room. There was no one who could have spoken to me. I honestly believed I was going crazy from lack of sleep. But when I woke up, I realized the voice was correct. Even with my lack of faith at the time, I knew God had helped me once again. And I was able to move forward when I thought everything was hopeless.

> *The Lord will fight for you; you need only to be still* (Exodus 14:14 NIV).

Then, my mother called and told me she had just been at a chamber lunch and sat beside the State Senator. She called him after, explained my situation, and asked if there was anything he could do to get involved and get this stopped. He was blown away at the situation and everything that had happened. He contacted our district congressman to help. Before I knew it, my discharge was stopped and I received a 6-month extension and was assigned a wonderful liaison named Delores to help coordinate all my medical appointments and communicate with my chain of command as my surgery was scheduled.

In surgery, they cut my head from ear to ear and literally pealed my skin from my scalp forward to access the location above my eye. Then they clamped off the artery supplying the blood to that area, removed the tangled mess of veins, and then finished by putting 70 staples in my head. They expected it would take me about six weeks to recover. My headaches pretty much went away and I was recovering really fast, but then other problems started.

I got really sick and diagnosed with pneumonia, so I was given strong steroids. Then my eye started swelling again, this time more severely. The AVF was returning. The doctors believed they missed some vessels supplying the main artery and needed to operate again.

The second surgery was done by going in from the front, at my eye. There was a high risk I could go blind in that eye. This surgery also appeared to be successful. I was nearly past the 6-month extension the Navy had granted me, so I had to get Congress to help me get another extension. At the end of that recovery time, the news was not good. My eye pain had come back, along with the swelling. AGAIN. The doctors had never seen this happen before and felt there was nothing more they could do. The pneumonia appeared to be worse, and I started experiencing severe lung issues. I was eventually diagnosed with eosinophilic pneumonia and placed on high amounts of steroids to try and control it.

I began the out-processing from the military. Part of my aftercare was attending pain management classes since I was still struggling so much, but I was done. I couldn't take anymore. I called my mom and told her I couldn't take anymore. She begged me to just go to the pain management class, promising she would get a flight out as soon as possible. I hesitantly agreed to go so she would not be so worried.

While at the class, I noticed a young man off by himself. I went over and started talking to him. He told me he had so much pain from an injury, but no one believed him. He said it wasn't like a lost limb that you can physically see. I shared my story and what I had gone through, and I told him to have his mother contact their district congressman. When he left, he thanked me and had hope in his voice. For the first time, I felt like everything I had gone through was for a purpose. If I had not had that experience, I would not have been able to help him, and he may have never gotten the help he needed.

Not only that, but we rejoice in our sufferings, knowing that suffering produces endurance, and endurance produces character, and character produces hope, and hope does not put us to shame, because God's love has been poured into our hearts through the Holy Spirit who has been given to us (Romans 5:3-5 ESV).

I ran into that young man one more time before I left the Navy, and he told me his mother did contact their congressman. They also learned that due to another situation with a young man from Georgia who had recently been brought to the Congress floor, some legislative changes were being made to help prevent this type of thing from continuing to happen.

Upon discharge, I had to start treatment at the VA (Veterans Affairs), where I ran into many roadblocks with doctors who did not believe I struggled with pain and headaches. My lung issues got so bad I was hospitalized twice and put on oxygen 24/7. Some days, I struggled just walking to the mailbox. Not willing to give up, I prayed, my family prayed, my mother's friends prayed, and we contacted our congressman once again for help. After four years of continuous prayer, I finally received some good news on my birthday: I was getting a referral to the Mayo Clinic in Rochester, MN. We researched surgeons and found one that seemed to speak to us. I wrote a letter explaining my whole situation and asked if he would accept me as a patient. And he did!!

In 2019, I went to Mayo to undergo all kinds of testing. They were so perplexed over my lung issues that they informed me there was no way they could do surgery on my head until they could figure out and improve my lung issues. After three weeks of testing and looking at all kinds of options, including considering a bone marrow transplant, they came up with a treatment plan. I spent the next year following their instructions and taking all the medications they prescribed. I finally got the call that my test and numbers for my lungs looked good enough for the surgery. After five years of prayer, on June 1, 2020, in the middle of the COVID-19 pandemic, I underwent surgery with one of the best surgeons in the world. The surgery was a success. Although I will never be back to 100%, that surgery took care of about 90% of my issues, giving me a better quality of life as I no longer suffered from daily headaches.

While everything didn't go the way I expected, my struggles helped change the path of my life. And I was able to see God at work as I had the opportunity to help others through instigating legislative changes. I will never know how many lives I was able to help by simply sharing my situation. Additionally, my initial injury forced me to do things differently, giving me a new understanding and appreciation for life. Then, the first two surgeries taught me that sometimes we must work hard, not just hope that everything in life will go the way we want.

Trust in the Lord with all your heart and lean not on your own understanding; in all your ways submit to him, and he will make your paths straight (Proverbs 3:5-6 NIV).

My last surgery taught me to never give up. Some things take time, so never give up. Just take one day at a time and keep moving forward, for with God, nothing is impossible, and we do not know His plan or His timing. Sometimes, the challenges in your life are there to guide you down that path you never could have seen.

"For I know the plans I have for you," declares the LORD, "plans to prosper you and not to harm you, plans to give you hope and a future" (Jeremiah 29:11 NIV).

No matter what your storm is, I encourage you to trust God. He is always in control.

NAVIGATING THROUGH TEMPTATIONS

by Ken A. Hobbs II

Temptation is something we all face. Whether it comes at us from the world, the flesh, or directly from the enemy, navigating through this storm can seem daunting. But we can get help in our time of need by going directly to God.

We can all investigate our past and find times when we've relied on our own strength to navigate life without God's help. No matter how long we have believed in God, we still face temptations. When we try to stand against temptation alone, we usually mess up. The Bible gives us hope. Instead of choosing to sin (and temptation is not a sin), we can look to God. He always provides an escape from temptation. It is up to us how we respond.

There are strategies you can use in your faith to help you combat tempting situations. First, it is important to understand, as Paul tells us in 1 Corinthians 10:13 (NLT), *the temptations in your life are no different from what others experience. And God is faithful.* He will not allow the temptation to be more than you can stand. When you are tempted, he will show you a way out so that you can endure. God will always give you a way to manage when situations arise in the waves of life that weaken you and try to take you out.

A great way to navigate this storm of temptation is by using your sword, the Word of God! It is what Jesus used to silence the enemy. Satan tempted Jesus in the wilderness by appealing to His appetite and emotions, recognizing that Jesus had, perhaps, been made weak by circumstances. But Jesus used a repellent against the lies that the enemy was bombarding Him with—the Word of God. By using this sword that we all possess, Jesus overcame the tempter and shut down the devil.

Navigating temptations can be intense, but that does not mean they have to overtake you. Every temptation is an opportunity to overcome and get victory over sin! The Word of God as our weapon is something we can always count on to resist temptation! The storm is real. When you play with temptations and find yourself in a hurricane, be honest before God. See the raging storm for what it is—deadly! Tell God you need Him. Tell Him you are having a rough time overcoming your temptation. Cry out to God within the forceful winds, pray, and let Him rescue you. Then, immediately find an accountability partner who knows what you are struggling with. Confide in them and ask them to be there for you when the temptation arises.

Believe that God has a way of escape for you. Temptation doesn't become a sin until you agree with it, so the way of resistance is the way of escape. Remember, God will never tempt you to do anything wrong. The devil and our flesh, which is sinful, tempt us to do wrong. God gives us a choice between right and wrong. Jesus passed the test by confronting the devil's lies with the truth of God's Word. We must do the same.

And remember, when you are being tempted, do not say, "God is tempting me." God is never tempted to do wrong, and he never tempts anyone else (James 1:13 NLT).

Pray that pride will not hold you back from looking to God for His help. As we look to God's Word to give us the truth, we need to navigate the temptation we battle daily, and one of the greatest truths is that God will forgive any of us who have fallen if we trust Christ for forgiveness. It may take digging back to incidents you fell prey to in order to see where extreme guilt took hold. You may still hold on to guilt, shame, or pride because you know you messed up in your life, making it easier to be tempted and fall again if it is not dealt with. Trust Christ alone for your salvation. When you confess your sin outright before Him, He forgives every fall into temptation. You will see the storms of this hurricane begin to dissipate and the seas calm.

God wants us to give all our battles to Him daily. He does not want us to be alienated from Him. Do not turn your head in shame if you're caught in the middle of a storm. Walking with God every day helps us to find the strength to meet the hurricanes in life. You will conquer the storm against temptation by giving it to God and not fighting alone. Remember, you have a Band of Brothers to hold you up.

. . . .

WAYNE F. SESSIONS

Wayne F. Sessions Jr. was born in South Florida. He attended college locally, then was commissioned as a United States Army officer and attended the United States Army Infantry Officer Basic School. He then attended the US Army Rotor Wing helicopter flight school and underwent additional flight training to transition in the AH-1S Cobra Attack Helicopter. He was transferred to Fort Hood, Texas, to lead and train a combat aviation attack Cobra (Guns) platoon. Later, Wayne was promoted to Brigade Aviation staff, coordinating and deploying Brigade aviation assets.

Wayne met his wife Paula while stationed in Texas. They have two children, Hunter and Claire. Paula has been a major part of Wayne's success.

Wayne returned to South Florida and continued his aviation career in the Army Reserves as a Medical Evacuation Pilot (Dust Off). He started a service company that was destroyed by Hurricane Andrew and eventually accepted a position with the fire department as a pilot for search and rescue trauma missions. His Son Hunter also serves in the same department.

Wayne is a member of the Chickasaw Nation and is on the Leadership Team of Band of Brother Christian Men's organization. He is an avid turkey hunter and fisherman.

JESUS, THE WARRIOR CHIEF

By Wayne F. Sessions

I grew up in Coconut Grove, Florida—a neighborhood on the bay in Miami. Growing up and living in The Grove as a young man truly was paradise. The Grove was an exciting place; something was always going on. We would hear and see Coast Guard seaplanes come in off patrol during the day. We would ride our bicycles in the marinas and help my father work on the family boat. My uncles would come over to our house, which was always a good time. And the fishing was great. I really did not have a worry in the world. Life was good. My family eventually moved inland to a bigger house in Coral Gables, still in the Miami area. Perhaps they had gotten tired of living so close to the water—including worrying about hurricanes and dealing with the cleanup and the invasion of land crabs caused by the nearly yearly occurrences.

I was a little older when we moved. That's when life and life lessons kicked in. While attending grade and high school, I did not like being couped up all day and only applied myself in the areas I took an interest in—like sports, metal shop, drafting, fishing, and, of course, girls. My parents picked up on the trend. Do not let me paint the wrong picture—I was not a delinquent, but I also was not an angel. We found things to get into.

My mother knew the interest I had in hunting and fishing. She pulled me aside one day before school let out for summer break and told me I would be spending the summer with my great-uncle in Oklahoma. That was where I started to learn about my family history and the chronological events that led up to my mother's wounds, which eventually manifested themselves to me indirectly.

My great uncle and I are members of the Chickasaw Nation Native American Society. The Chickasaw Nation was an unconquered nation within the United States, and it still holds that status today. The Nation's creed is "Unconquered and Unconquerable." The Chickasaws were great warriors and feared by other nations and Spanish explorers. My uncle and aunt were great Christian Chickasaw warriors who truly retained the Chickasaw credo in a humble and direct way throughout their lives. My great-uncle was an avid hunter and fisherman, and my mother was hoping he could give me sound life lessons because we had similar interests. Thus, my trip to Oklahoma.

Both my uncle and aunt were humble, soft-spoken people who were full of life. They met each other after World War II. My uncle was a war hero who fought in many battles. My parents informed me that when I stayed with my uncle, I should not mention the war, because his emotional and physical wounds were real and very apparent.

For example, my aunt would take us to a restaurant to get a burger with other family members, but my uncle would stay in the car. We would have to bring food out to him because he would not go into buildings. In his mind, that was where bad things happened. This was a result of his horrible memories of war.

My uncle had marched through Africa. In one battle, all his friends were killed; he was the sole survivor. He was later wounded as he fought in another very intense battle. He had made it through the battle, but when he stepped out of the tank, a land mine exploded and severely wounded him. He survived his wounds and their lasting effects and then was shipped back home.

Years later, I entered the story.

My summers with my uncle were priceless. We both constantly had the best time of our lives as we hunted and fished and just spent time outdoors. I think God was kicking me in the pants subtly and speaking directly to me, saying, "Wake up. There is something bigger than you—other people and serving."

God placed me in training mode to develop a servant's heart as I learned to serve and care for others by the example I was witnessing through my great-uncle and aunt's teaching. It was a great learning experience. To give you an example of the kind of Christian woman my aunt was, when I went home, she would constantly write me letters that were loving and packed with wisdom. Here is a prayer she gave me in one letter based on The Serenity Prayer :

> "God grant me the serenity to accept the things I cannot change. The courage to change the things I can and the wisdom to know the difference. Amen. Lord! Help me to remember that nothing is going to happen to me today that you and I can't handle together. Amen. Oh! Lord, help me this day to keep my big mouth shut. Amen.
> Tonka – Way – Con the Great One God. Amen"
> (In different native societies, meaning Great One)

This prayer hangs on my office wall.

That prayer is beautiful and scripture-filled, based in Proverbs and life.

This prayer is an excellent example of having a personal relationship with God. You and I also have access to this personal relationship when we allow Jesus in our lives. My aunt went to God with every daily life issue—big and small. She knew she needed Christ's strength and wisdom to fight the spiritual and physical battles we constantly face. No matter how severe or insignificant we may perceive our situation, God is there to guide, comfort, and mentor us.

I love those who love me, and those who seek me find me (Proverbs 8:17 NIV).

When words are many, sin is not absent, but he who holds his tongue is wise (Proverbs 10:19 NIV).

Reckless words pierce like a sword, but the tongue of the wise brings healing (Proverbs 12:18 NIV).

I continued to visit my great-uncle and aunt during my grade school years. It was a learning and training process for me and a healing process for my great-uncle.

Compared to what many others have gone through, my upbringing reads like a fairytale. Sure, I had ups and downs. But snap. What many men, even some who have written in this book, have gotten through is extraordinary—physical and mental abuse, abandonment, and worse. However, with His grace and strength, Jesus always gives His sons the ability to get through the obstacles placed in front of them. Sometimes, it is necessary to forgive someone who has wounded us—and when we go to God, He empowers us to be able to do that.

Create in me a pure heart, O God, and renew a steadfast spirit within me. Do not cast me from your presence or take your Holy Spirit from me. Restore to me the joy of your salvation and grant me a willing spirit, to sustain me. Then I will teach transgressors your ways, so that sinners will turn back to you (Psalm 51:10-13 NIV).

In many of these men's experiences, the fact that they have forgiven their transgressors brought them closer to God, brought the transgressors to God, and reunited relationships and families—no matter how egregious the act against them. That is the commanding strength of the Holy Spirit, and all things are possible through Jesus! Forgiveness is the greatest weapon we have in this world. The world tells us to seek revenge, but God insists we forgive; that is where real freedom and power live.

In addition to my great-uncle and aunt's influence, my heavenly Father and earthly father were major contributing factors in my life's direction. When I was younger, I did not realize they both were guiding me to a life of service, which I would ultimately achieve through my professions and lifestyle.

My father was a very accomplished man. I admired him immensely. To this day, I still think I could not live up to his standards. He was an American naval aviator night fighter pilot during World War II. After the war, he attended school to become an architect and was very successful. But his passion was art. So he gave up his successful and comfortable career to pursue marine watercolor landscapes. That took big faith and a lot of guts. He became renowned for his watercolor artwork, winning numerous awards, and is considered one of the watercolor greats of his time. And he made a living at it.

I could go on with more of his accomplishments, but I do not want to bore you, nor would he appreciate me doting on his accolades. But my dad was bigger than life. He was humble and a man of extreme integrity who was honored for his accomplishments.

My father also always looked out for the less fortunate or people in need. One Christmas, my parents held a Christmas party. Many people of prominence from our town attended. A conversation began between some men in our living room who were discussing their ranks and positions and what they did during World War II. Some said they were this and that. I listened, as my dad did. My dad said nothing. Then, one of the men asked my dad in a sarcastic tone, "What did you do during the war?!"

My dad paused and looked him in the eye. Then, in a humble, direct voice, he answered, "I was trained as a night fighter pilot In the F4U Corsair fighter plane flying off naval aircraft carriers."

All the men stopped talking. Their silence was due to their admiration of my father and what that accomplishment represented. The conversation ended. You should have seen the expressions on these guys' faces as they picked their mouths up off the floor. My dad was flying an elite fighting aircraft in an elite unit, defending his country the best way he knew how. It was truly an unbelievable accomplishment.

To say I was proud of my father was an understatement.

I was blessed with a loving father who was totally invested in me and my future. This was an extremely valuable lesson and a turning point in my life. It was time to buckle down and get to work.

I also have my heavenly Father and Jesus, who have guided me and given me an example to follow in my journey through life. Listening to the Holy Spirit and following the example of my earthly father has provided me with a pathway to wisdom and discernment, especially when I've needed to fight spiritual or physical battles I've encountered during my life:

> *He holds success in store for the upright, he is a shield to those whose walk is blameless, for he guards the course of the just and protects the way of his faithful ones* (Proverbs 2:7-8 NIV).

He mocks proud mockers but shows favor to the humble and oppressed (Proverbs 3:34 NIV).

All hard work brings a profit, but mere talk leads to poverty (Proverbs 14:23 NIV).

Whoever oppresses the poor shows contempt for their Maker, but whoever is kind to the needy honors God (Proverbs 14:31 NIV).

In my opening paragraph, I mentioned my uncles. When I was young, I looked up to them—they were cool, funny, and a lot of fun to be around. I always enjoyed their visits, but then they stopped coming by our home. I thought it was strange.

As I stated earlier, my father was compassionate, always looking out for people and intent on caring for and helping them. When my uncles stopped coming around, my mother told me they had been having a hard time with their young families and no steady income. So my father put together a business deal and was going to bring my uncles in as partners to let them get ahead and support their families. Long story short, my uncles somehow circumvented my father when it came time to close the deal. I was told that my uncles closed the deal without my father. Then they proceeded to call my parents and tell them, and I quote: "If you are to get ahead in this world, you have to screw somebody. Sorry, it must be you."

Needless to say, my parents were devastated. As it turned out, the company was highly successful—most Americans would recognize the company and brand. I have often wondered how the family would have changed if greed had not affected this transaction. My father shook it off and kept doing what he was excellent at. He continued with his art career and provided for us through that. But my mother harbored unforgiveness for years. She continued to tell me my uncles were not good people. It left an indelible impression on me, making me wonder, *Can I really trust people to do the right thing? Can I trust anybody in any relationship—business or personal?* This affected me for years and was a harsh lesson to understand or comprehend. I wanted to forgive and get to know my uncles again. But I was reminded we would not be seeing my uncles. Greed, pride, unforgiveness, and hatred are terrible things. They destroy everything they touch. Again, I go to scripture for the right answer, direction, and reassurance.

The Lord detests dishonest scales, but accurate weights find favor with him (Proverbs 11: 1 NIV).

A generous person will prosper; whoever refreshes others will be refreshed (Proverbs 11:25 NIV).

Get rid of all bitterness, rage and anger, brawling and slander, along with every form of malice. Be kind and compassionate to one another, forgiving each other, just as in Christ God (Ephesians 4:31-32 NIV).

I just recently finished a Bible study called *Forgiving Forward*, authored by Doctor Bruce and Toni Hebel. Their Bible study and book deep dive into what forgiveness really requires and its liberating influences. What I learned is that Christ has forgiven us before we have even sinned. Yes, there may be consequences. However, when we seek forgiveness, the sin no longer exists in God's eyes. You see, as humans, the world we live in tells us there must be conditions for forgiveness. For example, we might think, *If he or she only does this or goes through the process I have put in place, then I will forgive him or her. Maybe.*

But Jesus has forgiven us with no conditions.

If we forgive immediately, as Jesus does, the baggage of hurt and the memories of how we were wronged start to vanish. You don't have to carry any ill feelings, guilt, or anger. Let Jesus have it. Let me tell you that is hard to do. But letting it go and no longer carrying that junk around is so worth the emotional and physical relief you will gain.

I could write a novel about my life experiences. I have witnessed sin, unforgiveness, violence, and poor decision-making ruin people's families and lives. And I have also witnessed others stand firm for Christ as they follow His teachings and tenets and reap the rewards of peace and assurance.

Through it all, I have gained some nuggets of wisdom I'd like to share with you:

1. Take time to learn to be at peace with yourself, trusting God's purpose for your life.

2. Always go to God with constant prayer in the little and big things.

3. Serve others, trusting God for the outcome.

4. Work hard to forgive as Jesus did. It will unload a lot of baggage and provide healing.

5. Follow the examples of the great people God has blessed you with.

Additionally, I have learned that to develop my most important relationship—the one with Jesus, my Lord and Savior—I have to put some skin in the game. To do this, I practice:

1. Reading the Bible daily. It prepares you for life's battles.

2. Attending a Bible-teaching, Christ-oriented church.

3. Listening to others' stories—doing so puts things in perspective.

4. Upholding and relying on other Christians in fellowship by attending events such as those offered by Band of Brothers.

5. Sharing my experiences as God calls me to.

If I can help just one person by sharing these nuggets and practices I have gained throughout my lifetime, I have succeeded. God bless you.

Chisus Klaist Chihowa Holitopli
Unconquered and Unconquerable in Christ

ROBERTO RAMIREZ

Roberto Ramirez was born in 1972 in Habana, Cuba. He arrived in Miami, Florida in 1979 at seven years old and began studying martial arts at the age of eight, which prepared him to deal with anger. He attributes his calmness in times of turmoil to his training.

In 1990, Roberto graduated from Christopher Columbus High School. In 1994, he graduated from Spring Hill College, a Jesuit College in Mobile, Alabama. After college, Robert moved to Venezuela and worked in the seafood industry for eight years.

After his father passed away in 2000, he decided to transition back to Miami and start a new life. He moved his Venezuelan fiancé, Andreina, to Miami. They got married in 2002 and have three beautiful children.

Robert is an entrepreneur and has been in financial services for over 20 years. He attended the Band of Brother's bootcamp in 2015 and is part of the leadership team. He co-hosts The Conquer Series once a year, showing men how to overcome sexual addiction. He is a warrior for Christ and a devout father and husband. He can be reached at Ramirez.pfsrvp@gmail. com.

DEMONS DIE IN THE LIGHT

By Roberto Ramirez

My first recollection of hearing about God was when my parents baptized me in a Catholic Church in our province when I was six years old. During that era, Castro had prohibited baptisms. The only reason I got baptized was because my father and the priest were old friends. The church was dark, and we were the only ones there. There wasn't a celebration or party afterward. It was just something my parents wanted to get done. Although my parents grew up Catholic, we only attended church for social events, like baptisms and Christmas.

My parents met at a dance when they were 16 years old, and they got married 15 years later. When my father was 21, he fought against the Castro regime and was sentenced to 9 years in prison as a political prisoner. My parents stayed in contact through his incarceration and got married shortly after my father was released. I was born two years later.

When I was young, we lived with my paternal grandparents. Although my father had graduated as an electrical engineer, the government only allowed him to be an ambulance driver, and my mother was a nurse. Then, around 1975, my parents separated but never got divorced. My mother had caught my dad being unfaithful, and she left to live with her parents. I was three years old when we moved out. I don't have any memories of living with both my parents in Cuba. As a child, I couldn't understand why my father didn't live with us. He would come to visit three or four times a week, and I felt he was sad. I still remember the tension in the house when my father would come to visit. It always felt awkward. I was too young to know what was going on, and I started thinking I wasn't good enough for my dad. The enemy planted a seed of unworthiness that carried on throughout my adult life. I always wanted to prove to my father that I was a man he could be proud of. As an adult, I realized my father had wounds of his own. He also had an inner child who wanted to make his father proud.

In the late 70s, Jimmy Carter and Fidel Castro agreed to allow political prisoners into the United States. My father pleaded with my mother for us to leave the country as a family, which she agreed to, and on December 12th, 1979, we arrived in Miami. My parents, my paternal grandparents, and I arrived at my godmother's house in Hialeah and lived there for 30 days. It was a new start for all of us. My mother decided to leave the pain behind and begin a new future with my father for my sake. It was the best decision they had ever made as a couple. I was finally able to live together with both my parents, and it was amazing. My father had to maintain two jobs to make ends meet, and I was only able to spend time with him on the weekends. My mother was a stay-at-home mom while studying English to pass the nursing board and get licensed. I saw them work together as a couple, and we were happy. We lived in a 2-bedroom apartment; my grandparents lived with other relatives.

In 1981, the Mariel Boatlift occurred; my mom's dad, her sister, her sister's husband, and my two cousins moved in with us. We were now eight people living in a 2-bedroom apartment. My father was the only one able to work and ended up getting another weekend job to support us all. I would see my father at 6 a.m. when he would return from work and as I was getting ready to go to school. On the weekends, we would deliver *The Yellow Pages* as a family to make extra money. Times were tough, but we did things together. My father was our guide and stronghold. He kept us together.

Our situation got better as time went on. My mom started working as a nurse, and my father got an opportunity to begin studying psychology. He wanted to become a psychologist. As an intern, he began doing child consulting. Then, the father of one of his patients grew fond of him and proposed a business opportunity. It turned out the gentleman was a wealthy businessman who had a restaurant he couldn't take care of. He let my father know he had two years left on the lease and asked him to take over the business. My father saw a great opportunity and took advantage of it. I was 12 years old when I began working as a busboy at my father's restaurant. My father got the whole family to work there. He made money quickly and helped get other friends and family out of Cuba. In total, my father helped 31 people leave Cuba and start a new life in Miami. He was respected and loved by everybody I knew. I saw my father help so many people that I wanted to be like him. He will always be my hero.

During the restaurant years, the original owner introduced my father to other business associates. These business associates had an illegal drug trafficking business and were part of a Colombian cartel. My father became their logistics coordinator, and soon after the restaurant business was done, he opened a business importing fruits and vegetables from South America.

As a child, I saw my father go from rags to riches in five years. As far as I knew, he had gotten a break at a point in life and created a business that fed the family. As I grew into a teenager, my father and I bonded more. He was amazing—very intellectual and analytical. He knew how to analyze people and would share his thoughts with me. In all our conversations, I don't remember having a detailed discussion about God, Jesus, or the Bible. That was not something we spoke of, and we rarely attended church.

In 1983, we moved to a 5-bedroom house with a pool. We had a decent lifestyle as a regular, middle-class family. I had turned 15 and was learning to drive when, one day, everything changed. God opened my eyes to see reality. In September of 1985, at 5 a.m., there was a loud banging at our front door, and I woke up to see who it was. I was walking towards the door, half asleep, as I kept hearing screaming and banging. My father and I got to the door at the same time, and he signaled me to open it—he seemed more awake than me. When I opened the door, there were a dozen police officers with guns in my face yelling at me to open the front door gate. My father told me to open the gate, and he went back to his room. I later found out that he went to get properly dressed; he didn't want them to take him half-dressed.

When I finally opened the gate, I was told to lie on the ground and not move. My grandparents lived with us at that time. When they heard the commotion and came to the living room, they saw all the police officers in our home and were also told to lie on the ground. My father was put in handcuffs and taken away. My mother was crying and screaming; my grandparents were crying and very upset. I was so confused, angry, and totally disoriented. I remember that day clearly. I had so many questions, but my mother wouldn't tell me the truth.

Shortly thereafter, I learned the truth. Everything was exposed to the light. My father had been part of a drug cartel for several years and had led a secret life he kept from me. I felt like he had lied to us again. I feared I would not be able to be with my father again. The 5-year-old in me woke up and said, "Oh no, back to being unwanted." Those childhood experiences returned, and I got angry. My father was eventually sentenced to 25 years in prison. He was 46 years old when he was arrested.

I was not a happy teenager, to say the least, but I kept myself out of visible trouble. I didn't want to give my mother any more anguish. I was able to control and release a lot of my anger with martial arts. When I was eight, my father had put me in karate. That, along with my Sifu, helped shape me as a young adult. I thank God I had karate in my life during those times. Although my anger was under control, I started messing around with alcohol and sex, which led me down the wrong path. At an early age, women became an addiction for me. My Hispanic culture encouraged me to believe that the more women I had, the more of a man I would be. And I thought that would make my father proud. It wasn't about the karate trophies anymore; women became my trophies. The enemy worked on me as he had the men before me. I believed that my validation came from women.

My mother put me in a Catholic high school, and I began slowly to develop an interest in Jesus. I attended a Jesuit College, and my interest grew, but I wasn't ready to commit to a Christian lifestyle. Because of the shame I felt, I lied to everyone about where my father was. I was living in darkness. John 3:19 is clearly where I was: *This is the verdict: Light has come into the world, but people loved darkness instead of light because their deeds were evil* (NIV). I graduated high school and college, and my father couldn't be there with us. I was angry at how things had turned out, but I wasn't angry at God. I'd pray and ask Him why this was happening to us. Why did our family have to be apart? Why was there so much suffering in our home? I would ask, but I never listened for an answer. The more I asked, the angrier I got, and I would revert to drinking and finding women to have sex with. I didn't know how else to medicate the pain.

My mom made sure we would visit my father monthly as a family—wherever he was. I would travel with my mom and grandparents every time. Every visit, we would sit in a big room with other families around us and talk and eat things from the vending machine. It was an awkward and painful time.

Shortly after I graduated from college, my father was released early and returned home. He spent time writing articles and doing interviews about the evils of drug use and the problems we have with drugs in our inner cities.

While incarcerated, he came to the realization of how drugs destroy young men and their families. He met a lot of young men whose lives had been ruined because of drugs. He would tell me that he would always think of me; he never wanted me to end up like those kids. He saw the fruit of his previous work and was ashamed of being blinded by money. He was a man who learned from his mistakes and tried to make a difference. He tried returning to work and making a difference but had a heart attack shortly after getting released. For several years, he had to monitor his heart. Unfortunately, he had several medical complications and passed away six years after his release at the young age of 61.

I can say that the last six years of my father's life were when I really got to know him. He will always be my hero. He wasn't perfect and certainly made mistakes, but he taught me to be a good man. When I was a child, he never exposed me to his secret; he protected me from the evils of drugs and violence. Later in life, he asked me for forgiveness, and I understood he was doing everything for his family. I truly believe he loved us.

When we expose our demons to light and confess our torments, those demons die in the light.

My father didn't have an excuse for his actions; he fell, as many others have, for the love of money. But when he spoke about his mistakes and became vulnerable, I understood that the enemy had enticed him at his weakest moment, and he fell to the temptation.

Christ wasn't a part of our home during my childhood; that had everything to do with our problems.

John 3:20 (NIV) tells us, *Everyone who does evil hates the light and will not come into the light for fear that their deeds will be exposed.* That's what kept me in bondage for many years, living with a family secret. I felt I would be judged by others if my secret was exposed. That's exactly what the enemy wanted.

When my father passed in 2000, I was working in a shrimping company in Venezuela. I came home to be with my family. My mother and I needed some advice on handling his life insurance policy, so my cousin introduced us to a company that educates families about insurance and investments. When I met with the representative who explained my father's policy, I discovered my father had been lied to and had the wrong type of insurance for 16 years. At that point, I decided I wanted to learn how to help others with their finances—I had actually been looking for guidance and meaning in my own life.

I joined the company part-time; that was the beginning of my journey. God used this opportunity to open my eyes. I knew I was done with being part of the world. I wanted to find peace and stability.

My wife and I met in Venezuela and got married in the United States in 2002. As I worked with the financial company, God put men in my life who introduced me to Jesus. My wife and I got baptized together and began to create a married life with Jesus in our home and business. I decided that my kids would not have a childhood without Jesus. We chose to let Jesus guide us in every aspect of our lives, and we've grown in the process thanks to that decision.

Through our business, we've been exposed to Band of Brothers, which helps men understand and deal with their wounds. I've been able to understand the decisions my father made weren't meant to hurt us, but the enemy had blinded him with power and money. The enemy got to him at a moment of financial despair and enticed him. Ephesians 6:12 (NIV) states, *For our struggle is not against flesh and blood, but against the rulers, against the authorities, against the powers of this dark world and against the spiritual forces of evil in the heavenly realms.* Our real battle is against the unseen. I believe my father felt like many men who carry the weight of the world on their shoulders as they seek to provide for their families. I've learned from my father's mistakes, and I appreciate and love him for that. For God uses all things for His good. I know now that when I surrender to God, all my issues get resolved. *And we know that in all things God works for the good of those who love him, who have been called according to his purpose* (Romans 8:28 NIV).

God enlightens us to seek His wisdom and understanding. Proverbs 4:5-8 tells us, *Get wisdom! Get understanding! Do not forget, nor turn away from the words of my mouth. Do not forsake her, and she will preserve you; Love her, and she will keep you. Wisdom is the principal thing; Therefore, get wisdom. And in all your getting, get understanding. Exalt her, and she will promote you; She will bring you honor, when you embrace her* (NKJV).

God opened my eyes to a generational reality. The Bible mentions generational curses in several places (Exodus 20:5, Numbers 14:18; Deuteronomy 5:9). God warns of *punishing the children for the sin of the parents to the third and fourth generation of those who hate me* (Deuteronomy 5:9 NIV). My father, grandfather, and great-grandfather had their own wounds. They found comfort in alcohol and validation in women. They were victims of the enemy's attacks, which were never resolved because they didn't run to Jesus for comfort, strength, and wisdom. God made me aware of these generational curses, and I decided to break them. I strengthened my relationship with Christ. I released my anger and decided that to find peace, my relationship with Jesus needed to be more intimate.

I pray that my children see Christ in me. They will never have to feel ashamed of their father. My prayer every morning is for God to grant me wisdom and understanding and that I may never cause pain to my family.

I love the prayer of Jabez in 1 Chronicles 4:10: *Jabez cried out to the God of Israel, "Oh, that you would bless me and enlarge my territory! Let your hand be with me, and keep me from harm so that I will be free from pain"* (NIV).

And I love the end of that verse: *And God granted his request.*

I believe that every man's purpose is to be used by God to be a blessing to others. I fight off the enemy every day by finding refuge in Christ. I am, for the rest of my days, an instrument of His will. I have welcomed the light of God into my life, and with that, God assures me that all demons will die in His presence.

Navigating Your Business

by Asaad Faraj

Over the course of my career, I have often been asked to speak at financial conferences and business seminars. A few years ago, I had a God-given opportunity on a mission trip to address gatherings of small business owners from Third World countries.

In preparing for these seminars, I found myself running smack into an impasse. How was I going to teach business principles with my American viewpoint to these foreign businesspeople? Could I convey my message to people from completely different economic systems, not to mention reach across cultural and language barriers? On top of that, how would I be able to address all the diverse business issues they faced?

I realized that teaching conventional business principles wasn't enough. The message my audience needed to hear was one based on a biblical model of financial principles.

That was when a divine concept was revealed to me: God wants to be our business partner.

That's right! Regardless of what country we live in or what the economic climate is, God wants to see us succeed in business, and He presents keys to success in the Bible that transcend any perceived barriers.

God is not a man, so he does not lie. He is not human, so he does not change his mind. Has he ever spoken and failed to act? Has he ever promised and not carried it through? (Numbers 23:19 NLT).

God is the most trustworthy partner you could possibly enter into a business relationship with. Imagine having a partner who is incapable of lying, does not change His mind, never fails to follow up, and never breaks promises! That's what you can expect when you bring God into the equation.

In my book *Faith Over Finance*, I present a series of core principles entitled "Twelve Steps to Making God Your Business Partner." Each step details how we can invite Him into our business lives through actions such as setting up a tithing/offering plan, believing over business plans, asking for divine appointments, and praying for wisdom.

When you allow God into your business, you no longer have to fight issues that rise up against your family, finances, career, or health alone. He has an infinite ability to bless your finances, unbridled enthusiasm to empower your business growth, and an unmatched authority for giving guidance and steering you from harm. He's genuinely interested in every aspect of your business, whether you're making an investment, hiring new employees, leading teams, or launching new products and services.

In turn, God has enterprises that He wants us to invest in. These ventures include sowing/tithing, providing for the poor, taking care of widows and orphans, and spreading the gospel.

God does not want to be a silent partner in His relationship with us, nor is He an underling who does all our menial tasks. He expects us to accomplish certain things on our end. Just as it is in every good partnership across the world, the more the business profits, the more all the partners profit. This style of partnership favors God as the partner with the most incentive for the long term. This means that as your business grows, the more money you will be able to give to the kingdom of God.

Partnering with God doesn't involve sitting back in an easy chair and watching Him make millions for us. But it does mean seeking His guidance in everything we do in the business world and actively investing in the things He values. Partner with God in your business. It's the best business decision you can ever make.

· ·

BRUCE TANIS

Bruce Tanis has enjoyed a successful Wall Street career for over 40 years. He has held senior executive roles at leading investment banks as a trader, advisor, executive director, consultant, economic forecaster, and money manager.

Bruce studied pre-med sciences, political science, philosophy, ancient Greece, philology, Austrian economics, finance, constitutional law, and history of the US and Europe. He has worked with former members of the Reagan Administration to reform Social Security and with Steve Forbes to promote a return to the gold standard. And he has testified as an expert on the mortgage crisis before members of Congress. Bruce is a George F. Baker Scholar and was recently knighted as Knight of Grace in the Ecumenical Order of St. John of Jerusalem, Knights of Malta, a chivalrous order that has been defending Christianity in the world for 900 years.

Bruce is a speaker and radio personality speaking on a wide range of topics, including political and social theory, economics, history, music, wholistic health, and constitutional law. Bruce is also an avid traveler, guitarist, collector, singer, and writer. He is active in various charitable, philanthropic, and kingdom-building causes. He currently lives in Palm Beach, Florida.

One Word from God Can Change Your Life

By Bruce Tanis

All my life, I've identified as a Christian.

I was born into a Christian family and raised by loving Christian parents and grandparents who baptized me as a baby at Bethel Christian Reformed Church in Paterson, New Jersey. I thank God for the powerful words spoken over me. Little did I know the deep meaning and power those words would hold.

At an early age, I was fascinated by the Bible stories my mother and grandmother would read to me—especially the story of Sampson. One of my most prized possessions today is my childhood drawing of Sampson pulling down the pillars of the Temple of Baal. Sampson was like a superhero, and I admired his God-given strength and resolve.

My parents sacrificed a lot to afford a Christian upbringing and education for my two beautiful younger sisters and me. I was blessed to attend private Christian schools from kindergarten through college. I attended church, Sunday school, Catechism, and a version of Christian Boy Scouts called the Calvinist Cadets.

In our home, we sat down each night for a hearty, home-cooked supper, reading passages from God's Word and thanking Him for all our blessings.

Sundays were the Lord's Day, a special day in our home. Unlike other days, we weren't permitted to go out and play, ride our bikes, or make someone else work. We attended church in the morning and evening because my parents wanted us to receive the full message of God's Word from both sermons.

Train up a child in the way he should go, And when he is old, he will not depart from it (Proverbs 22:6 NKJV).

We often split our summers between an evangelical Christian camp in the Adirondacks and the home we rented in the Methodist beach community of Ocean Grove, NJ. Sometimes, we attended revivals, crusades, and gospel churches. The gospel music lifted my spirit, and all music would have an important impact on my life.

Over the years, I watched my father work hard to support our family, yet he still made time to serve as a deacon, elder, and treasurer in our church.

My beloved mother was a busy, stay-at-home mom with a side business. She had a kind word for everyone, finding time to counsel fellow parishioners, relatives, friends, and neighbors in our living room. There was always a warm cup of tea and a piece of cake awaiting anyone who needed to talk. One of my most endearing memories was when my mom broke out the Schofield Bible one afternoon and evangelized in our living room to two Jehovah's Witnesses who showed up at the door. She even witnessed to the Witnesses!

Be kind to one another, tenderhearted, forgiving one another, even as God in Christ forgave you (Ephesians 4:32 NKJV).

It was the sixties television generation, and when I saw the Beatles perform for the first time on the Ed Sullivan Show, I was mesmerized by their words and music. I immediately wanted to be a Beatle. I got a Beatles lunch box, a Beatles haircut, and begged my mom for Beatle boots!

The music of the sixties had the same gospel and spiritual roots I heard in church, and I found it captivating. What I heard on the radio and television drew me in so strongly that, by nine years old, I had picked up a guitar, and soon, I was playing and singing in a series of small garage bands.

Growing up in the 60s and 70s, I saw the peaceful world of my early childhood changing morally and spiritually. In popular music, we went from Pat Boone and the mop-top Beatles to the sullen, drugged-out Rolling Stones and Led Zeppelin.

As morals and music changed, the words changed, too. The rebellious, suggestive rock music lyrics and secular culture left a big impression on me. The new cultural revolution seemed fun and liberating and just a little edgy, enough to tempt a curious and impressionable young man like me. Little did I know then how powerfully media culture would affect me and an entire generation. Influenced by music, lyrics, movies, and television that normalized foul language, drinking, drugs, and adultery, many of us would make choices that would take us down a secular and self-destructive path away from God.

My parents had prepared me for success in life and set a wonderful example, but along the way, I started feeling confined under the strict Calvinist dogma. Compared to what I saw in the world, it seemed unreasonably restricted by a rigid, religious spirit,

I grew curious to see if things out in the world were different; it all seemed so exotic compared to how I was raised.

My curiosity began with music and fashion. Imitating what I saw around me, I began to dress, walk, sing, and talk like the secular world. I adopted the rock and roll rebel uniform: a leather jacket, boots, flannel shirts, and faded ripped jeans.

To my mother's horror, my language began to change. I began peppering my speech with profanity because I thought it was cool. I had no idea the power of my words, how easily words become habits in speech, and how difficult it would be to break those habits later.

Meanwhile, I was making new friends outside church and school. And not many of them were raised the way I was. They smoked cigarettes, used profanity, and took God's name in vain, something I was not exposed to at home. In my home and church, no one ever took God's name in vain. I never heard anyone use the name of Jesus Christ as a curse word in my early life, but these people did. I was inadvertently exposing myself to the world's temptations, not being fully conscious of the dangers and consequences bad choices and harsh, powerful words could bring.

"You shall not take the name of the Lord your God in vain, for the Lord will not hold him guiltless who takes His name in vain" (Exodus 20:7 NKJV).

You see, the enemy is cunning and creative. He starts by teasing us with little desires that seem harmless at the time. He normalizes evil words, deeds, and desires. Then he grows those desires slowly, almost imperceptibly, until they drive a big wedge between our relationship with God and others.

Be sober, be vigilant, because your adversary the devil walks about like a roaring lion, seeking whom he may devour (1 Peter 5:8 NKJV).

Looking back, I unfortunately mainly chose to ignore these warnings and prioritize music, money, worldly pleasure, and other temptations more than GOD. Like so many of my generation, I succumbed to the secular worldliness being promoted by popular media.

When I began to work, I took every dirty, sweaty, well-paying labor job I could to earn money and freedom. I worked as a farmhand, restaurant worker, dishwasher, roofer, construction worker, oil truck driver, and nightclub bouncer. I could have easily qualified then as the poster boy for the show, "Dirty Jobs." Here again, I heard foul language and curse words punctuating the conversations and jokes. It seemed so normal then, and unfortunately, it became normal for me too.

As I chased that more secular lifestyle, I lost a lot of friends and acquaintances to addiction, drugs, alcohol, motorcycle accidents, car crashes, and even suicide. I was deeply saddened and stunned by these events. I knew from all the young rock stars who were dying tragic deaths that the dangerous choices people made could ultimately destroy them, but seeing friends take this path was shocking. From my Christian upbringing, I knew that the path one chooses is very important. What I didn't fully comprehend was that these tragic events were a clear message from God that words and choices matter, and some decisions are irreversible. He was showing me you can't just drift through life aimlessly, recklessly, and profanely without any consequences, and that there is only one surefire way to not fall into that trap: walk closer with God.

My beloved Uncle Jack was a devout Christian and a successful businessman whom I admired, loved, and respected. One day, he intervened and knocked some sense into me. He pulled me out into the yard alone, looked me straight in the eye, and demanded to know exactly what I was doing with my life. He told me I needed to quit fooling around, clean up my act, and get to college. I got the message loud and clear.

Before I knew it, my parents were driving me halfway across the country to a well-regarded, private Christian college called Hope College in Western Michigan. The message? There's always Hope.

> *"For I know the plans I have for you,"* declares the Lord, *"plans to prosper you and not to harm you, plans to give you hope and a future"* (Jeremiah 29:11 NIV).

My arrival at my new, preppy, ivy-covered Midwestern college was quite a culture shock. Other freshmen were clean-cut and preppy: Top-siders, khakis, Brooks Brothers button-downs, and popped-collar Lacoste alligator polos were everywhere. They all spoke nicely and politely.

Not me. I was a long-haired urban rocker from New Jersey with a penchant for irreverence. My preferred wardrobe was ripped jeans, cowboy boots, a flannel shirt over a pocket tee with a pack of Marlboros rolled into the sleeve, and a beat-up old guitar. My language was somewhat unrefined, and I didn't even know what a Top-sider was!

It was a literal Psalm 40:2-4 moment for me. *He also brought me up out of a horrible pit, Out of the miry clay, And set my feet upon a rock, And established my steps. He has put a new song in my mouth—Praise to our God; Many will see it and fear, And will trust in the Lord* (NKJV).

My first semester was a disaster, as I found fast acceptance among the party crowd, but after a few wardrobe and attitude adjustments, I slowly adapted. I made the football team, played lacrosse, became a contributing editor of the campus newspaper, and had a DJ gig at the college radio station. I began to excel academically and was selected to be a George F. Baker Scholar, a prestigious academic honor affiliated with the Harvard School of Business.

On campus, there were plenty of opportunities for spiritual growth, but I still chose to lean on my own understanding. I rarely attended chapel, and I passed on an invitation to join Fellowship of Christian Athletes. I owned a Bible, but I didn't read it, and I rarely prayed. God lifted me out of the dangerous lifestyle I had chosen and placed me in a pristine, Christian environment, sending me signs that He had great plans for me, but I still stubbornly clung to the wider, easier path. I was pretty sure I was saved, but I was clearly not submitted. Dazzled by the world and its temptations, I was blind to the fact that submission was important to salvation.

Humble yourselves, therefore, under God's mighty hand, that he may lift you up in due time (1 Peter 5:6 NIV).

I graduated from Hope College as a George F. Baker Scholar in economics, history, political science, and philosophy. After my post-graduate studies in Europe, I arrived back in the United States with one goal: success.

Success to me equated to making money, so I dove into the exciting world of Wall Street with a new haircut, a new suit, and a new sophisticated attitude. I landed a great job with a major firm on the 72nd floor of the World Trade Center. My confidence was boundless. I thought I could sell brass knuckles to Gandhi.

Entering the fast-paced, big-city world of Wall Street largely without GOD, it is easy to be tempted to make bad choices, and I made a few, but I wasn't exactly the Wolf of Wall Street.

Over the next thirty years, I lived in and around New York City and created a strong identity for myself in business, but only God knew my real, spiritual identity, and He never left me. The purpose He had for me as a leader and builder of His kingdom was different than the life I was living. In retrospect, God allowed me to experience what I did to teach me important lessons.

> *Be transformed by the renewing of your mind* (Romans 12:2 NIV).

My story is not tragic, but it could have been had I not had a strong Christian upbringing. There were many crucial crossroads. Had I not gone to college and continued playing in bars, had I chosen to party and not study in school, had I gone off the deep end like some of my Wall Street colleagues, things would have turned out differently. But at each fork in the road, my moral upbringing and the hand of God would not allow me to stray very far. God had bigger plans, and He had planted those seeds long ago.

Eventually, I would find out what those plans entailed.

Amid lockdowns in New York, I made the decision to move to Florida. I began attending church, and I bought a new Bible. I felt I was headed in the right direction with these new Christian activities.

Then, suddenly, a close friend died. As a result of his death, another friend invited me to a Bible study, where I found peace, guidance, and fellowship.

Soon afterward, my parents became very ill. My parents spent nearly every day of their 65 years of marriage together. Now, they were deathly ill in the same hospital. Both nearly died, but by the sheer power of prayer, they improved. The doctors said it was a miracle. They recovered and came home.

But a few months later, I was reminded how precious and short our lives are when the Lord called my precious mother home. I rejoice, knowing that my beautiful mother is in heaven.

> *We are confident, I say, and willing rather to be absent from the body, and to be present with the Lord* (2 Corinthians 5:8 KJV).

I was crushed and sad. Once again, I found myself at a fork in the road with my faith being tested. I was walking closer with the Lord. What was God trying to tell me? Was there something I was missing?

I had no idea God would change my course again and answer that question in a very special way.

One evening, while attending an event in Palm Beach, I met a woman who told me about the incredible healing miracle she received from Jesus Christ of Nazareth and how she stood on the Word of the Lord to receive it. I was struck by her testimony and unshakable faith. It was as if God wanted me to hear an important message through her.

Soon, God would begin to use her as a vessel to teach me one of the biggest lessons I ever learned in my life. In speaking with her, I began to realize I sometimes spoke sarcastically, carelessly, and even harshly or profanely. I foolishly thought these were just words. Yet, all it took was a powerful Word from God to change my mind.

This was the Word she spoke over me: *Death and life are in the power of the tongue* (Proverbs 18:21 KJV).

She taught me life is all about the power of the Word of God and urged me to always speak life over every situation.

Prophetically, she also recognized by some of my words and actions that I was not fully submitted to God and admonished me to surrender my will to God's will.

That really opened my eyes.

I had never heard the truth spoken like that before, and it became the catalyst for me to rededicate myself to Christ and be baptized.

Instantly, my desires shifted. With the help of God, I mastered control over my words. My preferences changed. Even my taste in music wasn't the same anymore. God took a devout woman speaking His Word to get me to trade what I thought was happiness for real joy.

She made me realize that God spoke the world into existence with His Word. *In the beginning there was the Word, and the Word was with God, and the Word was God* (John 1:1 KJV).

She taught me that, in the end, only His Word will stand. *The grass withers, the flower fades, But the word of God stands forever* (Isaiah 40:8 NKJV).

Words matter. We reap what we sow.

So now, when I read Isaiah 55:11, which says God's Word will not return void, I realize the words spoken over me at my baptism so long ago may have seemed void for a season, but they surely didn't return void. Instead, they continue to bear fruit.

This is the most important lesson I can share with you: WORDS are powerful. If one WORD from God can change my life, it can change yours too. You can turn your life around, be healed, receive a miracle, and restore your relationships and finances, all with a WORD from God.

Even when we encounter evil, God's Word is our best weapon. *No weapon formed against you shall prosper* (Isaiah 54:17 NKJV).

The Word of God is sharper than any two-edged sword, and our duty as warriors is to spread God's Word and use it as a weapon against all evil.

I was always a Christian, but I walked in the world and yielded to its many temptations. I lost track of the Word of God and instead found traction in the world, often using my words carelessly. But don't think for one minute that words are just words and can't change anything, because they CAN. I am living proof that ONE WORD from God can change your life and that the words you speak can change your life and the lives of others for better or for worse!

You are what you speak, so SPEAK LIFE!

Doug Sahm

Doug Sahm's life started on December 13, 1977, in southern California. Currently, Doug lives in Jupiter, Florida, and attends Calvary Church. Doug and his wife Sara feel that their relationship continues to grow stronger, just like the faith that guides it.

Doug is a believer in GOD and believes that through GOD'S guidance, anything is possible. Family is the word that has become the backbone in Doug's life. For him, the meaning of "family" can include loved ones, friends, business partners, associates, and most of all, GOD. Faith is how Doug has been able to allow his "family" to grow, and by doing this, his life has become closer to GOD.

As his daughters Ember and River get older, Doug is watching them form relationships that, with GOD'S assistance, can help them form their own "families" of positive individuals. Through his expansion in faith, life's opportunities have truly begun to blossom. The words truth, love, help, trust, strength, listening, and forgiveness have all become leaders in the relationship that he has formed with GOD.

Healing Through Grace Is a Gift from Above

By Doug Sahm

Being alive is something that many people take for granted, which can lead to missing a lot of life's beauty. I used to feel I was owed freedom and success, and, for a large portion of my life, I allowed material things to determine what those words meant. The feeling of a hustle or a quick fix had me lost in a false world full of negativity and deceit. I had no connection to GOD's direction, and my life was nothing like it is now. Emotional freedom comes from faith, which is created through the Lord's gift of grace. Of all the opportunities we have, finding a relationship with GOD is a must. The Bible shows that GOD is always there for us, but we must believe it to see it. *"As for GOD, his way is all good: the word of the Lord is tested; he is a safe cover for all of those who put faith in him"* (2 Samuel 22:31 NIV).

As I begin sharing part of my story, I want you to ask yourself some questions designed to show you how looking at another person's faith can change how you see your own. Please take a moment and answer honestly, then read my story. At the end, I'll ask you again.

1. Do I trust GOD 100%?
2. Am I scared to let go of my past?

3. Am I an active believer?
4. Does trust come to me with ease?
5. Can I help others without having expectations of them helping me?

I ask myself these questions, and as my life gains years and I develop a closer relationship with GOD, my truth has begun to change its meaning to me.

When I was younger, the truth was a black-and-white description of what I was told and encountered. And although that is one way of looking at the world, when we bring GOD into the picture, we see beyond the black and white. I've seen this in action quite often as I've witnessed GOD'S grace when I've opened my arms to help someone else.

In my earlier days, the only help I looked for was that which I could take advantage of for my own benefit. That resulted in many missed opportunities and unfulfilled desires. In my old life, I lived selfishly, and my future was aimed at a barren land because GOD was not my leader. Then, one of GOD'S miracles occurred, and faith swept me up and into His arms, where He showed me that giving creates love.

When this began, I was scared, and I was still looking for my "prize," but it rarely showed up. It took me a long time to realize that the prize I was searching for was not physical; it was an emotional and spiritual one. Helping others strengthens my faith and my relationships as my heart opens. None of this could be possible without GOD's direction and without exercising true faith.

Now, every day, I ask GOD to show me how I can help someone else. I simply pray, "GOD show me how I can help someone else today. Amen." The Bible tells us how giving creates growth. *"A generous person will prosper; whoever refreshes others will be refreshed."* (Proverbs 11:25)

My vision of life has turned into something that I call a blessing and gift from

GOD. For me, the painful things that I have been through have now become tools for my future. With GOD's guidance, faith has healed and allowed me to help others find GOD's grace. The relationship that I currently have with GOD has changed the direction of what I do for others. Limitations are not part of what GOD desires, and through prayer, I am shown how I can help others.

The feeling of helping others was something my wife and I wanted to give our daughters. We tried to do that by giving them opportunities and choices to decide their own actions. In the beginning, they were hesitant to be open and help others; then, GOD presented them with an opportunity they could not resist. From that moment, their faith and how they see things in life has become a breathtaking gift from GOD. If you have children or friends who have almost found the joy of what giving can create, it is your job to keep them on track until joy finds them. GOD will then have a new warrior to help Him fight negativity through sharing His gift of grace. As life shows itself to me, I am always stunned by how small, positive actions can create such large spiritual explosions.

The blessings GOD provides are always happening around us, but we are usually looking in only one direction, so we don't see them when they pass by. When you look at yourself, do you see what you want others to be, or do you see things you can change to make yourself more like who GOD wants you to be?

To make changes in my relationship with GOD, I had to begin by working on forgiveness, trust, comparisons, doubts, and expectations. Those are some things that can block me from freely helping someone else. The Lord is my leader, and He constantly reminds me that I can help others, but I must choose to make the giving occur.

When helping others, I'd encourage you to try doing it in two ways. And then compare them. First, give help silently. And then help in a way that requires direct communication.

I have found that when using direct communication while helping, it is difficult not to look for a specific type of reaction, while silently helping can be a cheap way out. GOD has given us the ability to be gracious to others, and I feel that that does not mean taking the easy way out. Did Jesus take the easy way out, or did He give His life for us? What are you willing to give up? Are you willing to give your life for someone else? The Bible shows that the action of giving is a sign of true faith. *Do nothing from selfishness or empty conceit, but with humility consider one another as more important than yourselves; do not merely look out for our personal interests, but also for the interests of others* (Philippians 2:3-4 NASB).

The internal support that giving to others provides needs to be felt to understand its strength. Currently, some pieces of my life outside of my family are a bit uncomfortable, but GOD is helping me stay strong while I battle these chapters that life has provided.

Business is a complicated word with many meanings, and life is certainly showing them to me at a rapid rate. Some of the meanings are fabulous and have allowed me to flourish in physical and emotional ways. On the other hand, some things that have happened both to and from me in the world of business are not anything I can call fabulous. Without faith and GOD, a positive way out could not exist and would not even be visible. Looking at that statement lets me know that with the issues in business that are facing me, strength, honesty, humility, and forgiveness will be required from me to reach stability. The issues facing me are rooted in a family dispute regarding business directions, property, loans, communication, trust and the future of my relationship with people in my family. Why do things have to be like this? Now, that is a question I ask GOD countless times every day, and His response is that I should fix myself before I ask Him to fix someone else.

Help is a commonly added word in my prayers. But what I ask GOD to help me with always seems to change.

The type of things that I now need help in have become spiritual instead of material. That is a massive change from how I used to pray. With the ability to choose how we live and act, living by pure faith can be extremely challenging. The biggest emotional setback I encounter is also faith's worst enemy—that is fear. I don't fall into fear the same way I used to, but fear is a sneaky emotion that calmly waits for our most vulnerable moments and then strikes with no warning. The most common reaction I used to feel in response to fear was anger, because I thought that anger protected me from fear. That was so far away from the truth. Anger is a response, not a form of protection like faith is designed to be.

GOD desires us to trust Him for solutions to everything we encounter in our lives, and the directions He provides for us are not based on destruction but on repair. The fact that I can share this as part of my truth puts me in awe because before I allowed GOD to guide my life fully, all I knew how to do was fight. The Bible shows us how this is true through Jesus and His resurrection, which allows us also to be resurrected. *But because of his great gift of love for us, GOD, who is rich in mercy, made us alive with Christ even when we were dead in transgressions—it is by grace you have been saved* (Ephesians 2:4-5 NIV).

Countless things in my past and what I am sharing with you let me know that GOD'S grace is here for all of us if we believe. Open your heart, trust our Lord, accept GOD'S grace, and give thanks. In my life, those simple tasks have not always been easy, but they have become part of my relationship with GOD. Now that I trust GOD, trusting myself has become easier because of GOD's endless love for us.

This is the second United Men of Honor book in which I have shared some of my life and my relationship with GOD. The first book I wrote in was *United Men of Honor: Overcoming Adversity Through Faith*. In that book, I looked at how faith helped me recover. In this book, I have looked at how faith has protected me and how I can help others by showing them how to let GOD help them recover. The word that makes all this possible is the word GRACE. Grace is the most amazing way that GOD shows Himself to us. I used to only believe in it just a little bit, but then GOD repeatedly showed me how special it is, and my life began to change. From GOD's love, my desire to doubt has continued to lessen, and my heart continues to open. That seems like a simple synopsis, but with grace, you will see how easily things in life fit and how far into them you can go. *But he gives more grace. Therefore it says, "GOD opposes the proud but gives grace to the humble"* (James 4:6 ESV).

Now, I want to look at the word forgiveness and how it can strengthen your faith by releasing negativity.

Do you hold any old grudges and hard feelings, or do you work on getting rid of them? Many times, we forget we have the ability to choose how we handle our emotions, and we feel trapped. For many of us, it seems the easiest to release our negative feelings is to offer forgiveness. Releasing them creates emotional space, allowing us to replace negative feelings with positive ones and giving us the ability to grow emotionally.

Have you ever sat down and made a list of things you need to do? Most people have. Rarely do our lists include forgiveness. So, give yourself a gift and try making a list of what you need to forgive. Over the last year, I have started making lists of where I need to allow forgiveness, and that has allowed my faith to flourish. I certainly have not protected forgiveness, but I have allowed myself the ability to look at it in a much simpler manner. To forgive does not mean to forget. It simply means that you are willing to release the negative feelings created in you. Without GOD, forgiveness would be next to impossible because sometimes being spiteful is the easy way out. People often use spite as a shield to protect their emotions from further damage.

Old grudges and deep physical damages are the hardest to forgive, but with GOD's help, it can be done. A close friend of mine showed me an easy way to start making the tough forgiveness happen. He told me to allow myself the time I needed to offer forgiveness. I found that it can take just a couple of minutes a day to create the emotional space to forgive and experience unexpected positive feelings.

Did Jesus hide behind a shield, or did He give everything away for us? To give in spiritually means to let GOD fill your soul with the Holy Spirit. And when we do that, it feels incredible. *"I have filled him with the Spirit of GOD in wisdom, in understanding, in knowledge, and in all kinds of craftsmanship"* (Exodus 31:3 NASB).

Trusting GOD is how I have been able to truly love myself. Daily, I remind myself that I am GOD's child and that everything GOD has created is perfect. The only problem I find is that sometimes I struggle to believe it. But GOD knows the truth, so I am okay with my doubts. Feeling hope is part of the joy in my heart, and it is a relief that GOD freely provides me. The hope I feel is sometimes about me, but it is usually about my daughters. Every time I see them accomplish something new or overcome something that was difficult for them, I feel hope.

Hope fills my soul with joy. One thing I want you to look at is where your soul is. My soul used to be nothing but lost. At times, it can still wander. But GOD doesn't let it go very far now that faith runs my life. Honesty has become one of the tools I use to see exactly where my soul is in relation to where I am with GOD. Unfortunately, people lie and tell false truths that pull them away from where they were born to be in the arms of our Lord. Try looking at how you treat others and what they give back to you. Do honesty, trust, love, forgiveness, helpfulness, and genuineness come to mind? Or did you respond with some of the opposite things like lies, ill will, discrimination, hindrance, and questioning? Regardless of what your answer is, don't forget that you are also responsible for part of the answer.

To help your soul grow, allow GOD to penetrate your heart more deeply. And all your relationships will begin to bloom. Some verses in the Bible are awesome reminders of how foolish we can be. This one is one of my favorites. *"This is the message that we have heard and declare to you: GOD is light; in him there is no darkness at all. If we claim to have fellowship with him and yet walk in the darkness, we lie and do not live out our truth"* (1 John 1:5-6 NIV).

Now, ask yourself these questions again. But this time, let GOD provide you with the answers.

1. Do I trust GOD 100%?
2. Am I scared to let go of my past?
3. Am I an active believer?
4. Does trust come to me with ease?
5. Can I help others without having expectations of them helping me?

Trust the guidance GOD provides you, and know He is always there to help you during your deepest struggles.

Give GOD some extra time, and He will enlighten your life.

The next time you need help, turn to GOD, and He will guide you to what you need.

Don't be afraid of faith. Let GOD'S grace become what heals your heart.

And to that, I say, Amen.

NAVIGATING FAITH OVER FINANCE

by Asaad Faraj

Throughout our lives, many of us aim to ensure that our financial destinies will be successful and secure. For some, that means developing a beneficial savings plan. Others look to bring innovation to the workplace or start up a business. Still others invest their income in stocks and ventures.

Unfortunately, most people don't recognize that effort alone is often not enough to fulfill and sustain their financial visions. Paychecks can be reduced, businesses are subject to decline, the stock market is vulnerable to ups and downs, and even the most careful savings plans can fail.

When personal efforts or strong work ethics fall short, where can we turn? As Christians, we should be putting God in control of our money and applying faith over our finances.

> *Using a dull ax requires great strength, so sharpen the blade. That's the value of wisdom; it helps you succeed* (Ecclesiastes 10:10 NLT).

What is the dull axe mentioned in Ecclesiastes? It's your personal effort without the sharpening of faith—a condition that makes you work much harder to attain success.

Wouldn't it be much easier to have God, our almighty, loving Father and Lord, involved in your finances instead of going it alone? Yet many people—even Christian believers—never think of having faith over their finances or seeking out godly financial principles.

God wants all of us to prosper financially as well as spiritually. However, we need to make sure we're listening to the right voices in our lives.

Have you ever caught yourself declaring something negative like "I can't pay my debts" or "Saving and giving is too difficult for me?" If so, ask yourself an important question: "Who told me that?" Who told you that you can't make money, pay off debts, or give a tithe every paycheck? I'll give you a hint...it wasn't God!

To energize our faith, we need to filter out negative declarations that impact our financial lives. We should speak right, believe right, and act right when it comes to our finances. As children of God, we're no longer subject to this world's system. We're called to speak life to our financial situations and trust He will show us the path to financial breakthrough.

Secondly, we need to take inventory of what we have and avoid concentrating on areas of lack. Whenever you ask God for anything—whether it be with finances, healing, or spiritual guidance—He asks you for something in return. God wants us to help further His kingdom, whether that means spreading the gospel, helping those in need, or giving money to His storehouse. That's how we show our love and gratitude to Him and the great works He has done in our lives.

As a vessel for God, we must humble ourselves, confess our sins, and allow Him to use our talents for His glory. Humility enables us to surrender control of our lives to God in all areas, including finances, and to use what we have to bring change to the world around us.

God wants a reciprocal relationship with us. He wants to bless our finances, but He also wants us to invest our time, talents, and treasures back into His kingdom. He also wants us to listen to His voice and make proper confessions over our financial conditions. Those are the first steps to establishing Faith Over Finance.

> *"For I know the plans I have for you," declares the LORD, "plans to prosper you and not to harm you, plans to give you hope and a future"* (Jeremiah 29:11 NIV).

John Harwick Sr.

John Harwick Sr. is a 64-year-old retired electrical engineer and former Vice President of Engineering at a laser and electro-optics firm in Orlando, Florida. He and his wife of 39 years, Julie, now reside on an agricultural plot in Sorrento, FL. John and Julie have four adult children—three girls and one boy, ranging in age from 21 to 28. Their children reside in various cities in Florida and Texas.

Ecclesiastes 3:11 (NIV) says in part "…. He has also set eternity in the hearts of men…." This has certainly been the case for John, who has long believed that the only things in this world that matter are the things that we do for eternity. People are eternal. We are to love God and love people.

While working in his secular job, John has always put emphasis on working in his church. Since retiring at age 59, he has strived to serve where he can in full-time ministry. He currently leads Bible studies and small groups in the Orlando area.

John is a musician and has been involved in worship ministry in churches since the age of 14. His interests include video and audio production, baseball, football, tennis, martial arts, and MMA.

STEP BY STEP

By John Harwick Sr.

I have learned through the years that self-reliance does not serve me well in the storms of life. In a difficult situation, my first instinct is to take inventory of my own abilities. I remember a time years ago when I went through a literal storm in a small boat. I was out on the water with my wife, friends, and relatives when I saw a storm quickly approaching us. We immediately headed for home. I was a reasonable fair-weather captain but not at all experienced in storms.

As we turned a sharp corner, we were met with a wall of wind and water that washed over the top of the bow and put the boat under. I immediately looked to what I could do rather than what the boat could do. Swim! I was a good swimmer. My solution using my abilities was problematic. First of all, it would not get us home. Secondly, it would leave my in-laws' boat at the bottom of the Intercoastal Waterway. Did I mention that I borrowed the in-laws' boat?

Fortunately, a friend spending the day with us had navigated storms on the water before. He had knowledge of the boat's capabilities and experience harnessing its features. First, he removed all the obstacles, including me. He encouraged me to move my 6'2" 225 lb. frame to the back of the boat. Then, he adjusted the outboard trim and took advantage of its power with a shove of the throttle. Immediately, the bow popped out of the water. Next, he engaged the bilge pumps to help dispatch what water remained. We made it all the way back to the dock with the bow high above the rough water, cutting through the waves at an angle.

The difference between me and my friend in that situation was that I looked to my abilities while my friend knew and trusted the boat's abilities.

Trust does not come easily to me. I suspect that I am not that different from most men in that regard. I feel like I must be responsible for everything in life—my work, mortgage, utilities, and the general state of repair of the yard and house, just to mention a few things. Unfortunately, for a good portion of my young life, my need for control extended to a lack of trust in God.

I grew up in church, part of a mainline denomination based on ceremony and tradition rather than a relationship with God. From a very young age, I knew of God and had a reverence for Him, thanks to Sunday school lessons and sitting through long church services in a suit and tie with my hands folded neatly in my lap. In those days, there was no such thing as "Kids' Service," and I never connected the knowledge I was taught with practical applications for everyday life. Sunday morning was an obligation. The rest of the week was for "normal" life.

My pastor was a large man with a deep, booming voice and a dramatic, formal delivery. Often, his fists would pound loudly on the ornate wooden pulpit to emphasize the power and judgment of God. The bright lights coming through the stained-glass windows behind him gave him a saintly glow. That shimmering array of colors lent credence to his every word. I learned that God was someone to be revered. Dare I say feared? He was certainly not someone you spoke to daily, laying all your cares, concerns, and problems at His feet. I understood God's wrath very well.

I accepted Jesus Christ as my Lord and Savior at a Billy Graham film at the age of thirteen. I went to the film with my parents, who had accepted Christ a few months earlier. After that, our family changed churches to a more evangelical church. That was the beginning of a long growth process for me. I was exposed to many solid youth leaders. At least one of them was a college athlete that I very much looked up to.

Through many weekend youth retreats and Christian summer camps, I learned that, yes, God is just. But I also learned that God is love. And what the justice of God required, the love of God provided through the sacrifice of Jesus Christ. God is a God of balance, not one-sided fire and brimstone judgment. I also began to learn about the character of God. I learned of His goodness, graciousness, and holiness. I learned of His mercy. I learned that God is for us. I learned a lot of things about God. I gained a lot of knowledge. I grew into a "fine Christian young man."

After graduating high school, I went into ministry. I worked full-time at a Christian radio station and also worked at a Christian community center, leading young singles' groups and events. Looking back, I would give myself a grade of "A" for knowledge and learning. In some areas of application, I'm afraid I would receive something closer to an "F."

There was always that issue of trust. I felt the weight and responsibility of everything. It's not that I thought myself to be that capable. I actually believed the opposite—feeling it was only a matter of time until my incompetence would be exposed. Bearing responsibility, combined with feelings of inadequacy, led to a lot of anxiety. That anxiety sometimes would express itself as impatience or even anger and depression. These feelings were most pronounced when I would go through various "storms" in my life.

As a young married man in my twenties, I never really saw or considered the disconnect between who I knew God to be and my lack of trusting Him. God began the process of changing that in me through the influence of one of our church elders who mentored me. We often met to study and pray together.

One evening while we were meeting, He asked me a question I still remember more than 30 years later. We were talking about God's provision. He asked me if I believed that God was not only able but would meet all of my needs. I answered affirmatively. Of course, I did. The follow-up question was the most difficult. Did my actions in life show that I *really* believed what I professed? Did I really trust God?

In my heart, I knew the way I handled life's difficulties did not reflect what I claimed to believe. It seemed it was simply a memorized truth that I did not live. God would repeatedly bring that question to my mind over the next year or two as He worked in me to show me His love and provision. God graciously worked several undeniable miracles in my life to show me who He is, what His desires were for me, and how to navigate the storms of life. I wish I could write about all of them, but it would simply be too lengthy.

It was not too long after the trust question was first posed to me that God started repeating that question to me in my mind over and over as I encountered various "storms." Late one Saturday evening, the phone rang at about 11 pm. My mother was calling me to tell me that my father was not expected to live through the night. This was not a total surprise—he had not been well for years. But that call triggered a wide array of thoughts and emotions. I was certainly shocked at the prospect of losing my father. I was very much saddened. I felt relief and almost a little happiness knowing he knew Jesus and was about to be released from his illness. And I felt guilt at the thought of being relieved at his death, knowing my mother could finally be released from the burden of caring for him.

My wife and I lived about a 16-hour drive from my parents' house. Regardless of the late hour, I just wanted to get home to be with my family. We decided to leave immediately and drive through the night. I had a lot of time to ponder various issues on that drive. Do I trust God to be with me and my family in this situation? Do I trust God to work in and through all the details leading up to and following the funeral? Do I trust God to take care of and provide for my mother?

My mind raced as I drove through the Tennessee mountains on the way to my parents' house. I just wanted to get home. My racing mind influenced my speed as I found myself at 3 am with no one else on the roads driving like a NASCAR driver at Daytona. I braked leading into the curves and accelerated as I finished on the outside of the curves, on the winding mountain roads.

In my life, there have been a few times I felt God speak directly to me. One of the first times was on that drive through the mountains. I have never heard an external audible voice; it has always been in the form of a disassociated thought that was so foreign it could not have come from me. I was in the middle of a smooth recovery on the outside corner of a 70mph turn when I had a very clear thought. "You are going to lose a tire. And if you don't slow down, you are going to go right over the side of the mountain!"

Where in the world did that random thought come from? I was so shocked that I immediately hit the brakes hard and slowed down to the speed limit. Within three miles, I felt the car start to shimmy and swerve. Because of my reduced speed, I safely navigated to the side of the road next to a rock formation in the mountain. I got out to find the source of the problem—a totally shredded tire!

Sadly, the gratitude and miracle of not going over the side of the mountain quickly faded, replaced with anxiety and anger. I was angry my father was dying. And I was angry I was stuck at the top of a mountain at 3:00 on a Sunday morning in the middle of nowhere. On top of it, I only had a mini spare with a maximum rated speed of 40mph and a range of 40 miles. Why would God allow this to happen? Especially at this time! Didn't God at least *owe* me a smooth trip home?

In my mind, I kept hearing the question, "Do you trust me?"

I resolved to calm down, pray, and do what God put in front of me, step by step. The first step was to jack up the car, clear the trunk, and get out the mini spare. I considered it to be useless. It was in no way a solution to finish the long drive. However, I knew that putting it on the car was my only hope of getting moving at all. My heart sank as I dug to the bottom of the trunk and pulled out the mini spare. It was totally flat! (I had left in an extreme hurry and had not considered equipment or safety checks.) I had to use every ounce of my restraint to keep from heaving my tire iron off the side of that mountain. In my mind, I kept hearing the question, "Do you trust me?" Once again, I resolved to calm my anger and replace it with prayer. God brought to mind the fact that I had left my electric car tire pump in the back of the car.

I did not know the big-picture solution of how to get home. But I was beginning to learn to keep calm, pray, and trust that God would take me step by step. I plugged in the electric pump with no response. Again, I felt prompted to take one step at a time and find out why. I found that the cigarette lighter had a blown fuse. Now what? I felt a slight urge to throw the tire iron again, but not as strongly as previously. I turned to prayer and tried to resolve to trust Him.

Then, the thought came to mind to search the trunk. I was not sure what I was looking for, but I was trying to step one step at a time as God was leading. I continued searching for a couple of minutes, even pulling back the carpet in the trunk. As I did, I saw a single fuse lying under the carpet. It was the exact type I needed for the cigarette lighter. Within a half hour, the mini spare was inflated and on the car. We were on the road again. I was thankful to God that we were making progress. But I could not ignore the facts. We were driving on a tire that could go neither fast enough nor far enough. I was still in the middle of nowhere at 3:30 on a Sunday morning. I still had 500 miles to go to reach my ultimate destination.

I tried as best as I could to remember to be grateful for each step God provided. I gave thanks to the Father that we were driving again and for His provisions that had brought us this far. I prayed for the next step. I ended my silent prayer with, "In Jesus' name, Amen."

I immediately received the thought, "Look up."

"Look up?" I repeated to myself. What in the world does that mean? I took it literally and craned my neck to the top of the windshield as I was driving. As I looked up, I saw I was passing a faintly lit billboard advertising a brand of tires available at an exit in about 60 miles. That was my next step.

My car was a Honda; this was before Honda automobiles were as popular in the United States as they are now. I wondered if the size tire I needed would be in stock. I had doubts about the small garage in the middle of the Tennessee mountains. I doubted they would be open on a Sunday, certainly not at the hour I would arrive. Nonetheless, I knew that God was leading me step by step. I resolved to take the next step, even though it made no sense. I got off at the appropriate exit and rolled up on my tiny tire to a small garage shop at around 5:00 Sunday morning. I figured, if nothing else, I would just sit there until God gave me the next piece of the puzzle.

To my surprise, I could see a light on inside and a man walking around. I went up to the door, but it was locked. The man inside saw me at the door and opened it. He asked if he could help me. I explained the situation. He came out to look at my car. His first response was, "I don't stock these tires at all." Again, my heart sank. But then he had a sudden recollection. "I think you may be in luck." He went on to explain that a man had ordered a couple of the exact tires I needed a few weeks before and never came to pick them up. He was going to return them but forgot. He added that he did not work Sundays and certainly not at 5 am, but something woke him up early, and he could not go back to sleep. So he decided to come in and catch up on some work.

He invited us in, provided us with hot coffee, and offered a couple of couches in his shop to lay on. He told us to get some sleep and that he would have us back on the road within an hour. We did complete our journey that day and even had a brief rest. God also worked out the details of my father's funeral and affairs. And He provided step by step for my mother.

Looking back 35 years later, I am extremely grateful for the graciousness and wisdom of God. Each one of those steps was frustrating. At the time, I could not understand why God would allow them. Now, I clearly see that each obstacle was an opportunity for me to learn. I can now see how gracious He was with those teachable moments. Those miracles gave me more faith and trust in Him. Much as the Israelites set up monuments of stone to remind them of God's deliverance, I have built monuments of stone in my memories that remind me of the faithfulness of God. When I see a storm coming, I know, first and foremost, who God is. Remembering His deliverance in the past gives me faith in His provision for the present and future.

After decades of God maturing me, I wish I could say I have perfect peace and trust in God. I still struggle at times to turn things over to Him. I don't always trust Him fully for His perfect outcome according to His purposes. God has, however, to His glory, brought me a long way from where I was. I may never be able to claim perfect peace and trust. But I can say that I do have peace in all the storms of life, to the degree that I know God's truth from His Word and walk according to it.

MIKE CHILDS

Mike Childs was born in Georgia but has traveled a lot due to being a military dependent (AKA military brat) and a veteran. He bounced all over the southeastern U.S., to West Germany, then out to a couple of western states for a few years before returning to the southeast for the last 35 years. He attained the rank of sergeant before several injuries caused him to get out of the service.

Through Mike's travels, he attended 18 different schools in two countries, four states, and various cities on his way to getting his general A.A., B.S. in IIT (Interdisciplinary Information Technology), and MBA in Human Resources.

Mike is now married to a beautiful, God-fearing woman, Erica, and has a beautiful baby girl. God willing, they may have a second child.

Mike has been a volunteer in various organizations—Assistant Scoutmaster for Boy Scouts of America, Area Leader, and Division Leader for Toastmasters International in Pinellas County, and on the Leadership Team for Band of Brothers. Band of Brothers has been one of the most influential organizations in his life, showing him that men don't have to fight their struggles alone. www.BandofBrothersFL.com.

Mike is currently a Division Leader with Primerica. www.primerica.com/mchilds

PRAISE YOU IN THE STORM

By Mike Childs

On December 13, 2022, while I was at work, my wife called me to tell me that her water broke. My first reaction was, "Are you serious?"

She said, "Yes! It's like Niagara Falls here!"

I quickly ran out of my office, briefly telling my colleague I was taking my wife to the hospital. She was only 30 weeks along in her pregnancy, so I was calmly freaking out. I was thinking, *This is way too soon; I'm going to have to buy Barbie doll clothes for my daughter.* But I was calm because my brother was born a month premature, and he turned out just fine.

My wife was not yet having any contractions, so the hospital admitted her until our daughter decided to grace us with her presence. I went to work during the day and came to see my wife at the hospital each night. This went on for 12 days. We decorated her hospital room with a Christmas tree and some other homey touches to make the stay as comfortable as possible. We would watch shows and movies together and do things like diamond dots artwork to pass the time. One of the nurses even gave my wife a makeover so she could get dressed up for a nice Christmas photo in front of one of their huge Christmas trees.

Finally, on Christmas night, my wife began feeling contractions. Our daughter was still breech, and my wife was low on amniotic fluid. She was 4cm dilated when the obstetrician came to the room minutes after the contractions started. It was time for an emergency C-section. I barely had time to let anyone know the baby was on the way. Waiting around the corner from the operating room for the staff to prep her felt like an eternity. As I sat there, I said all sorts of prayers, including that God would guide the hands of the doctors and medical staff and provide a safe and successful delivery of our baby girl.

One prayer that came to mind was the 23rd Psalm. *The Lord is my shepherd; I shall not want... Yea, though I walk through the valley of the shadow of death, I will fear no evil: for thou art with me; Thy rod and thy staff they comfort me* (Psalm 23:1, 4 KJV).

There we were, in the operating room at 32 weeks along—eight weeks early, nervous as could be but also so excited for our daughter to be born. When the doctor removed our baby from my wife, she barely had time to lift our daughter up high enough for me to see her before handing her off to the neonatal team. Unfortunately, she didn't raise her up high enough for my wife to see her. I was sitting next to my wife up at the head of the operating table, holding her hand while watching the neonatal team prep our daughter. I finally realized our newborn baby was lying there lifeless while the medical team performed chest compressions and bagged her.

I could see the blue light flashing over the entrance door. Additional medical staff came in to evaluate and assist the first team. My daughter had coded at birth.

I had never seen chest compressions performed on anyone until I saw them being done on my newborn daughter. That realization hit me a couple of weeks down the road. As I watched, I somehow stayed strong enough not to say anything to my wife as she lay on the table, twitching from the anesthesia as the doctor closed her incision.

Several minutes went by, and my wife realized she couldn't hear her baby crying yet. She asked me, "How's she doing?"

I mustered up the strength to just say, "They're working on her." I couldn't, in good conscience, bring myself to tell her the whole truth about what I was seeing at that moment.

Twenty minutes passed, and the team finally got my daughter stable enough to call me up to the table. My first reaction was one of excitement, "Oh my goodness!"

Immediately, I'm brought crashing back down to earth with the somber tone from the nurse practitioner telling me something along the lines of, "I'm sure you've seen us working on your daughter. I'm concerned because it took us 20 minutes to get her to this point. She had a lack of oxygen to her brain that entire time."

It was at that moment I claimed that she was a fighter. Later, I was reminded of the scripture: *When the angel of the Lord appeared to Gideon, he said, "The Lord is with you, mighty warrior"* (Judges 6:12 NIV).

My wife and I were taken back to the recovery room while we waited for the doctor to fill us in on how our daughter was. It wasn't good news. Our daughter was not responding to the reflexes they look for in newborns regarding pupillary and gag reflexes. She was pretty much being kept alive by the machines; they told us we might have to consider taking her off the machines and letting her pass.

My wife then let out a blood-curdling scream, crying, "NOOOOOO!!!"

I started to cry with her and just held her. I just couldn't believe it. I didn't feel that my daughter was ready to give up on life so early. We discussed our options: letting her pass or asking the doctors to do everything in their power to keep her alive. I was leaning towards allowing her to pass because we were told she would remain in a vegetative state.

Before we made the official decision, my wife requested we have time alone in the room. She then asked for her phone and played the song "Praise You in the Storm" by Natalie Grant.

As the song was coming to an end, the neonatologist came back into the room with a shocked look on her face, saying, "She's responding. I've never seen this in the 26 years I've been practicing, and I can't explain it."

I just pointed to the heavens and said, "I can. Jesus!"

Then I looked at my wife and said, "Let's give her the fighting chance that she's asking for." We were both overjoyed because we knew our prayers were heard and answered, yes, and amen.

I strongly believe our daughter began to respond due to our faith in Jesus and my wife's initiative to praise the Lord in song. We had been willing to let our daughter go home to Jesus and wait for us rather than be selfish and keep her when the chances of having anything more than just a shell of a life were slim to none with no response to reflexes. It was truly a Christmas miracle that after 20 minutes of chest compressions, a lack of oxygen, and no reflexes, she made a turnaround.

> *Now faith is confidence in what we hope for and assurance about what we do not see... By faith Abraham, when God tested him, offered Isaac as a sacrifice. He who had embraced the promises was about to sacrifice his one and only son* (Hebrews 11:1, 17 NIV).

Unfortunately, the hospital we were in only had a level 2 NICU, so we were transferred to a hospital 40 minutes away that had a level 4 NICU that could support our daughter's needs. The transport team brought our daughter into our room in an incubation transport case so my wife and I could at least reach in and touch her to say, "See you soon."

When I arrived at the other hospital, I was taken to my daughter's room. She was on a CPAP (Continuous Positive Airway Pressure) machine, umbilical IVs, heart rate leads, and pulse-ox (pulse and oxygen) lead. She was so tiny and had so many things attached to her that it was hard to take in. When my wife arrived, I went up to her recovery room and brought her down to see our daughter. By the time we returned, they had also placed EEG (Electroencephalography) leads on our daughter's head and intubated her because she was not handling her secretions very well. They were also pumping a bunch of medications into her, a precautionary measure taken for premature babies who have such a rough entrance into the world.

Because she had no seizure events for the first three days, the EEG leads were removed. One thing down, many to go. During the first week, the NICU nurses invited us to be involved. They had us take her temperature and change her diapers, which was a chore with all those leads attached.

Finally, after five days in the NICU, the nurse asked if we wanted to hold our daughter. I said, "Of course," thinking in my head, *Does a bear go in the woods?* LOL.

Knowing that she didn't get that golden hour to hold our daughter at birth and that she would jump at the opportunity, I looked at my wife and said, "Honey, do you want to hold her?"

She had been calling her dad, but as soon he picked up, she immediately told him, "Dad, I have to call you back. I'm finally getting to hold her."

I couldn't let her miss this "first."

After one week, the medications decreased, the umbilical IVs were removed, and one of us could hold our daughter for a couple of hours each day—so we took turns. It required both the nurse and the RT (respiratory therapist) to transfer her from the isolette into the arms of whichever one of us would hold her. Things were looking up, but she was still desatting (having a de-saturation of oxygen level below 90%) 2-4 times per shift. She didn't know how to handle her secretions by swallowing yet, so she did what seemed the next best thing—holding her breath until she couldn't anymore. At least this prevented her from aspirating and catching pneumonia. She would dip hard and fast down to as low as 20%, and the nurse and RT would come rushing in to revive her. We made the best of that New Year's Eve—spending it with our daughter and even sharing some sparkling cider with the NICU nurses who were on shift that night.

After the second week, the intubation tube came out, and our strong girl was put back on the CPAP machine. We were now able to take turns holding her each day. At that point, I had returned to work as I was saving my PTO/

FMLA (Paid Time Off/Family Medical Leave Act) for when she came home so I could spend time at home bonding with my new family. I would take my wife to the NICU, go to work for a few hours, and then go back and spend a couple of hours with my girls before bringing my wife back home. I was on the road for 80 miles, 3-4 hours a day during the work week.

It was hard to leave my daughter each day, but it was harder on my wife when I would take her home at night. Luckily, the hospital had a secure streaming program called Angel Eye, which was like a long-distance baby monitor. That made it easier, but it was still difficult to be away from her. My wife would go to sleep each night with the Angel Eye camera on. On some level, it helped her feel like our daughter was in the room with us. The nurses encouraged the parents to go home each night or day, depending on their schedule, to ensure they got their self-care in.

During this time, what I had witnessed on the day of my daughter's birth two weeks prior sunk in. She had coded at birth, received chest compressions, and was bagged for air. I broke down crying in my wife's arms as I realized the gravity of what I had seen and experienced that night. Because of my recollection and my wife's own trauma, she couldn't bring herself to go to the NICU discharge class at this point. We waited until we were about two weeks away from discharge before attending.

In the class, they showed an instructional video on newborn CPR (cardiopulmonary resuscitation). There was a disclaimer in the introduction that the video included a real-life story about how CPR saved a young child. I had no idea it would affect me as much as it did. I felt like I was watching my daughter go through that all over again, this time understanding what I was watching. I kept my composure the best I could but was still crying and noticeably shaking during the story.

After about four weeks, our daughter was on high-flow oxygen. My wife and I were finally able to take her out of the isolette to hold her without the help of the nurse or RT. One time when I was holding her, she went limp. She was lying there in my arms, lifeless, having another desat episode. I panicked as I got up to put her back in the isolette to revive her. The nurses and RT came in to finish getting her vitals back up to 100% and evaluate her. After she was back up, they asked me if I wanted to continue holding her. The image of seeing her having chest compressions done on her at birth and the feeling of her lifeless body in my arms was too traumatic for me at that moment. I had to tell them no. I couldn't handle the idea of that happening again—not twice in one day, at least. It's one thing to pick up your child when they are sleeping and they feel like a dead weight, but when they are lifeless in your arms, it's a completely different feeling.

There was a difference of opinions among the neonatologists as to what our daughter needed regarding a tracheostomy, genetic testing, and a G-tube (feeding tube into the stomach from the outside near the belly button instead of down the throat). With the progress she was making, we didn't think any of it was needed. We did finally agree that the G-tube was necessary to be able to take her home soon and be able to feed her. We were tired of being in the NICU and didn't want to be there anymore if we didn't have to be. The pediatric surgeon said that if he felt she would be feeding orally within a month, he would not have recommended going forth with the surgery.

We had been asking family, church family, pastors, friends, and colleagues to pray for our daughter throughout this whole stay in the NICU. We also went into the hospital chapel daily, but one Sunday was different. We both felt a calmness, but since this was a major surgery, especially for someone so tiny, we were still nervous overall. When I knelt in the chapel to pray, I prayed our specific prayers, but I also felt compelled to say the Lord's prayer as I had been taught growing up in the Methodist church:

"Our Father, who art in Heaven, hallowed be thy name. Thy kingdom come, thy will be done, on earth as it is in Heaven. Give us this day, our daily bread. And forgive us our trespasses, as we forgive those who trespass against us. And lead us not into temptation but deliver us from evil. For thine is the kingdom, the power, and the glory, forever. Amen" (United Methodist Hymnal, #895).

I had a hard time getting through the prayer as I was crying from feeling the Spirit move through me that our prayers would be answered. And indeed, they were. Finally, after 94 days in the NICU, we got to take our daughter home. It was a lot to take in with all the DME (durable medical equipment) we had to take home. We were given an IV pole to hang her feeding machine, the feeding machine itself, oxygen tanks, a pulse-ox machine, and a suction machine. It hit me hard as I was putting all this in the car, but the day had finally come.

God definitely did perform many miracles during this storm in our life—from allowing our little girl to survive her traumatic birth and arrival eight weeks early to overcoming and reaching developmental milestones just as she should.

God gave my daughter a chance at life when my wife committed to praising Him through the most difficult storm either of us had faced. No matter what comes our way, as Christians, we can always praise our heavenly Father—knowing that He is good and worthy of praise.

Give praise to the Lord, proclaim his name; make known among the nations what he has done (Psalm 105:1 NIV).

NAVIGATING THE DESIRE TO CONTROL

by Ken A. Hobbs II

The Bible teaches us that God's sovereignty is an essential aspect of who He is. He has supreme authority and absolute power over all things. Yet, many of us struggle in our lives trying to take over God's absolute power. We battle in our flesh, and we strive for the desire to control. It is part of the curse of sin that is ongoing.

We can believe being in control will make our lives better, but that is a lie from hell. We want to decide for ourselves what is best for our lives and take over with force. But one day, we wake up to what God says and realize that life does not revolve around us, our thoughts, and our desires as we once believed.

Think about the enemy of our souls and how he desires to capture our hearts. He tells us that control will give peace, safety, power, comfort, respect, and so much more. But the more we feel out of control, the more we try to control. It becomes a vicious cycle. The enemy will use this against us. Since when do we validate the enemy and "give in" to him by believing we know it all? We do not know what is best for us. Only God, in His infinite wisdom, sovereignty, and love, deems what is best for us. Proverbs 3:5-6 (TPT) describes this very well: *Trust in the Lord completely, and do not rely on your own opinions. With all your heart rely on him to guide you, and he will lead you in every decision you make. Become intimate with him in whatever you do, and he will lead you wherever you go.*

Dying to ourselves and our desire to maintain control is not easy. It takes nobility and courage to admit, both to God and ourselves, that we have a problem we cannot manage. It is essential to take time with God and recognize that He is in control. We are not God. We are not all-knowing. And we do not reign over the Universe. Trusting God for your circumstances, relationships, and choices requires extreme focus and discipline. However, overcoming your own law and surrendering to His will can help you become confident—confident in knowing that His plan is the best plan. Keeping yourself in submission to God's will makes lasting differences in your life.

> But I discipline my body and keep it under control, lest after preaching to others I myself should be disqualified (1 Corinthians 9:27 ESV).

Submitting our control to God brings Him glory and allows Him to fulfill His purpose in us. However, when we think we have the best plan and try to control other people or the outcome of situations, God will always confirm that we are not in control; He is.

> For I know that nothing good dwells in me, that is, in my flesh. For I have the desire to do what is right, but not the ability to carry it out (Romans 7:18 ESV).

As you surrender control to God, remember to pray and seek Him first before making any decision, and be comforted knowing what He says in Isaiah 55:8-9 (NIV): "For my thoughts are not your thoughts, neither are your ways my ways," declares the Lord. "As the heavens are higher than the *earth, so are my ways higher than your ways and my thoughts than your thoughts."*

Please go before the Lord and talk to Him. Spend time doing this as you pray about relinquishing all control to God. Read His Word and understand that the more you know about Him, the more you learn His character. Listen to Him when He speaks and thank Him because He is so very good. Be assured that God knows what He is doing in your life, and watch as the big things you seek to control become little in His hands. God promises to cover everything you need.

· ·

BARRY ALSOBROOK

Barry Alsobrook has been an entrepreneur in photography and video production for the past 30 years. He has been involved in all aspects of church video production for many years and is known for his ability to connect people from various Industries and ministries who have accomplished some pretty amazing things for the kingdom.

In 2020, Barry launched TAKEN TV, reaching thousands of households for Christ. As a technology enthusiast and the sole person in charge of producing content for TAKEN TV, Barry has worked as both director and producer for a number of shows, including *The Hands and Feet of Jesus Show, Forever Young, Spiritually Fed,* and *Faith Today*. He is also responsible for live-streaming the ministry events of Dr. Chauncy Crandal and casting for the award-winning music video "Jesus Took It All."

Barry and his wife, Lora, reside in Port St. Lucie, Florida, and attend Christ Fellowship Church, where they are both actively involved.

Jesus, Take the Wheel

By Barry Alsobrook

My parents divorced when I was six—after my mother suffered through many years of mental and physical abuse at the hands of my father. After the divorce, my sister and I were uprooted from our small town in Georgia and moved to the much larger city of St. Petersburg, Florida. There, my mom purchased a home and started a new life—free of abuse for the first time in years.

My father was allowed to visit us. And on one of his visits, as my mom was just starting a new job, he took my sister and me. He returned to Georgia with us in tow while my mother was working. During that time, he told us lies to make us believe she didn't want us anymore. Sadly, we went about our lives with our dad for about a year and a half without ever seeing our mother.

We lived mainly with our grandmother during that time. Don't get me wrong, I dearly loved my grandmother and cherished every moment as we went fishing and just spent time together. She held a place in my heart that no one else could ever replace.

Eventually, my mother was able to get visitation rights. She would come and visit, and at some point, she was able to take us back to her home on the weekends. On one of those weekend visits, when my dad came to pick us up, he nearly ran down a guard at the gate, and a road chase ensued as we tried to escape, driving recklessly through the countryside.

After that, Mom brought us back to Florida to live. We changed our last name and constantly moved from place to place. My mother had a couple of relationships during that time, one of which ended with her getting pregnant. But continuous running and hiding didn't make for a good relationship, especially not a marriage, so that relationship was broken off before it had a chance to blossom. One awesome thing that came from this broken relationship, however, was my younger brother, who was born three months premature. But shortly after his birth, our world took another dramatic turn.

Just two days after giving birth to my brother, my mother was arrested. She had been approached by an organization offering to help with Christmas gifts and other benefits for us kids. As she and the representative from the organization sat down to meet, the representative graciously sent my sister and me to the store to get some ice cream. Unknown to us, my dad was in a car outside the store, waiting for us with his business partner. We did not recognize him—he had grown a beard and looked totally different. The two men came into the store and immediately grabbed my sister and me. We screamed at the top of our lungs; everyone in the store was horrified, thinking that two kids were being kidnapped, which we were.

My father took us and put us on a plane back to Georgia. During that same time, the man meeting with my mother revealed that he was not who he claimed to be but was a private detective hired by my dad to find us kids. He then had my mother arrested on false charges. She was put in jail while her newborn baby boy remained in the hospital fighting for his life on life support. After being in jail for three days, my maternal grandmother was able to arrange bail. Once the judge found out what had happened, he ordered warrants against my father in Florida, but they were never enforced in Georgia, and we remained where we were.

After a few months, my mother moved from the housing projects in Tampa to a new home. She got a job and kept visiting my brother for the three months he remained in the hospital—until he was able to come home with her.

My dad was still running his business and traveling all around the South. That life would soon come to an end.

My dad had a business painting and repairing large water towers—a very fitting job for someone who basically had no fear. Fighting and racing cars and motorcycles were part of his normal life. One day, he was doing an inspection on a tower about sixty feet above the ground when the safety equipment failed. As a result of this horrible accident, both his legs were crushed; he tragically lost his right leg. After a long hospital stay, he was eventually able to return home.

We continued to stay with our grandmother, occasionally spending the weekends with my dad. We were told repeatedly that our mother didn't want us and couldn't take care of us anymore because of the new baby. And we believed it because we longer heard from Mom. It was Christmas time after about a year and a half had passed when we finally got a phone call from Mom. She had been calling my dad's house regularly, but we were never there as we were usually at my grandmother's. My dad was sleeping on the couch, so I answered the phone. My mom and I both broke down crying as we talked.

After that, my sister and I pretty much demanded that our mom be allowed to come and visit. A couple of months later, she was able to visit us in February for my 11th birthday. The best present was that I got to see my little brother for the very first time. Following a lot of begging and pleading, my sister and I were allowed to fly to Florida for the following summer.

After that fun-filled summer, we were to return to Georgia before school started, but we again decided we wanted to stay with Mom. So, we loaded up everything we didn't sell or give away and moved to Miami. We changed our name again and lived there for several years.

While we were living in Miami, my dad suffered another tragic accident. He was struck by a drunk driver while riding his motorcycle through town. That accident resulted in the loss of his left arm. My sister and I only learned about this years later. Eventually, my parents reconciled. They were able to attend holiday dinners and events while being very cordial towards each other. Neither ever remarried.

There were many good things about living with my grandmother. One was that I always got to attend church, and at a very young age, I accepted the Lord as my savior. I had a very basic understanding of God's Word; I always had, even before I followed the Lord. The Word and the Holy Spirit always guided and led me to make the right decisions growing up. *Start children off on the way they should go, and even when they are old, they will not turn from it* (Proverbs 22:6 NIV).

Despite my childhood, it is amazing I never really got into much trouble. God was surely protecting and leading me from the beginning, and His hand continued to guide me.

I met my wife while living in Georgia. We soon fell in love, and she moved in with me. Together, we ran a children's photography business for a while. Then, we moved back to Florida in 2001, where we started a new photography business. We worked in marinas taking pictures of people boarding boats for sightseeing trips, dolphin watching, and dinner cruises. For several years, we did quite well with that business. Then came the downturn in the economy. No one was traveling, boats were hardly going out, and technology was advancing—so boat owners could buy high-quality equipment at very low prices and do their own photography and printing. Financial problems started to creep in as several projects that promised to be the answer failed to pan out.

In March of 2013, our home was invaded by a deranged drug addict who stole about $10,000 worth of jewelry left to us from our departed parents. There were also several other events that caused a lot of stress during that time. My now wife and I were both at our breaking points, but things hit her harder. She had told me on our first date that she was bipolar, but I really had no idea what that meant. Looking back now, I probably should have researched the issue a little more—maybe I would have been a little more prepared for what would happen 16 years later.

I don't know if you've ever felt like you were spinning out of control on a two-lane highway bordered on both sides by alligator-infested swamps with a semi headed right for you. That's what it felt like for me a few years ago when I experienced the most awful and terrifying break-up.

Do I turn left? Do I turn right? What do I do? I just screamed, "Jesus, take the wheel."

My whole world had come crashing down in just one moment. I always felt like I would be spending the rest of my life with this person—my soul partner. But somehow, we had lost that connection. It was like the enemy had crept in so slowly and built this gap between us. *The thief comes only to steal and kill and destroy; I have come that they may have life and have it to the full* (John 10:10 NIV).

The thief attacked with the speed of a venomous viper, and my life just started spinning out of control. Darkness was everywhere. It filled my mind, was in the songs on the radio, and turned all the beautiful memories we shared into unbearing sadness. The feelings of despair were so strong, so abundant. Couch surfing at my friends' houses became my new life. Long road trips to see family and short trips across Florida to some of my favorite places became my only time of peace.

I endured long and stressful days, searching for a place to live, but I couldn't find anything I could afford or that would accept my situation. Up to that point, I had been through some rough times financially and emotionally, and now, application after application were denied. A place of peace and solitude seemed so far away and so out of reach. One day, as my search was still not bringing the results I had hoped for, I cried out to the Lord with tears in my eyes and repentance in my heart for not being the Man of Honor I should have been towards her. I had loved her for so many years without being the man she deserved. I desperately cried out to the Lord, "Jesus, take the wheel." I had hit rock bottom. Darkness and despair were everywhere.

But soon after I cried out to the Lord, I began to see a glimmer of light.

> *I waited patiently for the Lord to help me,*
> *and he turned to me and heard my cry.*
> *He lifted me out of the pit of despair,*
> *out of the mud and the mire.*
> *He set my feet on solid ground*
> *and steadied me as I walked along.*
> *He has given me a new song to sing,*
> *a hymn of praise to our God.*
> *Many will see what he has done and be amazed.*
> (Psalm 40:1-3 NLT)

Jesus did take the wheel. He led me to the perfect place for me—a condo on the water.

Then Jesus said, "Come to me, all of you who are weary and carry heavy burdens, and I will give you rest. Take my yoke upon you. Let me teach you because I am humble and gentle at heart, and you will find rest for your souls. For my yoke is easy to bear, and the burden I give you is light" (Matthew 11:28-30 NLT).

But those who trust in the Lord will find new strength. They will soar high on wings like eagles. They will run and not grow weary. They will walk and not faint (Isaiah 40:31 NLT).

And my God will meet all your needs according to the riches of his glory in Christ Jesus (Philippians 4:19 NIV).

In my new home, Jesus transformed my life in a way I never could have imagined. This was a place of spiritual peace for me. Being near the water gave me what I needed, solitude and a beautiful location where I could walk in the mornings and be alone with God. He had provided what I needed to bring me closer to Him and help restore my mental health. The time that I was able to spend with God allowed me to deal with the hurt and the pain I was experiencing. This pain was the greatest I had ever felt, even greater than the loss of a very dear loved one. But when I allowed Jesus to take the wheel, He helped my pain subside, not go away, but subside. I wasn't angry anymore. I was no longer filled with rage. I knew I had to forgive and move forward. My love for this woman had gone from love to hate and back to a greater love than before. I began to see her through God's eyes.

It had become routine for our conversations to end abruptly, with a phone hang-up or an intense shouting match. But one call changed it all for me. After about a month of no communication, our call began with a lot of screaming and yelling from the other end. That is when the Holy Spirit came upon me, and I was very cool and calm. I stood my ground but in a very subdued manner, not giving in to the outrage coming from the other side. After a few minutes, the fury started to subside, and the atmosphere changed. The spirit of anger was now dealing with the Holy Spirit. Instead of being filled with anger and yelling, the scene became one of sobbing, repentance, and reconciliation. That call led to our first meeting in a little over a month, which went against all the advice from friends and family.

When we met, she looked like she had not had a meal in weeks. Her bones appeared to be protruding from her rib cage in a way I had never seen, except on one of those TV ads for starving children. My heart was broken at this sight and her condition, but God had gone before us. We met at our favorite place, an all-you-can-eat Japanese restaurant. God was clearly telling me everything was going to be alright. The next day, she moved in with me at the condo.

One thing I knew for sure was that if this new start for us was going to work, we needed to honor God in marriage. So, about a month later, we were married at the courthouse in Clearwater. We also found a great church and started attending and serving on a regular basis.

Looking back at all I've gone through, it is evident that God was in control all along. When we allow Him, He navigates our paths with His hands firmly on the steering wheel. As a child, He had provided His protection and, sometimes, deliverance so I could grow as He intended. As I began adulthood, He brought me a helpmate and gave me wisdom in the storms of finances and business. And when it really mattered, He was there guiding me with His peace and strength as I turned away from my worldly temptations and learned how to extend His mercy and grace to both me and the woman I so dearly love.

Through the tragic events in my life, God steered me into at least two awesome relationships: with Him and with my wife.

As you encounter storms, I hope you will think of my story and remember this one thing from God's Word: *And we know that in all things God works for the good of those who love him, who have been called according to his purpose* (Romans 8:28 NIV).

CRAIG E. PRATT SR.

Craig E. Pratt Sr. is the Founder and Director of TouchWorld Holdings LLC, a service provider in the behavioral health and wellness industry. With over 25 years of experience as a director of assisted living facilities, his passion remains in providing resources and support for those in need of achieving optimum mental wellness. Craig is also currently an academic instructor at Grace Place School, located in Broward County, Florida.

As a native of Miami, Florida, Craig has undergraduate studies in Business Administration from Nova Southeastern University. He is also a graduate of Connecticut School of Broadcasting.

Craig resides in South Florida as a husband and father to his three children. He has been invited as a keynote speaker and is eager to share his miraculous testimony of the good news of hope and inspiration. Contact Craig via email at TouchWorldCraig@gmail.com or call or text him at TouchWorld at (877) 842-3097.

FROM LIFE SUPPORT TO SUPPORTING LIFE!

By Craig E. Pratt Sr.

"Mr. Pratt! You did it! Oh my goodness, I'm so happy for you! You kicked COVID's butt!"

Those were the words I heard from the Intensive Care Unit's (ICU) chief pulmonary specialist, Dr. Sunil Kumar, as he hovered over my hospital bed. He actually used another word for butt. However, I'll keep it PG and family-friendly in this story.

As I struggled to open my eyes, slowly beginning to regain consciousness, I couldn't believe where I was or what happened. I turned and glanced around my hospital room and noticed several nurses applauding and smiling while informing me of how proud they were that I had fought and survived. I mustered up enough strength to try asking the doctor some questions, but as I began to speak, my voice was gone. I could barely utter a whisper. It was more like a muffled, rough howl. My vocal cords were stripped as a result of the tubes that had been placed down my throat. I was in horrible condition.

I asked the doctor, "What happened? Where am I?"

He said, "Mr. Pratt, you were on a ventilator—a life support system—for ten days. You flatlined (with cardiac arrest) three times! You were 100%

dependent on oxygen. It was a very serious situation. You are one of my patients who fought so hard to pull through. I'm so proud of you."

The weight of his words sent shock waves throughout my entire being! I had no memory of what happened.

The nurses advised me to relax and assured me that they would continue to take great care of me. One nurse said she spoke with my wife and family and told them all the tubes had been removed, and I was now breathing completely on my own.

I was astonished.

Wait! What, in the name of Shadrach, Meshach, and Abednego, is going on here?! Questions flooded my mind. I noticed as I tried to pull myself up out of the bed that I couldn't move. I was paralyzed. I couldn't feel my legs! I couldn't feel my feet! I could barely even lift my arms!

I had been diagnosed with COVID-19, acute respiratory failure, double pneumonia, asthmatic spasms, tachycardia (rapid or irregular heartbeat), and several other complications. Because of COVID-19 safety measures, medical staff would only enter my room every two to three hours unless there was a specific emergency. When they did enter the room, they were covered from head to toe in safety goggles and gear like they just returned from Mars! The weight of the experience was overwhelming.

I was heavily medicated. I had so many pills and injections I was like a human Walgreens or CVS. The medications had a tremendous bearing on my ability to recall anything that happened prior to entering the hospital. As the medical staff was leaving, I lay flat on the bed, unable to speak or move, feeling completely alone and, candidly speaking, terrified!

I stared up at the ceiling, and things began to come back to me. Suddenly, as Dr. Kumar was leaving, I asked a painful question I hoped wasn't true. "Hey Doc, did my mother really pass away? Please tell me it's not true."

I watched him turn to offer a word of comfort. "Mr. Pratt, please just relax, Sir. Please, you need to remain as calm as possible," he said. "We're going to take great care of you."

Then he walked out.

I can still hear the sound of that heavy door closing. "Boom!"

There I lay helpless. I was extremely cold and isolated. As I observed my surroundings, a treacherous sense of fear invaded my thoughts. I was in a tremendous storm! All I could do was lay there on my back, staring at the ceiling.

Suddenly, it dawned on me. That's exactly what I needed to do—Look Up!

> *I look up to the hills, but where does my help come from? My help comes from the LORD, who made heaven and earth* (Psalm 121:1-2 NCV).

Seemingly caught up in a complete nightmare, all I could hear was the sound of medical equipment. Beep. . .beep. . .beep. Every kind of electrical device was connected to me–tubes, wires, too many to count. I had IV monitors in both arms, some type of contraption connected to my legs, and an oxygen tube flowing from my nostrils. A tear began rolling down the side of my face as I tried to make sense of it all. I didn't even have the ability to lift my arm to wipe it off.

Reality set in as my thoughts became clearer. It was true. My mother, Carole Pratt, had died shortly before I was admitted. Moreover, I was unable to attend her private burial service because I was unaware, suspended in time, fighting for my own life!

The grief was unbearable. "Mom! You can't be gone! This can't be real!"

"GOD! Where are you?"

A litany of questions invaded my mind. *Will I ever walk or talk again? How is my family (whom I hadn't seen in weeks because of COVID-19 restrictions) handling this? Why am I going through this?* I was told it would take several weeks to months to recover.

But my faith began to stir. What happened next in that hospital room is quite honestly indescribable. A supernatural encounter with God!

> *I sought the LORD, and He heard me, and delivered me from all my fears* (Psalm 34:4 NKJV).

I began struggling, barely whispering a prayer that my precious mother taught me at a young age, "Our Father, which art in heaven. . .Hallowed be Thy Name. . ."

All of a sudden, it was as if the room began to become brighter and warmer! It was as if a subtle but apparent breeze began to blow across my room, blanketing me with a sense of comforting peace. My heart rate began to increase, and the beeping sound on the monitors became more rapid. Then, I felt or saw what can only be described as a huge, almost translucent, shining hand scooping me up! The entire hospital bed was encapsulated in the palm of this huge, mighty hand! A glorious light! The calm yet powerful voice I heard that night whispered to my spirit, "I AM with you!"

As I mentioned before, it's hard to explain, but it seems as though my entire hospital room was a tiny grain of sand in the middle of the palm of a huge hand. The wind blew through my room, and an indescribable peace overwhelmed me. A joyful disposition consumed my doubts and fears. I could literally feel my heavenly Father assuring me of His faithful presence! "I AM with you!" I truly believe I experienced a supernatural vision.

In the natural realm, I felt renewed energy. I thought humorously to myself, "Whatever medication they gave me, I'll take a double order again!"

My heart monitors began increasing so rapidly that the nurses came rushing into my room. "Mr. Pratt! What's going on? Are you okay? Your heart rate is increasing, and we want you to know that we're watching everything," they said. "Even though you feel alone, we're watching on the nurses' station monitors. Rest assured, you're in good hands!"

Wow! Yes, I was! They had no clue! And I was physically unable to tell them about the divine visitation that I just had!

Protocol requires medical staff to check my wrist bracelet to confirm correct patient information each time they enter the room. "You're Craig Emmanuel' Pratt?"

"Yes ma'am," I rasped.

"Emmanuel is your middle name—God with us!" one nurse said as she read my bracelet. Divine confirmation!

I must pause parenthetically and encourage those reading this testimony that the Lord is and has always been with YOU, too! He's as close as your next breath!

God is our refuge and strength, a very present help in trouble (Psalm 46:1 NKJV).

Let everything that has breath praise the LORD! Praise the LORD! (Psalm 150:6)

I find it ironic that COVID-19 attacks the respiratory system, often restricting the ability to breathe. Wow! Breathing is something we take for granted. You may find yourself in a storm at this particular moment. But take some time now and just breathe.

Breathe. It's a miracle we can breathe. There's power in the way that we breathe. This is why we have breath. So, let everything that has breath praise the Lord!

I will never be the same after that hospital encounter. My recovery from that night forward was simply miraculous. My health was restored expeditiously. Not many people can declare a 100% recovery rating with no physical limitations after flatlining three times and being on life support for ten days! I'm eternally blessed and thankful for the medical staff at Broward Health Hospital in Ft. Lauderdale, Florida. They are truly marvelous!

I recall being transferred from the intensive care unit to a regular patient room. Once settled in my new room, I could receive phone calls from family and friends. The first voices I heard were my supportive wife, Jennifer, and my three amazing children, Bree, Jordyn, and Craig Jr.—I hadn't spoken or seen them in weeks, so my excitement and enthusiasm took over.

"Daddy! We love you!!" Their voices were like food to my soul.

I tried responding, but again, I sounded like a wounded hyena. And they were laughing. They assured me of their support and gave their appreciation for all the nurses who called and FaceTimed them, showing me as I fought the battle each night.

> But we have this treasure in earthen vessels, that the excellence of the power may be of God and not of us. We are hard-pressed on every side, yet not crushed; we are perplexed, but not in despair; persecuted, but not forsaken; struck down, but not destroyed (2 Corinthians 4:7-9 NKJV).

The next call was from one of my sisters, Rebecca. I have three siblings. I'm the youngest and only male. Charlotte was at home praying while battling COVID-19 symptoms. Carla, I later found out, was actually just a few doors down from me in the same hospital. Go figure. Thankfully, her symptoms were not anywhere near as serious as mine. She prayed and gracefully recovered also.

However, Rebecca was one of my biggest cheerleaders during the battle. She actually showed up at the hospital parking lot and prayed while walking around the perimeter of the facility, sending up prayers of petition for my healing.

The nurse handed me the phone, and I heard Becky's voice, "Hey, Little Bro! You made it through the storm! God is going to bring you out completely whole again!" she said. "You know I have your back, right, Craig?"

She informed me that she called all my family members from across the nation to join a Zoom prayer call on my behalf. I had cousins from California, Texas, Georgia, New York, New Jersey, and even the Bahamas.

She had a family member praying each hour, 24 hours a day, until I was released from the ventilator and walked out of that hospital! Becky would call a few times a day with different friends or family on the phone to help encourage me to fight. Her faith level was astronomical and so inspirational.

A few days later, I walked out of that hospital—to the astonishment of the doctors. Praise God!

But little did I know, another huge storm was on the horizon!

About a year later, my cell phone rang while I was at work. It was my sister Becky. She didn't sound good.

"Craig, I drove myself to the hospital. I've been battling COVID symptoms. Please pray for me!"

Now, I was lifting her up in prayer. There was absolutely NO DOUBT in my mind that she would recover just like I did. I would call her and text her scriptures to encourage her to fight. We would pray together on the phone. The family held Zoom prayer calls again. She couldn't have visitors. The irony!

A few days later, Rebecca was placed in ICU on a ventilator. She died on August 28, 2021. The pain of her loss is still, at times, incomprehensible!

Once again, I found myself overwhelmed with grief. I hadn't come to grips with the loss of my mother, and now one of my beautiful sisters was gone! The storm was raging! More questions of despair and unbelief!

"Why God? Why did you take my loving sister?" I was grappling emotionally. Imagine the dichotomy of my emotions as I called out to the Lord for help in understanding. "I made it out...but..well, she made it IN!"

Better to go to the house of mourning than to go to the house of feasting, For that is the end of all men; And the living will take it to heart (Ecclesiastes 7:2 NKJV).

I had the humbling yet amazing privilege of speaking the eulogy at my sister Rebecca's homegoing service—one of the most difficult tasks I've ever undertaken. I spoke from Ecclesiastes 7:2, teaching that death is an appointment we all must keep.

Attending the funeral of a loved one reminds us of a sobering fact: We must never take anything or anyone for granted. Becky, as well as my other sisters, were instrumental in my ability to acknowledge a need and dependence upon the Lord. Becky was forthright in her convictions and was a warrior for the kingdom. She was the assistant director for Hope Women's Pregnancy Center in Broward County, Florida. Throughout the course of my life, I remember Becky challenging me to uphold a righteous and respectful character and always reminding me that the Lord is an ever-present help.

As we laid her to rest next to our mother and father, she had to be lifted up high into the mausoleum vault. Now, whenever I visit their resting place, I have to...Look Up! Just as I had to do in that hospital room. Look and Live! The memories from her encouraging conversations fuel my passion to move forward with optimistic expectations of reuniting again!

Yes! I encourage you always to look up. Know you are never alone. If you find yourself in a storm, remember this: For every eternal purpose, the Lord designs everlasting safeguards.

Scripture reminds us, *"Before I formed YOU in your mother's womb I knew YOU!"* (Jeremiah 1:5 ESV).

Although we may feel ambushed by the storms of life at times, our Creator never is!

I have one question for you: Who's the Captain of your ship?

You have tremendous purpose, and the Lord will be faithful to complete it in you.

Once again, Who's YOUR Captain?

I must admit, I'm no match facing these storms on my own. I depend upon the God of my salvation. He's my Captain. He brought me out with a mighty hand—just like the three Hebrew boys I mentioned earlier (Shadrach, Meshach, and Abednego). They were thrown into the fire. But there was another in the fire with them (Daniel 3).

Each day, we are blessed with brand new mercy. I have a renewed appreciation for life. The simple things aren't as simple as we think. The challenge of learning how to walk and talk again was overwhelming. There were times when I couldn't feed or bathe myself; I was fully dependent on the medical staff for assistance. Now, I take long showers, singing like a kid at Christmas time! Thankful. . .so thankful.

> *For in Him we live and move and have our being, as also some of your own poets have said, 'For we are His offspring'* (Acts 17:28 NKJV)

Let's be mindful to appreciate life and take nothing for granted, knowing we're never alone in our storms. I understand that we all experience what seems to be insurmountable odds at times: sickness, death, poverty, divorce, financial ruin, loneliness, and abuse, amongst many other things that cause discouragement. And there will be situations that we don't understand. That's why we need to refer to the manual, the Word of God, to help us navigate through each storm. He promises to provide His peace to guard our hearts and minds during situations we don't understand.

Even now, I'm still yielding to the sovereignty of God concerning my sister's death. A short while after we laid her to rest, I discovered the last birthday card Rebecca gave me. It was handwritten! She said that, for some reason, she felt like writing to me this time, and she encouraged me to go forward, remembering all that I had survived. "Go forward, Lil Bro... Do all that God has called you to do!"

Wow! What an awesome keepsake I have. Her words are dearly placed upon my heart. She is the inspiration for my forthcoming book entitled *The Supreme Vaccine!: The Vaccination of Reconciliation Back to Our Heavenly Father.*

Finally, my brethren. I'm a preacher, and I'm starting to get happy now! But I'll leave you with this: We can't always react emotionally according to our situations. We must rather respond according to our revelation. Whatever situation we are in, however chaotic or resulting from self-inflicted, foolish mistakes or something beyond our control, we must depend upon and rely on the revelation of God's promises.

No one! I believe no one is outside of the grace of God.

For whosoever shall call upon the name of the Lord shall be SAVED (Romans 10:13-15 KJV).

Seek the LORD while He may be found (Isaiah 55:6 KJV).

A broken spirit and contrite heart you, God, you will not despise (Psalm 51:17 NIV).

He is also able to save to the uttermost those who come to God through Him (Hebrews 7:25 NKJV).

Look Up! Give thanks! Move forward with purpose and gratitude, relying on His promises! The Captain of your soul will guide you safely through the storm. I'm a witness.

Going from Life Support, to Supporting Life!

NAVIGATE YOUR MARRIAGE

by Asaad Faraj

Marriage is sacred to God. It is so significant that He analogizes the relationship between Christ and the church to that of a husband and his bride! The ultimate purpose of the church is to LOVE Christ!

> *Three things will last forever—faith, hope, and love—and the greatest of these is love* (1 Corinthians 13:13 NLT).

The ultimate purpose of a husband is to love his wife. Love should be our highest goal!

> *Dear friends, since God loved us that much, we surely ought to love each other. No one has ever seen God. But if we love each other, God lives in us, and his love is brought to full expression in us* (1 John 4:11-12 NLT).

If you are married or desire to be married, it is extremely beneficial to be familiar with Ephesians 5:21-33 and read it often, for it is God's design for marriage.

The Apostle Paul teaches that staying faithful to our marriage commitment actually requires a kind of death. We have to die to ourselves so we can be one with each other. *And further, submit to one another out of reverence for Christ* (Ephesians 5:21 NLT). This is what Jesus did. Jesus laid down His life as an act of submission to God and as the ultimate sacrifice for us. As Paul says, *Jesus gave up His life for the church* (v.25).

Being a godly husband and a godly wife requires us to treat our spouses in a way that is counterintuitive to our respective nature. *So again I say, each man must love his wife as he loves himself, and the wife must respect her husband* (Ephesians 5:33 NIV).

You see, nowhere in scripture does God command a husband to respect his wife or a wife to love her husband. That is because it is very natural for men to respect and women to love. However, it takes a transformation of the heart and a renewal of our mind for a man to love his wife and for a wife to respect her husband. God's advice for husbands, spoken through the Apostle Paul, tells husbands to love their wives *to make her holy and clean, washed by the cleansing of God's word* (Ephesians 5:26 NIV).

I never knew a practical way to implement this until a few short years ago when I asked my wife if it would be okay to read a chapter from the Bible to her every night before we went to sleep. Now, we both look forward to it; we've found there's no better way to end the day.

When you love your wife as Jesus loves the church, she will see an example of God's love for her right in your own home. The next time you feel agitated, annoyed, or frustrated, imitate God's love for you as a sinner. Show your wife love via mercy, grace, and forgiveness.

> *In the same way, you husbands must give honor to your wives. Treat your wife with understanding as you live together. She may be weaker than you are, but she is your equal partner in God's gift of new life. Treat her as you should so your prayers will not be hindered* (1 Peter 3:7 NIV).

God is so concerned with how we treat our wives in marriage that His response to our prayers depends on our actions. Marriage takes two people each giving 100%. When push comes to shove, put on love—that is how God commands us to navigate marriage.

. . . .

JEFFREY LEWIS

In 1964, Jeffrey Lewis was born in Bergaw, North Carolina, to Alton Ray and Maryland Lewis.

Jeffrey accepted Jesus Christ as Lord and Savior in the spring of 1988. He married Avril S. Lewis on October 26, 1991. They have two children, Briana C. Bervine and Jeffrey K. Lewis, and four grandchildren—two grandsons, Ali and Aiyden Bervine, and two granddaughters, Ayla Bervine and Bless Lewis.

In 2002, Jeffrey Lewis became the pastor/founder of Keys To Life Ministries Healthy Church.

He is the former Camden City Drug Elimination Coordinator, contracted by N.A.I.S.A., and a retired state of New Jersey Corrections police officer.

Jeffrey's God-ordained mission in life is to teach people how to gain access to total victory in every area of life through a relationship with their Lord and Savior, Jesus Christ, the Word of God, prayer, and living out key kingdom principles.

And I will give unto thee the keys of the kingdom of heaven: and whatsoever thou shalt bind on earth shall be bound in heaven: and whatsoever thou shalt loose on earth shall be loosed in heaven (Matthew 16:19 KJV).

THRONE OF MY HEART

By Jeffrey Lewis

> *"I took you from the ends of the earth, from its farthest corners I called you. I said, 'You are my servant,' I have chosen you and have not rejected you. So do not fear, for I am with you; do not be dismayed, for I am your God. I will strengthen you and help you; I will uphold you with my righteous right hand."* (Isaiah 41:9-10 NIV).

Like many other Christians, my life appeared desirable to those who looked from the outside in—early retirement, financial stability, a comfortable home in one of my city's best communities, children who were upstanding in the community, a beautiful wife, and an influential church on the verge of exploding. After all, I was great at casting vision while projecting what I felt would encourage others to become followers of Christ.

On one hand, I really felt like I was in a very good place. It felt good knowing that I was a pillar in the community. On the other hand, I knew something wasn't quite right. However, I chose to ignore what I knew was the "warning of the Holy Spirit."

The warning of the Holy Spirit is the essence of the heart of God that enables relevant and applicable information to matters or circumstances needed to facilitate living a holy life before the Lord as He continues to reveal His will for your life.

There were things that the Lord wanted me to be aware of that I mistakenly yet willfully overlooked because things were going so well.

On Sunday, November 14, 2021, something took place that would begin the necessary reset in my life and, more importantly, in my heart.

That Saturday, my son and I drove well over 500 miles from our home in Sicklerville, New Jersey, to Dayton, Ohio. Our plan was to spend quality time together as I was on my way to celebrate the marriage of my pastor and his beautiful bride, and my son Jeff was scheduled to visit his daughter in Columbus, Ohio. Then, we planned to reconnect on Monday morning to take the long ride back home together.

I was scheduled to stand in the place of my pastor and share the Word of God with his congregation that Sunday morning. I anticipated a powerful move of God, just like we experienced every time ministry took place at Revival Center Ministries. Yes, I had it all planned out. The sermon title was supposed to be "You Are Never In A Position To Lose." My focus scriptures were Romans 8:31-39.

What, then, shall we say in response to these things? If God is for us, who can be against us? He who did not spare his own Son, but gave him up for us all—how will he not also, along with him, graciously give us all things? Who will bring any charge against those whom God has chosen? It is God who justifies. Who then is the one who condemns? No one. Christ Jesus who died—more than that, who was raised to life—is at the right hand of God and is also interceding for us. Who shall separate us from the love of Christ? Shall trouble or hardship or persecution or famine or nakedness or danger or sword? As it is written: "For your sake we face death all day long; we are considered as sheep to be slaughtered."

No, in all these things we are more than conquerors through him who loved us. For I am convinced that neither death nor life, neither angels nor demons, neither the present nor the future, nor any powers, neither height nor depth, nor anything else in all creation, will be able to separate us from the love of God that is in Christ Jesus our Lord (Romans 8:31-29 NIV).

As usual, everything was planned out perfectly. Yet, God knew something I didn't know: He knew my plans would not be my reality.

As I previously stated, I was supposed to drop my son off in Columbus, Ohio, and continue my journey to Dayton. However, the Lord decided that my son was to remain with me and go to Dayton. Jeff's willingness to obey the voice of the Lord is certainly a part of the reason I'm still alive today.

It's important to realize that our obedience to the Lord is not always about us.

After a long 9.5-hour drive and a very busy day, we arrived at our hotel. I immediately got in the bed and went to sleep.

Around 11:30 p.m., as I awoke from my sleep, I was a little surprised at how exhausted I was. I noticed that I stumbled when attempting to stand and take off my trousers. I simply attributed it to exhaustion. Nevertheless, I got back in bed and went to sleep. During the night, I awakened several times. Each time, I noticed that I seemed a little bit more out of it than usual. When I awakened around 6:30 a.m., as was my normal practice on a Sunday morning, I attempted to sit up and get out of bed. The struggle to get up seemed like I was having a nightmare.

Not wanting to awaken my son too early, I continued my efforts until I was successful in sitting up. Once I got to my feet, I noticed that my walk from the bed to the bathroom was challenging. Slowly, I made it to the bathroom. I became even more concerned as my attempt to urinate in the toilet was less than accurate. However, I continued to press through my morning routine of brushing my teeth and then taking a shower.

My attempt to step in the shower was cut short when I realized that I was not able to lift my leg over the edge of the hotel tub so that I could step into the shower. I then accepted the reality that something was wrong. I shuffled my way back to my bed and called out to my son, "Jeff. Jeff. Jeff." He did not respond. I'd find out later that I wasn't speaking as loud as I thought I was.

After gathering myself, I once again called out to my son. He suddenly jumped out of his sleep and said good morning. As he looked into my face, he said to me, "Dad no matter what, please do whatever I ask you to do."

Before I knew it, we were in the SUV, he was on the phone, and suddenly, we were pulling up to the hospital emergency room. Not long after, I remember seeing everyone around me moving with urgency and concern. Feeling exhausted, I went back to sleep. As soon as I awakened from what I thought was a short nap. The soothing and assuring voice of the Lord said to me, "This is not from me. However, I will get the glory out of it."

I need those of you who are navigating through any type of storm to remember that every storm does not come from the Lord. I also want you to be reminded that the Lord will stand by his Word even in your most difficult season.

> The Lord himself goes before you and will be with you; he will never leave you nor forsake you. Do not be afraid; do not be discouraged" (Deuteronomy 31:8 NIV).

At that time, my son Jeff spoke words of strength to me. He stated, "Dad, this is not how the story will end. You're going to be alright."

In that moment, I watched my son step into a man of faith who would take the authority of God as an intercessor and leader. He refused to bow down, give into, or be persuaded by anything contrary to the will of God for his father's life.

This became very evident to me as I lay there listening to the doctor as he gave Jeff a bleak report. I heard the words, but I could not respond to them. The doctor stated that I had a stroke that covered a significant portion of the right side of my brain. He further stated that my condition could remain the same for the rest of my life. I was reminded that when Jesus healed people in the Bible, He restored them to complete health. That's what He could do in my life. Still, I'll be honest and tell you that hearing the doctor's words was very difficult.

Immediately, Jeff called my 76-year-young prayer warrior of a mother and told her what the doctor had said. I'll never forget that she chuckled and informed us that she had been in prayer at 6 a.m. that morning when the Lord told her, "I already healed him." She said that at that time, she had no clue who the Lord was talking about, but when she got the call from Jeff, she began to rejoice because God had already given her a word promise.

Days later, I was released from the hospital in Dayton, Ohio.

Several days after I arrived home, my recovery became a major concern. I was still unable to sit up on my own, nor could I read, stand or walk. In addition, anything I ate had a very unpleasant taste, and it was difficult to chew and swallow. Holding anything in my left hand was absolutely impossible. I'd spend days unable to drink anything without a straw. I had sudden episodes of crying and couldn't figure out why. My faith was being tested. As difficult as it was, I became determined to show gratitude to the Lord. I thanked Him for my life and the privilege of seeing another day according to 1 Thessalonians 5:18. *In everything give thanks: for this is the will of God in Christ Jesus concerning you* (MEV).

Many times, I thought, *If this is your will for me, I don't want it. But I'll accept it.*

Without the ability to read, Psalm 23 became my focus.

> *The LORD is my shepherd; I shall not want. He makes me lie down in green pastures; he leads me beside the still waters. He restores my soul; he leads me in the paths of righteousness for His name's sake. Even though I walk through the valley of the shadow of death, I will fear no evil: for You are with me; Your rod and Your staff, they comfort me.*
>
> *You prepare a table before me in the presence of my enemies: You anoint my head with oil; my cup runs over. Surely goodness and mercy shall follow me all the days of my life, and I will dwell in the house of the LORD forever.* (Psalm 23 MEV).

Four words out of those six verses would always stand out, even when I would listen to a song my son introduced to me during my recovery process. Those four words are still resounding in my soul: "I SHALL NOT WANT."

After quoting that scripture to myself one day, the Lord filled me with a level of faith that calmed my fears. He did it through my 6-year-old grandson Aidyn. Aidyn came over and said to me, "Pop Pop, don't worry. I'm going to show you how to play basketball again, and Jesus will help you."

The faith that filled me that day came with a river of tears and joy that was unmatched. I went to sleep that night believing something amazing was about to happen.

A couple of days later, I was sitting in a chair in the guest room of our home. I was slumped over, looking out of the window. Suddenly, one bird landed on a branch in the tree, and everything went silent. Then I heard these words, "When you give me back the throne of your heart, I will heal you." I immediately knew that it was the Lord. I was deeply humbled.

The next morning, I awakened early, still unable to sit up. Moments later, I heard the firm, loving voice of the Lord say to me, "Sit up."

Nervously, I began to rock myself until I was sitting upright. I was thankful and satisfied that I was sitting up. I then heard His voice again. This time, He said, "Stand up."

I must admit I was a little apprehensive. However, I did what I heard. With three strong rocking motions, I sprung to my feet, fell forward onto the wall, and began to fall toward the weak, almost lifeless left side of my body. The Lord then gave me strength on my right side to pull myself up on the wall, as I caught my balance.

After a few minutes of struggling to remain standing, I heard a third command from the Lord. He said to me, "Walk."

I took my right leg and swung it past my left leg while dragging the left leg and foot for about three steps. Suddenly, I could feel new strength in my left leg. I walked from the guest room to my son's room with no assistance— twenty-one glorious, slow, and unstable steps. I knocked on my son's bedroom door. He opened the door, and we began to praise God. My wife soon joined us. After about ten minutes of celebrating and rejoicing, I became exhausted. I walked back to the guest room and climbed into bed for a nap.

After several hours of sleep, I awakened and was startled. I no longer had the ability to sit up. It was at this time I heard the voice of the Lord again. He repeated what He initially said, "When you give me back the throne of your heart, I will heal you."

My response was different this time. I confessed, "Lord, I don't know how to give you back the throne of my heart because I don't know when I put you off the throne."

This is when the Lord revealed to me that I had been depending on my own resources that he blessed me with. He also showed me certain decisions I had made without consulting Him. Those decisions weren't bad, but the problem was that I had eliminated the Lord from the process. I unknowingly was abandoning Proverbs 3:5-6. *Trust in the LORD with all thine heart; and lean not unto thine own understanding. In all thy ways acknowledge him, and he shall direct thy paths* (KJV).

Like so many, I was unaware I was trusting my own ability and leaning on my own understanding. I might have acknowledged God in a few things here and there, but my total dependency on the Lord was lacking.

You see, if we are going to keep the Lord on the throne of our hearts, we must understand that the heart is the seat of the will. It is also the throne of one's life from which choices and actions originate. If we or anyone else sits on the throne of our hearts, then we, as children of God, can be led astray by the deception of the enemy. If we are not diligent in protecting our hearts, we can easily end up like the Galatian church. *You foolish Galatians! Who has bewitched you? Before your very eyes Jesus Christ was clearly portrayed as crucified. I would like to learn just one thing from you: Did you receive the Spirit by the works of the law, or by believing what you heard? Are you so foolish? After beginning by means of the Spirit, are you now trying to finish by means of the flesh?* (Galatians 3:1-3 NIV).

Through my experience, I discovered that countless others also started out with the right motives and a desire to do nothing more than honor the Lord with their lives. However, just like me, they also found themselves in the midst of a storm that challenged everything in and around them. What seemed secure became fragile as instability began to shake the foundations of everything around.

If your world is shaking, make sure the Lord is sitting on the throne of your heart.

You are more than the sum of every high and low of your life. You belong to God. And as such, you can be certain that everything will be alright—because God is with you in every storm.

Navigating Your Relationships

by Asaad Faraj

Life is about relationships. We have all heard the Golden Rule, "Treat others the way you would want to be treated." That is the rule of thumb for Christians and unbelievers alike, and it comes from the Bible. *"Do to others whatever you would like them to do to you. This is the essence of all that is taught in the law and the prophets"* (Matthew 7:12 NLTSE).

Our God loves relationships! He wanted a relationship with us so badly, John 3:16 tells us, that He sacrificed whom He loved the most, His Son Jesus, to come to this earth and die for our sins so that He could adopt us into his family. A life centered on God has purposeful, authentic, and rich relationships. But all relationships can become difficult, draining, and even confrontational. So, how does God call us to navigate our relationships?

FAMILY RELATIONSHIPS

God's plan for His people is for us to be in families structured within His design and biblical principles. Most people would say that the people they love most are their families. Sadly, most people would admit that our choice of words and tone when it comes to the people closest to us don't always reflect how much we love them. This should not be.

A gentle answer deflects anger, but harsh words make tempers flare (Proverbs 15:1 NLT).

CHILDREN'S ROLES

Children are given two primary responsibilities in the family: to obey their parents and to honor them (Ephesians 6:1-3). Obeying parents is the duty of children until they reach adulthood, but we are to honor our parents for a lifetime. The fifth commandment says, *"Honor your father and your mother, so that you may live long in the land the Lord your God is giving you"* (Exodus 20:12 NIV). The Bible does not make an exception to this commandment. Most people would say that if your parents abused you, neglected you, or mistreated you, then you are exempt from honoring them. The Lord will honor boundaries that you put in place with your parents but will never bless dishonoring your parents.

NON-FAMILY RELATIONSHIPS

Above all else, we are to love those God has put in our lives.

> *We love each other because he loved us first. If someone says, "I love God," but hates a fellow believer, that person is a liar; for if we don't love people we can see, how can we love God, whom we cannot see? And he has given us this command: Those who love God must also love their Christian brothers and sisters* (1 John 4:19-21 NLT).

DIFFICULT RELATIONSHIPS

We all have difficult relationships—including with people who continually hurt or disappoint us. Anyone reading this can think of a person in their life, such as a coworker, boss, neighbor, or acquaintance, who truly gets on your nerves. So, what can we do about those relationships?

I like to pray for what I describe as a "Saul-to-Paul conversion," for God to change their hearts to align with His! Let's consider the apostle Paul. Before the road to Damascus in Acts 9, Saul (as he was known) was determined to persecute all Christians. Saul is the absolute last person I would want to have as my next-door neighbor. But after going to cities and persecuting Christians, Saul was radically saved and heard the Lord speak to him. God then radically changed his heart, and he ended up writing 2/3 of the New Testament.

I challenge you to pray for your enemies and for people who have hurt you to have a heart change that looks like a Saul-to-Paul transformation!

> *The king's heart is like a stream of water directed by the Lord;*
> *he guides it wherever he pleases.*
> *People may be right in their own eyes,*
> *but the Lord examines their heart.*
> *The Lord is more pleased when we do what is right and just*
> *than when we offer him sacrifices.*
> *(Proverbs 21:1-3 NLT).*

Praying Proverbs over your relationships is one way to allow the Holy Spirit to infiltrate you and set your will to obedience in Christ. As Jesus teaches in Mathew 5:44, *"But I say to you, Love your enemies! Pray for those who persecute you!"* (NLT).

THROUGH IT ALL, TURN TO GOD

Our God is perfectly sovereign, which means that He placed you in and among the people in your life purposefully. When you turn to Him, respond obediently to His will, and allow Him to guide your thoughts and actions, He will fill your life with purposeful, authentic, and rich relationships—even through the storms.

. . . .

Bob Tardell

Bob "Buzzy" Tardell was born in the Bronx. His early years were very tumultuous, but with the love and guidance of his grandmother and mother, he aspired to achieve things that were seemingly beyond his reach. Their passings when he was young motivated him to never give up in overcoming challenges, regardless of the odds against him.

Bob was blessed to be married to the love of his life for forty-two years until her death in 2013 from cancer. His love and bond with his daughter and granddaughter are special and fill his heart with joy.

Most of his career was in the optical industry, and to this day, he serves on the board of directors of his prior company, from which he retired in 2017.

In 2022, Bob was introduced to Jesus and, ultimately, gave his life to HIM and was baptized on June 11, 2023. Every day is a beautiful day and an opportunity to spread HIS love to others and live a life fulfilled and with purpose.

LIVING IN FEAR—
LIVING FEARLESSLY

By Bob Tardell

Among I have been consumed with fear for most of my life. This impediment began at the age of four, and now I am seventy-seven years old. On June 11, 2023, I was baptized—and by virtue of my faith, trust, obedience, and commitment to Jesus, my burden of fear has now finally been lifted.

> *This is the day the Lord has made. We will rejoice and be glad in it* (Psalm 118:24 NLT).

My biggest challenge in undertaking this endeavor to help you understand my journey is adequately describing the depth and profound effect that fear, chaos, traumas, and losses have had upon me and, literally, how I survived many life-threatening events to get to this stage of my life. I used to attribute my ability to overcome all those struggles to my own inner strength and desire to live. But now, after all these years, I finally fully grasp and understand with clarity that HE was watching over me, and there has always been a definite purpose to my life.

I grew up in the Bronx. My family consisted of my parents, Henry and Harriette, and my brother David. Additionally, my mother's sister Lilyan, my Uncle Harold, and my grandparents, Jesse and Daisy, all lived within one block of us. The public school I attended was just across the street from my grandparents. It was an extremely dangerous neighborhood.

My family was of Jewish heritage; Jesse was Orthodox. He was my only family member who had any significant attachment to religion. Uncle Harold, of German ancestry, was an agnostic and became a role model for me. Even though he was not very affectionate, he filled the role of a surrogate father, as mine was truly a despicable human being. The spirituality, or lack thereof, is referenced because it had an influence on me as the years passed. I felt no connection to Judaism and, due to my uncle's influence, adopted being an agnostic.

When I was four, several things began happening that would impact my life. I began having nightmares of being buried alive in a grave in a remote forest. The feeling of suffocation would often wake me, causing me to gasp for breath and sweat profusely. My visions of screaming with no one around were frightening and left me in despair. These nightmares haunted me for decades, even after I learned some deflection mechanisms.

I also became extremely claustrophobic, which later made me uncomfortable giving presentations in school or being in any situation that caused me to be near others, leading me to feel an extreme sense of being closed in with no escape. The inevitable onset of sweating only exacerbated the situation. In college, I even had a total meltdown during a speech, which actually caused the entire class to walk out. It was embarrassing and devastating.

Another trauma I underwent at a very young age was, due to a miscommunication with my mother, I ran across the street without looking, only to be struck by a car. I survived but had damage to my eyes that triggered double vision that continues to this day.

This same four-year-old walked into the bathroom one day, looked into the mirror, and asked, "How did I get in this body?" Apparently, I was able to distinguish the difference between mind and body and spirit but could not connect the dots. The message was there but not received or understood due to my youth. But if nothing else, that experience opened the door for me to question so many things, which was a blessing and a curse. My thirst for knowledge has been a lifelong quest, but with that, the level of frustration in seeking answers without success was extreme.

Our neighborhood was overrun by gangs of all ethnicities, a melting pot of sorts. On two occasions, a knife was held at my throat while I was pinned to a chain link fence. That lack of control, knowing my life was in someone else's hands and held at their discretion, was paralyzing. This became a major issue that enveloped me; in the future, I did all I could to prevent something like that from happening again. My phobia was so pervasive that I sat on the aisle whenever possible, and in movie theaters, I would sit in the last row so no one could sneak up behind me. I lived in fear that, out of nowhere, someone would slit my throat. Although totally irrational, my fear was quite real and ever-present. It seems almost incomprehensible that I could not share these events with my family. Before this, however, there was an incident in which I told my father something was occurring, and by the time he checked it out, it was already taken care of. So, my father questioned the validity of my word, assuming I had lied. That shut me down. After that, I figured he would not give credence to those later episodes.

My life was spared on many other occasions. There were at least five car accidents where I was struck from the rear, sandwiched between two cars. I was also hit on the driver's side when someone jumped a red light. And

I experienced two near-drowning episodes.

How did I stay alive? Were these all miracles?

Ultimately, we moved to the safer confines of Queens, but remained close to the rest of the family. As my Bar Mitzvah approached, my grandmother Daisy became ill and entered the hospital. We visited her on a Saturday with assurances that she would be released the following day. We traveled back to Queens only to receive a call on Sunday that she had died. Her death was attributed to a medical error by a nurse.

After Daisy died, my grandfather gave all her jewelry to her sister instead of to his two daughters, my mother and aunt. The result was such acrimony that the family became irreparably divided. All the holidays our large family of over twenty members had spent together were gone forever. My many cousins were now out of my life. I only ever saw one of them again when she attended my mother's funeral seven years later.

My grandparents had celebrated their 50th wedding anniversary just before Daisy's passing and my Bar Mitzvah. It was a beautiful occasion, but just six months later, my grandfather announced that as an Orthodox Jew, if he could still satisfy a woman, it was his obligation to remarry. My whole life was turning upside down. I had a father who was despicable and a grandfather who broke my heart and whom I resented to my core. My family was getting more and more splintered.

The fear that gripped me was reinforced many times. In second grade, I had a crush on a classmate named Pamela, but when third grade began, she didn't return to school. I learned that she had gotten ahold of her parents' lighter during the summer and burned to death.

Francis, another classmate and friend, lost a brother who drowned in a tub at the age of two. Then, I saw in the newspaper that a boy had drowned in the creek behind our school. I later learned that it was Francis. Pamela, Francis, and Francis' brother all died while I was still living in the Bronx, which compounded my fear of my own demise.

My father, Henry, was selfish. My earliest recollections of him date back to when I was three. My parents never shared the same bed. Many times, they refused to even communicate with each other while in the same room, making me the conduit to do so. It was bizarre and disturbing. My brother David and I never asked for anything, my mother never got gifts, and my parents never went out together or socialized. We lived modestly; my father spent any extra money on his obsession—stamp collecting. When we lived in Queens, my mother slept on the living room couch while my father was in the master bedroom with his stamps on the floor and covering the other side of the bed. One day, he walked into our bedroom to tell my brother and me we were idiots and would never amount to anything. He recommended we find an easy job in the future, one that would not require great intelligence and without too many responsibilities, as we would be incapable of handling them.

At the age of eighteen, I found out my mother, with whom I was incredibly close, was terminally ill. She had been unaware of how severe her condition was; perhaps it was denial. The last year of her life was brutal; she was heavily medicated and would moan throughout the night. She did not sleep at night but would fall asleep out of exhaustion each morning. She passed away when I was nineteen.

Although my father professed his love for my mother in the last year of her life, within one week of her death, he told me he was having an affair with the woman who lived in our apartment building. Attempting to put his prowess on display, he described all their sexual activities. I shut him down immediately, using some well-chosen words to express my utter disgust.

After that, he started drinking heavily and sleeping around and remarried thirteen months later. I was left to my own devices and wound up living hand to mouth in ten places in a little over three years.

In 1968, a friend set me up on a blind date with Steffi, a recently divorced woman who had been in a terrible marriage. Her now ex-husband had wanted a child to avoid being drafted to serve in the Vietnam War, but he cheated on her as soon as she got pregnant. When I met Steffi, her daughter was eleven months old. We hit it off and were married 363 days later. Six months later, she noticed a loss of peripheral vision. We went from one doctor to another until a neurosurgeon told us he believed she had what they referred to as a pseudo-tumor in her brain. She was put on steroids for three years, which affected her adrenal and pituitary glands and nearly caused Addison's Disease. The medical bills mounted to $18,000. I was making a gross of $7,800 a year.

Throughout the ordeal, Steffi's doctors warned us that if she became pregnant, her metabolism could change, causing blindness or even putting her life at risk. Allison would be our only child, and we were certainly content with that. The three of us built a wonderful life together. We dedicated our lives to each other, and the bond could not be broken. My wife became a therapist and a knowledgeable expert in so many subjects. She left me in awe. She was respected and dedicated to helping others who suffered from panic, phobias, and anxiety. She became an interfaith minister and volunteered at the local hospital chaplaincy, assisting terminally ill patients.

I furthered my education and worked as hard as I could to support our beautiful family. Unfortunately, it would take almost twenty-five years to become debt-free. The best part of our lives was that we were in it together. I was blessed for over four decades with the woman I loved who changed my life. Tragically, Steffi was medically misdiagnosed six or seven times. The last time was fatal. She died on August 6, 2013. I cannot wrap my head around the fact it has been over ten struggle-filled years without her.

My profuse sweating, claustrophobia, anxiety, and fear were detrimental throughout my career. Despite excruciatingly embarrassing moments, I persisted, but my self-consciousness never left me. In 1971, I took a position in the optical industry, where I spent my entire career. Over the subsequent thirteen years, I had sixteen different bosses in total that I had to report to. It was challenging and certainly fear-inducing. For the first five years, my issues were less on display as I ran an office with just three employees and nothing especially stressful. But when the branch offices were to be shut down, eliminating my job, I was offered a sales position. The very thought was terrorizing for me, but I accepted the role so I could bring in an income for my family.

I did have many uncomfortable times. However, my ability to bring in sales elevated me to be the top producer in the entire company among fifty sales reps. Although my skills were far inferior to the other reps, the street smarts and instincts I'd gained growing up in the Bronx made me quite effective in building relationships with the largest customers within my territory. I was given a few promotions, which I thought to be miraculous. As my authority increased, I achieved the goal I had set for myself to be a manager, avoid those daily confrontations of being face-to-face with a doctor, and have those horrendous sweats and insecurities affect me. It was absolutely mystifying to me that someone with few skills, whose instincts were to shield myself from all the torturous times, could rise within any organization. It was simply miraculous to me—I could not attribute it to anything else. But although my title was wonderful, the compensation was meager.

With minimal funds, I eventually partnered with someone to form a company. From 1989 until 2017, we led stressful lives buying and selling contact lenses globally. In 2010, Homeland Security falsely accused us of knowingly buying stolen products, and the company was placed into what the bank refers to as Work Out and Recovery, which is essentially a liquidation process. The likelihood was heavily weighted to the bankruptcy of the company and me personally. We overcame the false accusations and were told by the bank that it was the very first time any company had gone through this process, which lasted close to fifteen months, without going out of business. With our assets severely depleted, we were saved when we secured an SBA loan that reversed our downward spiral. We sold the company in 2017. Due to the fact we never bought products directly from manufacturers and did not have contracts with buyers or sellers, we were referred to as the grey market. It was never realistic or feasible to even conceive of it. Were all these events pointing to miracles or perhaps something else? The pain of my Steffi not being around to see this happen after our struggles still runs deep.

On September 2, 2022, I sought out medical treatment. On that date, I met Janet Berrong, a founding member of Women World Leaders. It was highly unusual, but we engaged in an interesting conversation that created an incredible connection. I cannot precisely detail how it unfolded, but we began discussing spirituality. The glow on Janet's face, the expression of joy, and her love for Jesus intrigued me. She poured more and more information my way, and we began attending church services. I felt like I never had before. I then participated in Pray South Florida, a 2-day event where I met the most beautiful, caring, and giving people. I knew this community was where I belonged. It was a revelation. I witnessed Dr. Crandall in his magnificence, which brought me to tears. It was unforgettable. The effect of ministry as Janet and I leaned over a young man overpowered with pure joy was something to behold. We lifted up this young man three times before leading him back to his friend, who was so overcome with emotion and asked to be prayed over. Janet and another woman, Rachel, did so. The woman cried and cried—it was so joyful as a horrific burden was lifted from her.

It has been over a year since that fateful day I met Janet. She introduced me to Jesus, and I have since dedicated my life to Him. I am fully committed and will be His obedient messenger as I have put all my faith and trust in Him.

Back in 2013, I began an existence of hopelessness, with no true joy or happiness. I planned to play out my days without purpose until my time had expired. I had the company to occupy my mind, but when that ended in 2017, things really got dark, with so many voids in my heart and mind that could not be filled.

In 2019, I typed an email to Steffi, which, of course, could not be sent. I described how tired I was of living. I expressed that I had lived a full life and, other than seeing how our daughter and granddaughter would evolve, I was pretty much resigned to hanging around without anything to look forward to.

In 2022, my entire outlook and perspective changed. And it all revolved around Jesus. I wanted to be baptized and thereby affirm my own dedication to feel worthy of being His messenger and vessel to spread His love to others. And so, I had my life-altering baptism on June 11 at the home of Kimberly and Kenny Hobbs. It was a very intimate day. Janet baptized me, making it the most beautiful, glorious day.

I now pray every single day, asking Him to watch over those who need help, whose lives have touched mine, and who may be struggling. I also ask His guidance in how I can help others, expressing my love and devotion to Him so they, too, can be joyful and have hope for the future. I want to let them know that they are not alone or forgotten.

I know that all the miracles I experienced throughout my entire life were truly Jesus watching over me. I have grown to accept and embrace everything that has happened, as it all led me to who I am today. I approach every day as a beautiful day and an opportunity to connect with people and share the love in my heart that comes directly from the Lord. I know that whatever words I say or actions I take do not come from me but through me, as He guides me every day of my life. I live each day to the fullest. Most of all, I now live my life without fear. I have a purpose, and I am happy and joyful every single day. Praise the Lord!!!

AFTERWORD

As you step out fully equipped to navigate your storm from the waves of life that toss you about, the authors of this book go with you. May their stories remain in your memory and resonate in your mind when you need them to. Our writers will continue to lift you up in prayer. It has been their commitment in authoring this book. We never need to face the waves of uncertainty alone because God's Word tells us He will never leave us or forsake us (Hebrews 13:5).

Whenever you face a storm, may the scriptures you have read throughout this book bring you confidence in God's power. Hold them close to your heart and whisper them back to God, knowing His promises are true. He wants you to believe Him with strong faith. He's got you. Don't lose heart; He's got your back! And with Him, you've got what it takes! The Word/ Bible is your sword to fight spiritually, but it is also your strong rudder to guide you through any storm that comes your way. You are NOT alone. You are part of a Band of Brothers; no man fights alone.

"Peace, I leave with you; my peace I give you. I do not give to you as the world gives; do not let your hearts be troubled and do not be afraid" (John 14:27 NIV).

> *"When you pass through the waters, I will be with you; and when you pass through the rivers, they will not sweep over you. When you walk through the fire, you will not be burned: the flames will not set you ablaze"* (Isaiah 43:2 NIV).

Suddenly a furious storm came up on the lake, so that the rains swept over the boat. But Jesus was sleeping. The disciples went and woke him, saying, "Lord, save us! We're going to drown!" He replied, "You of little faith, why are you so afraid?" Then he got up and rebuked the winds and the waves, and it was completely calm. The men were amazed and asked, "What kind of man is this? Even the winds and the waves obey him!" (Matthew 8:24-27 NIV).

> *I saw the Lord, and he answered me; he delivered me from all my fears* (Psalm 34:4 NIV).

Cast all your anxiety on him because he cares for you (1 Peter 5:7 NIV).

Please write these scriptures down, take them with you, and even commit them to memory. Make them part of your emergency storm kit. You will need them when there is a storm brewing on the horizon.

Even as a man who may feel unshakable, be aware that dangerous storms can take a great toll on your spirit. Arming yourself with scripture will provide a light that will beckon you to God's side through any storm. When the wind begins to whip up around you and darkness quickly closes in, God's Word will remind you where to seek your refuge. There is no weather too rough for the One who created it. Again, God has you. Keep your focus on His light, and allow Him to navigate you through any storm.

God already has a plan charted for your future. He sees what is ahead of you, and He can handle it all. He will carry you through every storm despite the enemy wanting to wreak havoc on your soul. Ask God for strength and endurance to steady your boat through the rough waters. Always remember God is preparing you for what is next, even though you may not yet see it. You can do all things through Christ who strengthens you, but you must take the first step through faith to believe it! Get yourself equipped to head through the storm. You can do this! The faith God called you to have in Him claims this: *"With God all things are possible"* (Matthew 19:26 NKJV). BELIEVE IT!

You will keep in perfect peace those whose minds are steadfast, because they trust in you (Isaiah 26:3 NIV).

"God's voice thunders in marvelous ways; he does great things beyond our understanding. He says to the snow, 'Fall on the earth,' and to the rain shower, 'Be a mighty downpour.' So that everyone he has made may know his work... to water his earth and show his love" (Job 37:5-7, 13 NIV).

As we close this book, remember that God never promised us this life would be easy, but He does promise that He is bigger than any storm we face. And He's always working for you and for your good. One thing we can count on for sure is that even though things may go wrong in life, God never fails. Though the storms may turn deadly, and destruction is everywhere we can see, the clouds will begin to clear, and the sun WILL shine again. His Words and His promises are true, and He will never let any of us down.

God promises to bring good from the storms of devastation. Be sure you place your trust in God and find safe harbor in HIS ARMS, believing the rain cloud over your life will dissipate, the shining light that penetrates darkness will break through, and the SUN WILL SHINE AGAIN!

Let us hold unswervingly to the hope we profess, for he who promised is faithful (Hebrews 10:23 NIV).

If God has moved within you as you've read this book, prompting you through the power of the Holy Spirit to be brave and share your story, we want to hear from you. We will help you get your story to the world. Contact us at www.unitedmenofhonor.com or @UnitedMenofHonor on social media.

UNITED MEN OF HONOR. TOGETHER WE CAN.

MORE FROM WPP!

World Publishing and Productions was birthed in obedience to God's call. Our mission is to empower writers to walk in their God-given purpose as they share their God story with the world. We offer one-on-one coaching and a complete publishing experience. To find out more about how we can help you become a published author or to purchase books written to share God's glory, please visit: www.worldpublishingandproductions.com

The authors of *Miracle Mindset: Finding Hope in the Chaos* , have experienced the wonders of God's provision, protection, and guidance. These stories and teachings will ignite a spark within you, propelling you to encounter the marvel of God's miracles, even in the chaos.

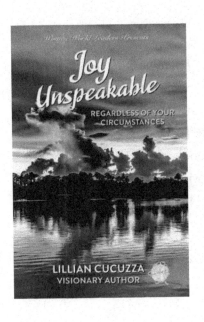

With *Joy Unspeakable: Regardless of Your Circumstances,* you will learn how joy and sorrow can dance together during adversity. The words in this book will encourage, inspire, motivate, and give you hope, joy, and peace.

Surrendered: Yielded With Purpose will help you recognize with awe that surrendering to God is far more effective than striving alone. When we let go of our own attempts to earn God's favor and rely on Jesus Christ, we receive a deeper intimacy with Him and a greater power to serve Him.

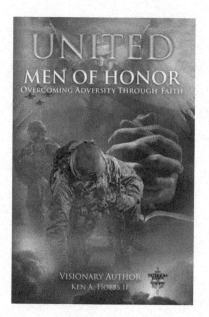

United Men of Honor: Overcoming Adversity Through Faith will help you armor up, become fit to fight, and move forward with what it takes to be an honorable leader. Over twenty authors in this book share their accounts of God's provision, care, and power as they proclaim His Word.

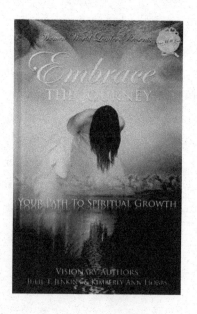

Embrace the Journey: Your Path to Spiritual Growth will strengthen and empower you to step boldly in faith. These stories, along with expertly placed expositional teachings will remind you that no matter what we encounter, we can always look to God, trusting HIS provision, strength, and direction.

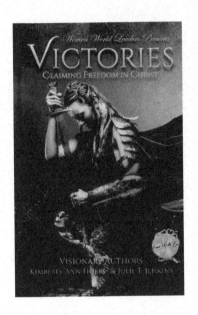

Victories: Claiming Freedom in Christ presents expository teaching coupled with individual stories that testify to battles conquered victoriously through the power of Jesus Christ. The words in this book will motivate and inspire you and give you hope as God awakens you to your victory!.

The world has become a place where we don't have a millisecond to think for ourselves, often leaving us feeling lost or overwhelmed. That is why Max Gold wrote *Planestorming!*—a straightforward guide to help you evaluate and change your life for the better. It's time to get to work and make the rest of your life the BEST of your life.